Special Edition

A Handbook & Field Guide

With a Special Chapter on
Advanced Psychic Healing

By

I

Acknowledgements:

I would like to thank everyone who has contributed to the workshops and classes their time, resources and personal support during the past years of teaching abroad and during the production and constant vigilance in writing, publishing and producing this book. Also to all the practitioners, teachers and holy masters who have changed the world for the better with their presence, service and teachings and have made a personal impact on my life and the lives of countless others with continued inspiration for creativity, service, and healing.

All Paintings and Illustrations by Bill Foss
© 2015 Bill Foss All Rights Reserved

ISBN-13: 978-0692466414 (White Wizard Publishing)
ISBN-10: 069246641X
"Journey to the Akashic Records" Revised Special Edition
© 2015 Bill Foss World All Rights Reserved

Table of Contents

Dedication

May this Book Serve You
In Your Search for
Greater Understanding
as You Look Into
Dreams, Visions and Intuitions.
With Eyes that can See
and Ears that can Hear,
For You, the Reader,
And to All the
Workshop Sponsors & Participants
the World Over, Thanks for Helping to Make
This Book a Reality,
I Hope It Serves You Well, Enjoy!

JOURNEY TO THE AKASHIC RECORDS

A HANDBOOK & FIELD GUIDE

By  BILL FOSS

Note: The information and exercises contained within this book are not intended to replace psychological counselling or medical attention. If you feel the need for help, contact a qualified service professional in the appropriate field. Do not attempt to engage in the meditation, visualization, or energy exercises in this book while operating tools, heavy machinery or a motor vehicle.

VI

Introduction

$\mathcal{S}$ince times memorial there have always been mystical pathways into other realms of existence. Contact with guides, angels, masters and healers, both mortal and immortal. Throughout history there have always been way showers for the tribes as 'Shamans'. Seers and witches for the villages and the people. Healers and mystics sprinkled along the countryside and even grand oracles in the community temples of ancient societies. These variations of the grand play of consciousness, spirit and the multi-layered streaming realities dancing together simultaneously, synchronous and even seemingly chaotic at times all point to the vastness of mind through individual, group, and universal expressions.

Within this vast grandeur of possibilities and probabilities streaming through all of the layers of dimensional realities comes the realization of the existence of an ancient system, place, vortex in a reality all it's own. The Akasha or 'sky library'. Also known as the Akashic Records. This energetic field of knowledge has been used throughout history by the great wizards and magicians. The masters of earth and beyond, esoteric groups and individuals dating back to Atlantis and Lemuria used this system for everyday connections and was also used in the mystery schools of Egypt and other ancient cultures.

As I began my journey home or my 'remembrance program' as I like to call it, I was guided to a great teacher, and as I read his book about the Records, I realized that a recent prayer that I had set into motion was now being answered at the next level. My prayer had been most intently asking God to be shown 'how it all works', 'the Meaning of Life' and the 'Secrets of the Universe'. As I continued to take in more and more information about the Akashic Records, I realized that I already knew this, all of this. So I intently practiced continually at reading the Records and accessing the various levels of knowledge. The Akasha is so vast it could literally take lifetimes to process all the data, knowledge and information streaming there. For this reason, systems were developed over the course time for the entry and access of these great banks of knowledge.

Through my personal study of the Akasha I have come to learn much about my own self, my life's path, my soul's journey and what my other selves or past lives have been. This has been a steadily unfolding process for me with some accelerated spikes along the way. I truly believe that if I'd known certain things about my past lives, the in-between life times or the future, I might have sabotaged my own realization, enlightenment and the chance to help others.

As it now stands I continue to receive information and energy from the Records, and as I've come to understand the dynamics that exist within the mystical realm of the Akashic Records I've had the privilege of helping 1,000's of people in the workshops to better come to know and understand themselves at ever deepening levels through the processes of this work. And it just keeps getting better, every time another person in the classes finds a key that unlocks their own mysteries of understanding their true nature my heart opens with gratitude. Sometimes when we're in a journey, I get the clarity of the timeless moment as I'm facilitating a group of students in one of the guided Akashic Journeys. I realize that I'm getting to spend a few special moments with them in their lifetime, and that this moment is special in connecting to the Records for them. In this way I've found it truly gratifying to work with others. To help you get your own answers and understanding.

So with all this said, I truly hope you enjoy the book and that it brings you insight and joy, realization, healing and creativity. I hope to see you at one of the workshops or in an Akashic Reading or Healing/Clearing session. Many Blessings on your Life's Journey and I'll see you in the Records! Best Regards, Healing and Success,

Bill Foss, 11/22/2013

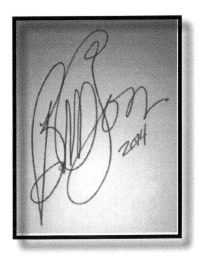

*Within the book are terms, word variations and sentence structures which may be new to you and are not considered proper English or grammar. This is used purposefully to fully convey the ideas, teaching style and to illustrate that which is beyond the physical.

Enjoy!

Babaji
Immortal Master of the Himalayas, my Friend
and guiding Light

SPECIAL EDITION

JOURNEY TO THE AKASHIC RECORDS

A HANDBOOK & FIELD GUIDE

WITH A SPECIAL CHAPTER ON
ADVANCED PSYCHIC HEALING

BY  BILL FOSS

The Tao is said to contain the manifestation of 10,000 things while it also remains empty. Both principles are true and yet one does not supersede the other.

Chapter 1

Description of the Akashic Records

The **Akashic Records** is many things. I will describe it to you here in this chapter in simple ways as well as in depth and detail so that your mind can get pictures, connections, and intuition about this vast storehouse of knowledge. From this information your mind, senses and being can start to grasp, envision and eventually learn to assimilate the energies, wisdom and knowledge of the Akashic realm.

Available from within the Akashic Records is the living etheric energetic record or signature of every past, present, and future moments of every person, place and thing that is associated with, or has ever been created, or whosoever has incarnated here on this planet. The records of all things animate and inanimate are held within these great banks of knowledge.

All considerations, variations, and streams of creative invention and endeavor. All things in manifest form and that which has yet to be created. All possibilities and probabilities. The energetic, foundational reasoning behind, around, inside and surrounding the ideas and situations of why things are the way they are in the world today. The views, insights and knowing of why things have played out the way they have so far and the constant streaming, forming, re-forming and morphing considerations of the

1

future. We use the word 'consideration' as a focus on the idea that these possibilities can take a certain shape or they can stream out in other surrounding directions as a focal point of energy manifesting from the quantum field of possibilities in a general or specific way. So you see the possibilities are truly endless. Not only within realms of visionary thought but with ways that it can create itself in the external world of reality. In accordance to that idea, there are certain tendencies of people's minds, thoughts and emotions to elementally create within certain or more specific patterns of manifest realities. Certain spiritual paths have specifically or even more loosely translated variations of these dynamics. The Tao is said to contain the manifestation of 10,000 things while it also remains empty. Could that translate in todays world as the manifestation of 100,000 things or even a million things? Quite possibly. Both principles are true and yet one does not supersede the other. The Tao is often thought of in relation or perspective to one's life, path, thoughts and feelings, and surroundings or possessions. Not that it was intended to be perceived only for those reasons, yet, these are the unspoken quick references that come up from within a person's mind. Tibetan Buddhism has similarly different approaches to thought, feeling, thinking and acting. These are approaches to the spiritual path based on reference points of consciousness from within and without that creates itself as a streaming manifestation of being and doing through the individuals and groups who experience it. Again...considerations.

Ancient Egyptian mystery schools such as the **Order of Melchezidek** priesthood. This ancient group's roots comes directly from their ancestry in **Atlantis**. The knowledge, wisdom and power to manifest, manipulate and create from cosmic energy, the stars, constructed power sources and energy technologies from light and sound. Rituals to open the senses into the Akashic Records or Akasha. Yet another example of spiritual and energetic situational development from the ethers into reality by using the ethers themselves. The Hermetic approach of the **Kyballion** speaking of the ancient wisdom and right, clear or exacting usages of the energetic laws and principles. There are true spiritual masters, sages and adepts living outside of communities of the known world, relying on the inner wisdom of the good, humble or resourceful usage of true knowledge and powers.

Such is the way of the ancient **Siddhas** or 'Enlightened Ones' of the Indian continent. They were known for their connections into the Akashic Records and writing it all down on Papyrus leaves. They were known to have extended their lifetimes or even experience immortality by usage of certain herbs, tinctures, meditation, breathing processes and solar gazing to reach an ascended state of moving into and through the ethers and fields of other dimensions while existing either continually or intermittently in physical reality. Great considerations made earthly manifest.

Is any one consideration greater or less than any other? In some ways comparatively speaking, yes, and yet nothing exists as the whole of creation without the variations of different ideas, people, ways of living, flavors, colors, and all different shapes and sizes. It is all important in and of itself speaking of and to itself through the lense of consciousness that continually grows, moves, creates and diminishes as the never ending ever unfolding process of the cosmos, Creator and supreme dance of creational consciousness. The pure 'ISness' of it all. The I Am, **I Am that I Am**, I Am that, the Tao, the Alpha & Omega. And yet our reference to all of this is through our mind and our senses. Through our minds, hearts, emotions and energy centers we are having the experience of witnessing all of this.

When we access the Akashic Records we are expanding into what we are already part of; multilayered, multidimensional

3

beings having an experience of reincarnation. We expand our view and learn to focus in on certain points of our personal or collective group history and evolution so we gain expanded reference points to this witnessing process.

In history whether referring to the Atlantian, Lemurian, Egyptian and Indo-European sourcerers (sourcers), priests and seers, or the siddhas and masters of India, or the magicians of ancient mystical Tibet. The commonality that they all have shared in one aspect is this ancient mystical system for journeying into the 'sky library'.

In ancient Hindu tantric traditions there are a set of elemental **yantra** symbols called the **Tattvas**. There are 5 symbols representing the elements: earth, water, fire, air and...akasha. Akasha is said to be the combination of the other 4 elements. So these symbols are used for meditation of the mind, energy centers and senses to gain heightened awareness into creating one's own path or learning the higher precepts such as opening the heart to love.

The Akashic Records have a location(s). They lay within the etheric field of the planet starting at 240 feet from the surface and remaining upwards to 1-1.5 miles from the surface. The actual field can be accessed anywhere here around us in the physical air space, though it is more easily accessed through travelling to these higher altitudes via the mind, soul or astral body, where there is no hustle and bustle from the surface, especially in city areas, and less to no electronic (EMF) interference. You can also access through the starlight energy entering the atmospheres. This acts as an amplifier or buffer of energy and can even give you insight to other lives in other star systems or act as a gateway. Often times during a journey we will move up, out, over the planet where we can be away from surface interference and access the energy of the Akasha. Also places on the planet where the earth energy is high in natural energy vibration such as at the ocean, on top of a mountain, in the woods. These are all good to great energetically clear areas to access, though it can be done from anywhere at anytime. Each planet has it's own set of Akashic Records. Each solar system, star system, galaxy, and so on has it's own set of records.

There are primarily 3 ways of accessing. Through the sky or etheric field, through the mind, heart and physical body, and through the earth. There are primarily 2 sets of Records. One that acts as a more general set of records and can be accessed through the astral realm or 5th dimensional and then there is a higher more advanced set of Records accessed by the masters. This part of the Records takes more practice to access and is generally reserved for the pure of heart. This portion, higher set, or 'upper chamber' is located between the 10th,11th, and 12th dimensions or on both sides of the 11th dimension. 11:11.

As we think of the 'Keeper of the Records' and the surrounding angelics of the light of Creator God that protect it. This Ancient Temple of Knowledge is kept well guarded. Not in the ways of forceful strength but in more subtle ways. The ways of the higher mind, of Creator God and of creation. The same ways that have kept it hidden or tucked away from the mainstream of primitive lower mind group consciousness of humanity. So in the middle ages, the time of separation, there were mystical groups of seers, astrologers and magicians and individuals such as **Nostradamus** who were accessing the Records for many reasons. Anything from foretelling the immediate and long range future of the world to looking at weather patterns and astrological movements in relation to planting crops for harvest seasons to the development and movement of societies. **Leonardo da Vinci** was part of a study group who accessed the Akasha and as an individual and artist detailed his inventions in the cascading nonlinear information of creative possibilities, variations and considerations. People of society, at that time, in general and dare we say much like modern times, were not so much concerned with the higher mind, meditation, astral projection or finding the 'real' truths as to why things are the way they are. As usual society was more concerned with prophecy only when it echoed of some great impending doom of the future or when some fear-based dark force or evil spell was upon them.

Often times for the whole of humanity there is little attention or interest in anything to do with operating from a self realized vantage point or being clear enough to connect to higher realms. The main concern has been from the lower mind set that something has been hidden from them. Though the spiritual masters, teachers, watchers are still persistent in guiding humanity towards the truth and the light. The natural laws of the Universe include growth, change and evolution, and hopefully we are moving along those lines as a race for the betterment of the collective Self and planet. No matter how much we have stagnated, been kept in the dark or naturally resisted the higher road through the ego of lower self servient survival tactics, there is always hope for great movement for the human race to reach it's magestic and masterful potential.

In Truth, and I use this word purposefully, we have available to us the opportunity through studying the Akashic Records to find, witness, experience and know the true dynamics behind and within our world, and the human race with all it's incarnations and creations. There were those then who knew the Truth in the past and there are those of us now in current times who continue to hold that torch for humanity as more and more of us wake up from our sleepy dream.

We use archetypical symbologies to systematically move into these realms to access the Records. This moves and directs our mind and consciousness up into these finer, more pure states of being and to the *non-location location* of the Akashic Temple of Records and then brings us back out and home again. This is a silent key for accessing. Moving in through relaxed processes of visualization and meditation and then back out. Much the same way we would move into sleep and then back to waking state reality. Though the areas and places we visit are actually in the dream state accessed during **R.E.M** (rapid eye movement) states of consciousness between sleep and the waking state.

These Akashic Temples and Records have been visited by all of the great ones over history. The masters, the mystics, magicians and seers. Creating these non-physical locations by the continued streams of visitation to these places. There will be an afterlife-like feeling when you actually access this realm. Primarily because the Records are used between lifetimes by all the Souls visiting the earth plane, Creator God and the Angelics of the Light of God in charge of transporting Souls into the Records to review their lifetime(s) for lessons learned, victories, regrets and missed opportunities.

Maybe there is a central lesson to a certain Soul's purpose and it plays itself out in recurring multiple life themes in order for a soul to have the opportunity to experience the lesson more than once if needed from different angles until the goal is met and the experience of the lesson has been understood with wisdom gained. There are Keepers of the Records who tend to this realm. Special angelics or Gate Keepers guard or stand watch outside the harmonic entrances into the Records. Inside the Records there is a Watcher, a Keeper of the Records. This Keeper may take on an earthly or a more other-worldly presence. When visiting the Records you may connect with the Keepers or it may be that you have your own individual experience alone, though, they are still there guiding you. You may be accompanied by your guides, angels or family members. It is a special place to visit.

The Akashic Records could be referred to as a way station for all the souls who have ever visited the earth plane. Coming here from other star systems the souls check in to receive their agenda of life times, lessons to work on, and through experiences they come to know themselves as a fingertip or expression of Divine Source, Creator God, and an expression of divinity through the experiences and challenges presented by earth life incarnations. Souls check in between lifetimes and even in dreams, out-of-body and near death experiences to gain perspective on what is occurring and how to proceed. They receive the harmonic resonance or information that it's time to go back to their life and their journey is not over yet or it's time to move on to their next scheduled adventure.

In this way the Akashic Records is really all about the Souls of humanity and our journey here and beyond. Our evolution both as energy beings and as a race. The Records are similar to the other realities and dimensions in that there is so much cascading information within it, streaming, moving, storing itself in the energetic field of the earth and within all living things.

A place that you are connected to in every moment of every lifetime that records the dynamics of why we are here. Organic in nature, it is a special place to visit. With the importance of learning our earthly lessons and working out our karmas, so is it special that we can have a pathway up into this realm to experience what we experience between lives while still in human form. This is where the magic lies. This true and simple process through continual practice will provide ever unfolding worlds of knowing for the Real You in expanding and simplistic ways that we will attempt to write about here for pages to come. Once you experience this 'place' within you and without that you are connected to it will start to transform you. Remember the Matrix movie

"Would you like the red pill or the blue pill?" With one you wake up and with the other you fall back into sleep.

The Akashic Records have been looked at by those in connection to conspiracy or secret groups controlling the world or spying on other governments. And to this I say, the vibration of the conflicted reasons for which they would try to gain access will only continually thwart successful attempts to gain the purest of prophecy or information.

There is a special language or alphabet of Akashic symbols. These are not angelic symbols. These symbols for some are easily read and translated into earth based language or knowing within the mind. They have surfaced in temple carvings such as Egyptian hieroglyphs and art forms throughout the world. Once you have visited the Akashic Records you will recognize writings, symbols, and art forms including paintings that have the visual information or vibration of the Records. You will just know. We will cover this in detail in Chapter 5.

Many of the things here in this chapter of description will be touched on and expanded in other sections, as well as in preparation for your Akashic journeys. I hope you enjoy the Journey. Suit up, we're going in!

The Elohim hold space for the Akashic Records by surrounding it and holding fields of emanating energy which allow for the great storehouse of knowledge to remain undisturbed. The Great Keeper of the Records, an ancient Elohim master spirit timelessly stands within the Great Hall of Records.

Chapter 2

History of the Akashic Records

The History of Akashic Records is very interesting indeed. It seems to have more than one source of it's creation. Each planet, each sun, star, moon, and heavenly body or star system has it's own set of Akashic Records. So as we look from this perspective the Collective Akashic Records of the Universe are layered. The Earth's set of Akashic Records are what we will primarily work with. This immense set of Records with it's collections of each person's Book of Life or Individual set of Akashic Records of each person who has visited this planet is connected to all other sets. Classified in groups by each Soul's sets of lifetimes, by types of events, historical sequences of time, certain types of Souls, Inventions and **Sacred Geometries** and many other ways of categorizing the groupings, streaming from a continual Source of pure Creator Energy. When we access lifetimes from other star systems we do it primarily through the set of Akashic Records from our world and then out from this address. Much in the same way, we move from waking state reality up into the Akasha and then back out and down to our current standard operating vibrational frequency. And even though we may step back down in frequency certain adjustments, integrations, healings and clearings have happened naturally just by our visiting of the Records.

It is sometimes hard for us to imagine a time when magic was the common technology. Though if you think of it in that way, there wasn't yet in that time period cars, planes and computers. No electrical power lines covering the earth, and no satellites. The energy waves were much more clear and organic. **Magic** or the use of energy to create from Source was more practical than most of society gives it credit for. In the distant past it was even then considered to be an ancient practice and study. Some would consider it then in the same ways we view and use trades, commodities and technologies today.

From it's resourcefulness came the naming of nations, blessings and sometimes saving of the crops, changing of weather patterns, healing of the sick, protection against dark agencies, and the list goes on. Immaculate conceptions in the days of yore were more common place because the energy was so much higher and clearer. Forms could be easily instantaneously manifested or morphed out of the ethers because there was no power grid, or limiting beliefs. Pure positive potential was at hand. In other related ways these special moments and manifestations can happen anytime, anywhere and in any age depending on what Spirit and Creator are up to.

As we look back further into the times of Atlantis, earth experienced a more advanced civilization than the archaic period of the Middle Ages (as earth recovered from the desolation that took Atlantis). A more unified age was experienced until by way of the grand procession of the cosmic seasons, separation and duality became prominent again.

This great race of people and their ways of organic power and energy have had mystical connections into the Records.

The Atlantian technology was called Selfic and was based on organic plant life being turned into an energy source and harnessed with crystals to create morphagenic fields that could then be amplified by human thought waves and mind power for many different applications. There were also great monumental power beacons to bring down cosmic energy and to transmit it out through their cities and beyond. Grand temples stood both above ground and below. The use of energy symbols and the elements were common. There were power sources made of geometries and crystals which human mind power could be harnessed to and create waves of signals for broadcast. At that time on the planet the energy was clearer, purer and higher in vibration lending itself to a more inter-connectedness with all people. What we now consider in this day and age as direct psychic connections through our third eye centers. There were no secrets. Everyone lived in a harmonious flow of vibration even if there were ebbs and flows within the social consciousness and inter-connections.

The Atlantians had such a connection with the Akashic Records because they literally enhanced it's nature by way of their own ways of thinking, feeling and existence. They were living the same dynamic in the physical 3rd dimensional reality that flows through the Akashic Records. We may individually or collectively and either knowingly or unknowingly experience this dynamic from time to time as an enhanced version of the 3 dimensional world including moments and extended periods of 4th and 5th dimensional awareness and it's corresponding energetic principles.

This is one reason why we can so vividly access the Atlantians through the Records (as they can access out across different time lines also). They were using sound to bring matter into manifest form from the ethers through group chanting and the focusing of intention plus they had the power sources to support their intentions. Levitation of large stones into place or other monuments and manipulation of the elements to create forms out of the ethers was a mystical art of both mastering energy and becoming a trade smith of etheric energy for the community.

We are moving back into a time when the energy will be much higher again and many great things will be achieved and witnessed.

The Egyptian society developed out of a string of tribes making it's way to survive the destruction of Atlantis as it was destroyed. The reason for the destruction was at the time of the last great shift, as the poles shifted and the Atlanteans were using Selfic mind power to focus amplified mind power towards balancing the earth and her atmospheric fields. If a little was good, more should be better to stabilize the planet. It was a gamble and it didn't work. There were great separations in consciousness from unity to duality starting to naturally occur as the great cosmic seasons changed as well as the rift of the natural fields of the earth being cauterized by these Atlantian beams and waves of energy as they attempted to intervene.

The surviving Atlantian priests of early Egytian colonies with the help of aliens were able to set power sources in place to help stabilize and rebuild humanity and the group mind field as well as the minds of every member of humanity which had been almost completely wiped out when the magnetic poles of mother earth shifted drastically and quickly. One of these power sources is the great Hall of Records hidden in secret chambers at sacred sites in Egypt. There were many other interesting and powerful technologies that we do not know of in the mainstream, though if we look within the Records it is all there. This earthbound Hall of Records contains several different power sources which in turn are linked to the original Akashic Records. The power sources included a great set of crystal spheres and a DNA chamber based on the same geometry we know as the **Kabbalah** diagram. The Atlantian artifacts have been found as far west as South America. Was this an Atlantian outpost or part of the great continent as it moved apart? And there is now a set of pure crystal pyramids which have been found on the ocean floor in the area known as the Bermuda Triangle and another set off the coast of Portugal. We can imagine the power fields that these structures are able to create. Many air and sea vessels have completely vanished in the ocean vortex of the **Bermuda Triangle**. Were these powerful pyramids originally on dry land or were they placed knowingly underwater to harness the pure living consciousness of the water to create vortexes, portals and gateways? There are other systems and structures underground of which some have recently been unearthed, which form a network around the planet.

The **Lemurians** were a simple and joyful people, they too used the Records in an even more organic version of society. As an advanced tribal culture with their great temples made of wood and stone. As they created, they literally were connected elementally or organically to the Earth and in turn to the Akashic Records. It was a constant stream they could continually access. This access was done by way of a simple 'knowing' much like the Alantians whose priests termed the path of study called the '**Knowing Way of Truth and Light**' or simply the 'Way' which has translated itself into the messages of many post dated sacred texts including the Bible. Jesus the Christ channelled Creator God in the scriptures interpreted as: " I Am the Way, the Truth and the Light."

Ancient Lemuria was what we would consider to be Asia. If you have studied Chinese medicine or any of the Asian spiritual paths you will notice that they are uniquely different than other approaches. There are many detailed and hidden things known about the human body in a similar yet different approach than the Hindu based energy centers of the body called chakras. Some knowledge is similar or even overlapping while other information is completely different. The Asian mind approach is very practical and structured when it comes to thinking, intentions and life. They are true thinkers driven by the mind. The practice of using the Chi or Ki (energy) was what we would consider to be masterful. Words and symbols appearing in the air as they spoke. Their connection with the earth and the ethers were so harmonious that it was as if the Akasha were streaming and being written simultaneously in their presence.

Fragments of history remain as the face of the Earth has shifted many times over and our true history has been either hidden, lost or rewritten. We can access the true history from within the Akashic Records. Many of us have keys to certain or more prominent information stored within our own Souls and our DNA. This information can be accessed by entering deeper states of meditation often lying just beneath the surface of our conscious minds.

The **Elohim**, a hierarchy of powerful creative angels in charge of creating the Universes and all of the heavenly bodies and planets on behalf of Creator God, had been given the blueprint to create the Akashic Records by authority of **the Council of Twelve**. A group of 12 Master Spirits governing and guiding the higher dimensions of pure light and pure laws. As the Elohim show me pictures, I see rainbow shards of rainbow spectrum light touching down or reaching us in consistently concentric locations in the atmosphere and the surface of the Earth. Energy that is holding a space for the dynamics of not only physical reality to occur and re-occur, to form and re-form but quantum opportunities and considerations for continuing realities. These Elohim angelic energies are high in vibration and very diversely unique.

The Elohim hold space for the Akashic Records by surrounding it and holding fields of emanating energy which allow for the great storehouse of knowledge to remain undisturbed. The Great Keeper of the Records an ancient Elohim master spirit timelessly standing within the Records and greeting all of the visiting souls, masters and angelics who have ever come to access information, knowledge and wisdom for healing and knowing of the souls.

In reference to the intricacies of this great sprawling storehouse of knowledge (the Akashic Records) we may liken the precision and workings to that of the physical body with all of it's finely tuned interacting parts and rhythms, both physically and energetically. Within the higher realms of creation there are many, many places and beings that are so high in vibration that their considerations will never be realized in the physical realm of humanity. So high in vibrations that they are not recognized in name or form by us yet they exist. Such are the higher holy **Bhoddissatvas** created and recreating themselves within those higher realms. Their pure essence is of such high order and vibration never to be realized upon the earth plane, yet we know of their existence through the higher order of mystical religions such as Tibetan Buddhism and it's predecessor, **Bon**. Some say there is no real reason for such high 'holier than thou' beings to practically exist and contribute to creation, though there is always syncronicity of all things at work and everything has a reason, benefit and contribution.

Since times memorial this sacred library or study was given special space for all of the Souls to visit and to interact with Creator God, the masters and the high councils. To look into their own challenges and lessons, observations and life's experiences by what they had experienced during incarnate lifetimes on the Earth and other planets, or in other dimensions. In this way the evolution, and learning of Creator's energy of Souls as expressions or fingertips of the greater I Am is guided and protected, even governed by higher laws and guidelines of harmonic vibratory frequency.

This is a main reason why many of us are not privy to the information. It is harmonically specialized to those who are guided to it to use it and access it. Though, in light of that, Everyone is depositing information into the Records continuously and we all have access to it in any moment when we are ready. Souls from other galaxies, star systems and universes visit here to look into the catalogue for having an earthly experience. From the earth experience these higher beings can have just that, an earthy experience. They're able to roll up their sleeves, dig in and get dirty, and then take a cosmic shower cleansing the unwanted harmonic karmas and consequently either get back in the earth game by way of reincarnation, or move on to other systems of creation having had the earthly(earthy) experience.

The history of the creation of the Akashic Records is two fold. Put in place by the far reaching cosmic hands of Creator God as a dynamic energetic ever resonating dimensional storehouse of blueprints. Created in another way to self perpetuate the continuing unfoldment of creation itself and as the great Observatory of Souls with all it's many facets, ever documenting, way showing, healing and teaching in all of the special and intricate ways that are unique to the Akashic Field and Hall of Records.

© 2014 Bill Foss

Mother Meera
living master, avatar and incarnation of Divine Mother energy
30" x 40" acrylic on aluminum

19

Think of, search for and contact the pure forms of Christ, Creator and the Masters. Listen and receive connections, messages and blessings from them.

20

Chapter 3

Non-location Locations

Within the vast reaches of the etheric library of the Akashic Records lives and streams what I call 'non-location locations'. Seemingly an enigma wrapped in a riddle, yet a way for the mind to focus and expand into the momentary data streams of ideas.

Let's talk about different aspects of this. The idea is that there are remote locations that we look at or into when we access the Akashic Records or our personal Book of Life within the Akasha in general. Similarly to remote viewing, we are transported to a different time and place.

Remote viewing is an isolated aspect of accessing the Akashic Records. I use the word 'isolated' because the protocol for many (not all) of the 'ministers' of remote viewing is to move in the direction of taking emotional, inspirational or spiritual responses and the stimulation of these attributes out of their process. In this way they hope to have a clearer and cleaner look at their target location. There are advantages to this and a yet more controlled environment of hopeful visual information. We could go on and on about 'looking at looking'. One question you may want to ponder: What is your reason for looking? If your reason is in question, then the information that you get might naturally be skewed. Not always though possible.

In our exercises we do not isolate emotional, spiritual or

inspirational input, because we understand that these are voluntary and involuntary responses that we have culminated from other moments, places and other lifetimes. This is part of us, and it brings us back to ourselves in a more expanded way of accessing moments in this and other lifetimes where we were also generating a plethora of thoughts, feelings and expressions. Though we also understand that we can remove ourselves from the emotions and bodily sensations and watch or participate in our own Akashic movie without being encumbered by any emotional charges keeping us clear of conflict for more precise viewing and streaming of the Records. So you may not want to be overcome by the emotions and bodily sensations of the other life times, moments and time lines, though you want to have access to it all. This is more of a complete recall.

In this streaming of our senses to these non-location locations, we are transported remotely to the destinations of times and places that we intend to visit. We simply intend to look into them and then we are there. This is one of the intricate aspects of access with the creative and intuitive mind as well as the senses. We will talk about this in other ways in following chapters.

Here, a key point to be touched on: conflict. If there is energetic, mental or emotional conflicting ideas, thought patterns or sensations in the body generated by stress, tension, fears or anger it can hamper or limit the access, the streaming or the amount of information that a person is able to retrieve, have the experience of, or remember. The creative mind in conjunction with the ego can colorize and even polarize the information and intuitive sensory experience giving it a more psychic or astral plane flavor. In this way we are only touching distantly into the full spectrum of information that is available to us.

Pertaining to various aspects of the creation of these

locations in ancient cultures and spiritual paths, there were deities set into place in many cultures, including **Hinduism, Buddhism** and **Christianity**. These deities acted as power generators, power sources and pinnacles of virtue to live by. Let's look at the Hindu deities. These 'virtuous ones' are reflections of actual beings and people as well as mythical beings that were created to represent certain distinct virtues of God or Creation by those who knew to do so. As the beings were created, exaulted and respected as one of the many aspects of Creator God, they were actually given energetic life. This was during another clearer and higher energetic time on the planet and in a part of the world (the Middle East) where *mantras* (energetic tonal sound prayers), *mudras* (energetic hand and posture flow gestures) and stories, teachings and verses were passed down through generations. The energy of each deity was gathered, conjured and gained momentum over time. Most all of these deities were placed in the form of statues in temples of meditation and worship. As hundreds of thousands, millions even into countless numbers of prayers, mantras, and meditations were offered to the deities or aspects of God.

This aspect of God directly shined these energies of blessings, healings and manifestations back to those who directed energy towards them. This is the quantum energy of manifestation creating an experience through the harnessing of love, devotion and other positive emotions. What a powerful dynamic! Think about the amplification of energies and the possibilities on a quantum level. Shining energy back to the ones saying these prayers and to all life with the virtues that they focused on of each deity truly blessing humanity en masse.

Catholicism, during the Roman Empire during the last period of separation, borrowed heavily from spiritual communities by using these same principles of focusing energy. A separation of the energy by focused intention on the homogenized rewritten life of a spiritual leader or mascot, built an empire with cathedrals in their name, then killed all who opposed in crusades and in so doing influenced generations with ideas of an external God.

With God, Spirit, Creator now separate from the people, also came 'living in sin' as unclean, unworthy people. The controlling of the masses by fear and force cultivated disempowerment for future generations of humanity. The ways of the old religion or spirituality were taken away. The artists of the times were commissioned to paint religious leaders with the Son of God as if they were somehow related to Him or acting on His behalf. In fact it was illegal for a time to paint anything that was not regulated by the church, though, not heavily enforced. Artists make lousy slaves, and so a wide array of well crafted paintings continued. Paintings at that time were all that existed as far as communications and advertisement. Was the crucifixion the image of a spiritual saviour that took on the karma of the world... or the subconscious mascot as an example of what happens to those who oppose?

Sex was deemed dirty and unclean because the leaders were in conflict with their own sexual tendencies behind closed doors. Celibacy was supposed to be protocol for the priests, though, they had no energetic preparation for this.

The sciences of eastern kundalini pranayan in preparation for celibacy found in Kriya yoga and tantras for the transmutation of base chakra energy works very well for this, and perhaps today people are starting to move towards the investigation into practice as a helpful aid of celebacy. Christ knew well of these techniques through his study of spiritual practices in multiple cultures during his travelling years.

When human sexual energy is denied it takes on strange

forms and some priests and nuns have struggled with their sexuality because of it for generations. Truly, one cannot deny a part of oneself, they can only work with that part to change it, integrate it, love it or transform it. This can be a struggle for saints, priests or the average person. It's part of the human condition and as we recognize it and heal it, we transcend to new levels of social behaviour and family.

Deity-like saints were created or exalted in the image and likeness of God, prayed to, painted, told stories of and generations later we have more of a controlled conservative version of spirituality and it's mascots which conveniently regulates the usage of spiritual energy. The real goods were kept in the basement. (Vatican Library)

Although, you could access a limited version of God by way of your local governing church officials. Some of the same officials who used magic and witchcraft behind doors in secret rituals to control the masses and bring themselves power. This often included sexual abuse of adults and children, not to mention their sacrifice in order to disempower others and steal their soul or core energy. This entailed activating unholy energies. Angelic magic and Satanic rituals were also used behind closed doors. Some say this still goes on today and though it's rarely talked about, people and society are becoming wise to it. Many church officials have been reprimanded and even imprisoned for unjust and sexual acts against their congregation members and other church employees, not to mention all of the missing children.

The movies "The Da Vinci Code" and "Angels and Demons" are a look into syndicated religious organizations. Also the movie "Stigmata" has some strong messages.

Energy can be focused to generate, amplify and control. And after all, even tyrants need good art! As this happens, different versions, levels and variations of God among other things are created. And if a person only believes that they have limited access to this version of God, Spirit or representative of the Divine then by certain universal laws this is the case and is allowed to be. In our world and the world of spirit Creator God can and will supersede this when and where necessary during periods and places of these controlled separations.

If you want to ultimately control someone or even vampirize a whole race of people, separate them from their true understanding of their spirit, their soul, and their relationship to their Creator. We have seen this movie as a race and it's time for a healing change.

All this said, I do know wonderful practicing Catholics who are devoted to service and to God. There is good in everything, and we know that. We're looking through a bird's eye view of the whole spectrum. So if you are Catholic, I honor you and your spiritual studies.

Don't let the bad decision making of a few gone astray influence your study or worship. Your light and love is needed to heal, balance and clear through compassion, acceptance and forgiveness. As with everything else in this book, take what serves you and leave anything that doesn't.

So can you imagine different versions of God? Can you imagine different versions of Christ which have been created? Or **Mother Mary**, or **Mary Magdalene**? What is the real truth of the way the person actually was and what misinformation has been mythically adopted about them as supposed truth? Was it intentional or simply because humans were involved with the interpretations over generations? Possibly both. In this way different versions are created. What is the difference between the Catholic God, the Buddhist version of God or any other version?

So could you imagine that there are different energetic versions of Christ because of the focusing of mind, heart and prayer energies and all of the beliefs in the ways that surround Him? The preconceived versions of the Master serve the conservative community needs for a spiritual mascot. So if millions of people focused on a certain version or aspect of Christ or another master would that version be created on the astral plane? Yes. Can the same thing happen with different versions of God? Yes. So you would have two versions of God. A supposed and 'real to some degree' version which might be governed more by emissaries of the Light of Creator or those intercepting the prayers. Then there is also the original truth of Creator's existence available to us simultaneously as well.

If you write Santa Claus a letter is he really getting it? Or is it Mrs. Claus or the elves reading and replying to your inquiry? Hmmm? Confusing isn't it! Bypassing the parameters of these preconceived versions of God and the Masters can be virtually unknown to an individual's consciousness until they move past the governing properties of limited thinking and find some real truth through their own path of self discovery. Think of, search for and contact the pure forms of Christ, Creator and the Masters. Listen and receive connections, messages and blessings from them.

As we discussed non-location locations, the creation and/or fabrication of versions of God, deities and spiritual teachers, we are getting a glimpse into certain aspects of creation and the processes of manifesting. In much the same way non-location locations are generated by the continuous visitations into these realms. Archetypical symbols, places and beings are generated creatively by the mind. There are several levels involved with this. The laws and quantum mechanics of energy itself creating, re-creating and spiraling into etheric and physical existence.

As the ancient wisdom keepers continued to visit the great banks of etheric knowledge of the Akasha, they created streaming pathways which have been continually accessed.

We also can create new pathways in new moments every time we are writing our life times of responses into our Book of Life within the Akashic library. When we focus our conscious mind towards these moments we create portals of etheric energy into these non-location locations of the store house for great teachings and experiences of the Souls. Do you now understand how these dynamics can work in reference to the original creation of the Akashic Records? When we focus on things with our mind we strengthen them and other times even create them. We visit through these portals into the Akashic Temple, a mysical place created and / or strengthened by the visitation of the group mind, soul and spiritual essence of those who have definitively cared to do so. Again noted here: the Akashic was inaccessible to the masses for various natural reasons and other times for specifically esoteric reasons. Often confused with forms of magic and witchery because the Akashic is an element which has been used by those who also practiced ancient arts of sourcery and magic as wells as spirituality in other cultures.

Though, the Akasha is much more than that and has been used by great artists, inventors, humanitarians, and spiritual teachers. So in this way the Akasha has true spiritual properties of Cosmic Source Essence. Leonardo da Vinci naturally accessed the Records and is quite apparent in his intuitive, creative and inventive drawings. Sir Winston Churchill was said to have accessed the Records. All of the great teachers, saints, seers and masters are accessing the Akashic Records whether they are conscious of it or not. Masters like **Babaji** and **Christ** access the Records naturally, constantly connected and streaming through them on the other side. Much like being in more than one place at the same time with a 360 degree view. **Merlin** the great magician of King Authur's court also accessed the Akashic Records.

In defining the ways of the energetic pathways into

realms beyond and the creation or recognition of teachers and deities we have sought to expand your view or mental ideas and pictures of the elemental patterns that are the basis for the very existence of the Akashic Records and the expansion and additions to it, of it and from it. The silent passage ways into silent places that are viewable and experiential. The non-location locations of the Great Hall of Records, The Souls, and the lifetimes and moments of soul life experiences in lives taken up as human form upon the earth plane.

The creative process itself can go on and on. It's never ending and always beginning. This has given us all the great art over the centuries of time.

Chapter 4

Pathways In the Akasha

Within the Akashic Records there are ways to access even deeper areas and parts of the great libraries of knowledge. As we look towards accessing the Records, there are several intentional ways to do this and even more natural ways to 'look into' and perceive the pathways that connect us into the Akasha. As Souls in human form we are all connected to the Akashic Records in every thought, word and deed of each lifetime, even in the deepest levels of sleep. We are likewise still connected to this great repository of knowledge even as we transition between lives into the 'in-between'.

The pathways into the Akashic Records can be experienced in multiple ways:
1. A stream into the Records.
2. A stream from the Records.
3. A field of energy that you merge with as you expand your energy.
4. Accessing the Records from deep within the Mother Earth.
5. Accessing the Records from your own Heart, Mind, Soul, Body, Energy fields, chakras and/or DNA.
6. Accessing from another person's Records with permission (as a personal guidance or healing) session.

A Stream Into and From the Akashic Records

When I teach a class on how to access the Akashic Records, we practice the process of journeying up and out of the body with our consciousness. We start the class or the journey process itself with a 'Grand Invocation' prayer. This humbly announces and actually commands the ethers to open and align themselves in ways that call the Ascended Masters and spiritual helpers, including the Keeper of the Records to all be present and create a stream, window or doorway into the ever-after. We then move into a guided and hypnotic style of relaxation and meditation, and as we become more and more relaxed, we become open and more present to the spirit guides which have gathered around us in the Invocation prayer. This synergistic conjuring brings silent open passage ways for the Soul and the mind to have an experience with the masters, guides, angelics and ancestors in the Akashic Records and the energy of the pathway itself which leads us into the Records.

Pathways are created into and from the Records as we endeavor to create. All things creative, whether art, music, poetry or sculpture. What other things would you consider to be creative? The sciences, mathematics, numbers, and geometries are all given to us from the Akashic Records. Ancient **Mandalas** or **Yantrams** for meditation, tantra and energy techniques were streamed from the Records into the 3D material world by way of a deep connection to these streams of creativity. Building, design, and architecture, writing, dance, and holistic medicines are all 'considerations' we have dreamed into existence. So in essence everything we do is creative. This is our nature in mind, body and spirit both individually and as a collective. Often many of us have thought if we could only paint, draw or play an instrument then we would be doing something creative. We are a creative race and it is our nature to be naturally creative. Everything in life is a creative process and uses creative energies. By simply acknowledging the thousands of hours that went into making an ancient tapestry or a new pair of socks; the textures, colors, patterns and materials you are aligning yourself with creativity. Driving, working and going to school to learn all involve creative processes within the brain, body, heart and soul of an individual. At this level we become more aware and we become more creative with everyday life in general. We become more alive! If you tap into the Akashic field of creativity then you will naturally start to expand your thoughts into new ideas. It's a never ending, self perpetuating stream of thoughts, words, forms, visions, ideas, and physically created art forms and objects which is always constantly creating itself through you as you. Simply amazing! If you are an artist you know what I'm talking about. If you've been driven to continue pondering what color and finish you want to paint a chair or a room you know what I'm talking about. The creative process itself can go on and on. It's never ending and always beginning. This has given us all the great art over the centuries of time.

Akashic Field of Energy

The ancient adepts from different cultures who practiced this art of divining information from the Akasha developed various ways of using their senses. In these ancient times when technology and progress were different in it's various stages of development these techniques were viewed as an art form, a science, as spiritual rituals and even as a spiritual technology, if you will.

The Egyptian priests connected with the afterlife and the Akasha through the Great Hall of Records. There are two important references that overlay each other.

A. There was a physical geometric power source set up by the priests with the help of off world intelligence to balance and restructure the energy fields and magnetic poles of the planet.

B. The pyramids were also a natural key for this as they used their own geometric shape to bring down cosmic energy to stabilize the group mind field of the remnants of civilization that had failed after the earth passed through the last photonic shifting of the poles.

As the earth passed through the photonic light beam shining out from the Great Central Sun with the 'changing of the guard' and completion of the previous age, the new age now began as the grand astrological cyclical rotation and procession of the ages took place.

The Geometric power source or hidden temple hall included two sources used to restructure, balance and bring back on line the group mind field and every human mind field on the planet. I see one such chamber as a physical geometric template of what we now know as the Kabbalah diagram. This chamber was made for reorganizing the DNA of the human race through energetic sessions with the priestly class and the royal families.

The other power source was a great collection of 12 concentric crystal spheres, one within the other which vibrated or resonated tones of energy for all of creation to sync into harmony with. Similar devices and chambers were also used in Atlantis for a myriad of different creative functions. So there is the physical recognition of actual power sources in a place governing or synthesizing creation including the human mind fields, human chakras, and balancing humans and the planet energetically so that the enjoined Souls as humans could continue to have the experience of incarnation here on the planet.

This geometrically driven Hall of Records is a physical representation to a much greater etheric Hall of Records, the Akasha or Akashic Records contained in the living field of the earth. The ancient Egyptian priests would use meditations and rituals containing techniques for opening the senses or the *upper openings of the body*. They called this interestingly: **Art**. So as they opened the upper openings of the body they would not only travel to the celestial Akasha, as we think of a direct stream of astral projection, they would merge with the field of the Akasha by expanding their fields and delicately holding the intention for the Akasha to come down and to merge with them through the 'upper openings of the body.' This is likened to ancient forms of manifesting which involve holding a direct individual intention for creation and simultaneously letting it go and moving into oneness or expansion into the fields of creation. There are several versions of this.

This ties together the idea of the physical manifestation of the power sources and their connection into the cosmic etheric version of the Akashic Records contained within all creation and, specifically for our studies here, within the etheric field of the planet. They used star gates both physically and by way of the Akasha to project to other star systems in meditation for the passing of people's souls into the afterlife and to bring souls to the earth from different star systems to Atlantis. Other sources were implemented in these practices, techniques and procedures such as gold jewelry, crystals, and tinctures which were also used later in Egypt.

In essence it is possible to expand one's field and merge with the Akashic field. As you merge out with your energy fields, senses, mental intention, body awareness, and soul, the Akasha like wise will merge with you. So you are traveling into it and it is traveling or responding to meet you.

Accessing the Records from deep within Mother Earth

Akashic Energy can also be accessed from the Earth itself. Each planet has it's own set of Akashic Records as does each solar system and other celestial bodies, galaxies, etc. The Earth is a sentient being. It is very much alive and is the living 3 dimensional yet multidimensional and organically natural elemental being that the Akasha is part of. The Akasha (father sky) is in the Etheric field of the planet (mother earth) and as so, they represent that first stage of a duality. The earth is primarily feminine energy or Yin and the sky is primarily masculine energy or Yang. Though the etheric field of the planet (sky) referred to as positive/masculine is actually the energetic, and auric field of this feminine planet. So as a result this part of the sky's atmosphere is Yin (feminine) as well. This etheric field supports the planet through the suspension of the upper atmospheres and also permeates deep within the earth connecting with the elemental energies and primordial elements of the earth herself.

Let us remember the ying and yang mandala of Asian descent. The Black and White swirling in a concentric circle with opposing or alternating black & white circles within the 2 larger colors making up the circle. In some depictions there is another yin/yang illustrated within the circle of each opposite color dot of the black and white swirls illustrating the infinite balance and order of earth, sky, positive and negative, male, female and so on. See Fig. 1, 2

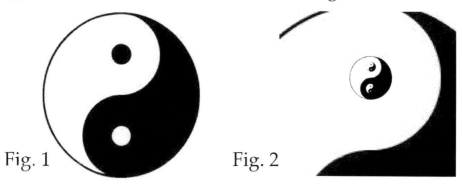

Fig. 1   Fig. 2

Ying Yang examples:

Husband-Wife, Sun-Moon, Fire-Water, Father-Son, Mother-Daughter, Light-Darkness, Heaven-Earth

In Ancient Hindu **tantras** or techniques we find the Tattvas. A set of archetype symbols composed of primary colors and shapes which represent Earth, Water, Fire, Air and the fifth tattva is Akasha, the composition of all the other elements together. These powerful and simple archetype symbols are used to influence certain parts of the intellect, emotions, soul, and body in the world. See Fig. 3, 4.

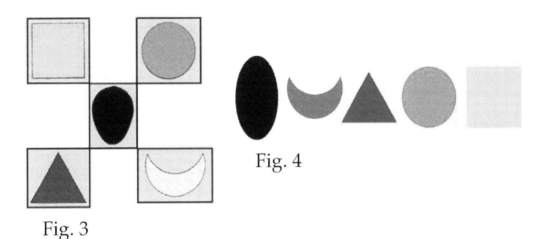

Fig. 4

Fig. 3

There are many stories of the Inner Earth and the amazing 'other worldly' attributes to this amazing planet.

In other parts of the world such as with the Indo-European and Celtic tribes, their knowledge of the inner earth and the elemental kingdom was expansive. In ancient times when magic was a science, energy was used to 'see' by the seers, to 'source' by the sourcers, and for a myriad of other uses including gathering of knowledge, reading the stars, healing the people, and even conjuring or creation of beings composed of elemental energy from the earth itself to guard villages, forests, crops and sacred ceremonial places. Directly calling on the forces of nature or the elements to affect powerful change.

Wizards such as Merlin used these energies to connect deep within the earth and was known for using the forces of nature for a multitude of changeful happenings and manifestations including the creation of Stonehenge.

It is possible to travel *down* deep into the earth as well as *up* into the sky to access deep levels of conscious awareness. Many different hidden truths, secrets and ancient knowledge lay hidden in the Records of Earth waiting for us to look into it and to experience it in a more full body sentient journey deep into the great mother. We may uncover things of our own nature which are more primal or elemental. Things that we may have been in a naturally hidden and primal involuntary denial about. We may also see, witness or connect with some of these elemental earth creatures here in 'middle earth' or even Merlin himself. Imagine seeing Druidic keepers walking through the caverns calling up pure light from their staffs to show the way through hidden tunnels underground.

Accessing from Another Person's Records with their permission for Guidance or Healing

As you continue to practice reading the Records you may want to give sessions for others whether practicing with friends or reading professionally. It is a good idea to always ask permission from the person you are reading for instead of just snooping around. Snooping may cause skewed information and be more akin to the ego and psychic activity such as mind reading and connecting through the astral plane. Accessing the Akashic Records for another person by opening their 'Book of Life' is an excellent way to practice the technique of reading and focusing consciously your awareness within the vast Akasha.

Each and every one of us has our own 'Book of Life'

within the Akashic Records. This is a stored personal book and record of files for each Soul's journey including all the lifetimes of that Soul. So if John Smith was born, lived his life and then passed, as the Soul left his body, depending on the Soul's purpose, let's say that same Soul re-incarnated as Sally Davis. Then we, as readers, and as a reference point you would go to the same Book of Life for both incarnations. You would not need to search continually, you would simply connect through that person as they have given you permission to do so.

Is permission always needed? It is best, however it depends largely on what your intentions are. If it is for the purpose or competition, personal gain or confrontation then you could simply visit the lower vibrations of the astral plane for this kind of stuff.

What are your intentions? Are they for the highest good? Are they to help others heal or know who they are? To learn more spiritually and in turn help others to awaken to a better way of living? Then by very nature of your purpose you can have access the Records or an individuals's Book of Life because you develop a relationship with the higher realms in the understanding that you are truly here to help and the information is given or naturally streamed to you. So let's say someone was in the hospital and unconscious or in poor health. If your intention is to help them heal, you can take a look and see what the injury or sickness is about and then pray for them or send healing energy so you can help them in the best way possible. If someone has passed on you can access their Records or simply open to the Akasha and guide them to it. I have had the opportunity of working with others who have crossed over in leading them into the Akashic Records so they can get an idea of what to do next. When someone goes out of body they could be disoriented and searching. Often this is the case.

A person's spirit guides and/or guardian angels can help them find the Records. Family members and ancestors often assist in this way. We find our way into the passages of our Book of Life where it is harmonically written what we have learned, what our lessons are for the future lives and what we have accomplished, or our missed opportunities.

You will sharpen your Akashic skills by reading for others. In some ways it is generally easier to read for others than it is for yourself. We will discuss this in another section.

Sometimes you will get information about others that you can't do anything with because your natural psychic abilities are increased with your Akashic practice. It may cause disruptions in someone's life or family were you to naturally bring forth unasked for information. As my grandfather used to say: "Unasked for advice goes as far as the hat brim". Use discernment and discretion when communicating what you see, feel and come to know.

Ocean Seaboard Healing with a Staff
Summer 2013 Seal Beach, CA

When we visit the Great Hall of Records it should be done so in reverence. We are asking to be shown the ways that it all works. We are asking to be shown the understanding of our own Soul's purpose. With great knowledge comes great responsibility.

Chapter 5

Interpretation of the Akashic Symbols

Within the Akashic Records exist hidden levels of information. Is it Purposely hidden? That is to be discussed. One of the special qualities to this grand library of information is that it has special light energy codes of holographic symbols which translate to us on a soul level through the higher mind.

We can find these special **cuneiform** symbols deep within the layers of the Akashic Records. They come to us through visions we have of archtypal images of the library filled with books, scrolls, or written records. We sooner or later come to see a symbol(s) which represents our Soul, or a special symbol that's transmitting energy to us from the higher realms of the Akasha. When we have a special experience of connecting with sacred soul signature symbols from within the library or our personal book, special transmissions of energy take place. We are being shown these symbols for a reason. It opens us up and helps us to connect within ourselves and to the world on a deeper level. It may help us heal certain physical maladies, give us energy, healing of past life events, or to be clear indicators of karmas.

As we journey into the Akashic Records or any other type of visionary work including astral projection, lucid dreaming or clairvoyance, we may be looking for a profound experience. This can be a double edged sword. We should have a pure intention with our journey work, and yet, hoping for a profound experience can keep it from happening through subtle levels of anticipation being directed by the ego. We'll get into just how subtle these blocks or 'conflicts' can be and how they can keep us from having a visionary or sensory experience. As we let go, relax and release any investments we may have in the process or let go of the outcome, we may start to have experiences such as tapping into these soul symbols. When we are doing visionary reconnaissance work a certain symbol or geometric pattern that we tap into can bring us continual moments of observation and information. This is often accompanied by energy sensations which may be openings, expansions, clearings or healings. These very subtle moments of accessing the Soul Symbols can hold great keys to our journey, healing and understanding.

You may also see, experience or access other more familiar symbols from the earth plane which are already known, written or illustrated. This is also an opportunity for insight. Stop, look and listen. It may hold a key that gets you to the next doorway in life. This is happening at very subtle and deep levels. As you intuit the messages from the symbols you hold the key to the next door in front of you. It could be a life experience, a new job, a relationship or any of the wonderful colorful adventures that make up our lives. By working at this level you have opened a new pathway of understanding both of yourself and the cosmic highway of information that's available to you.

Has this information been hidden from us? In a word, yes. It is hidden by the mysterious nature of its dynamics that helps us to search it out and connect at deeper levels to have a richer experience. There have also been times for society in the world when we as a race have experienced duality or cosmic separation at it's peak. In these times it has been harder for humanity to feel a connection with each other, the earth, spiritual world or even a sense of oneness with each other. Likewise in other times we do feel the connections as we move into the grand procession of cosmic unity. These are the times when it is easier and more natural for us to tap into our intuitive nature and see into the ethers. To be able to use the ancient tools of sacred wisdom for understanding higher levels of truth.

You will naturally know if you see a symbol that is new or foreign to you. Maybe it is a known symbol from another race, culture or religion. Maybe it is Latin or another language you may need to research in order to find it's reference. With some of the symbols, you will just have an instant or inner knowing that they are not from any written language and are emanating energy as you will feel it. As you view and perceive these symbols you can ask to be shown the meaning they hold in translation for you. This is the point at which you start to build an energetic story, a new way of communicating messages at deeper levels of understanding.

The Akashic Living Language of Light is akin to the Angelic language though not the same. They are both uniquely different. The one thing that they have in common is energy. They both emanate energy. The angelic language has been used by adepts, alchemists and esoteric spiritual groups to call or conjure the angels. To bring their energy to the earth plane for a specific blessing, manifestation, protection or healing. **Alchemists** such as **St. Germain** and **John Dee**, or groups such as the **Rosicrucians** and the **Templars** used angelic writings, markings or symbols to designate their places of ritual or messages including protection. One thing that has been questionable with the rites of conjuring the angelic realm is that sometimes those who were involved with invoking these energies did not fully understand enough of who or what they were conjuring. At times some have searched blindly for power or simply to have an experience. Such was the case with John Dee. Often when the conjurers of rituals are uncertain or invitingly too open to having any experience of energy at all, then calamities can occur and a mixed bag or a cast of both light and dark beings can come through the ritual. Know what or who you are working with and have a purpose or focus. The Akashic doesn't not hold or embody the same energies as the angelic realm, so there is no need for concern, though, there will be remote reference to it.

There were great splits or conflicts that occurred in the angelic realm. Universal laws and vibrations being compromised. Much like the lawyer who makes his living from looking more deeply into the ins and outs of using the laws and even getting past them, this also occurs quite heavily in the upper realms. A great battle between light and dark continues in other dimensions among other things.

The Akasha and it's language have remained hidden or esoteric for good reason. It holds the universal keys to creation of this world and record of the signatures of every soul that has visited the earth plane both physically or etherically. When we visit the Great Hall of Records it should be done so in reverence. We are asking to be shown the ways that it all works. We are asking to be shown the understanding of our own Soul's purpose. The harmonic signature which makes us unique and has created all of the unique attributes and life path situations that make us who we are. This is a special place and like any other sacred temple whether physical or etheric, it should be treated as such. With special treatment comes the assurance that the knowledge, intentions and everything surrounding the Akasha will remain pure. With great knowledge comes great responsibilty. As we hold this intention and understanding, the idea is not to create subtle road blocks of grandiosity, the idea is to resonate with the silent and vibratory clarity and purity of the act of connecting and for what reasons.

As you look at the symbols they can be moving with energy or streaming with light. If they are stationary that is fine too. As you look into the symbols, study them closely and listen, watch and feel for the message or vibration of the symbols. If you remain vigilant while 'looking in' and listening the answer will surely come by the simple reason that you are already being shown the information. Again, stop, look and listen. Be silent and watch.

Let's take a look at some examples of the Akashic language. Some or all of the symbols may look close to other words, letters or symbols in that they are the vibratory language that all written languages come into form from. When you are divining for the symbols or language you may get other languages such as angelic language or an alien dialect. Simply ask 'What is the origin of this dialect?' Then accept and trust your answer. It is connected through the Akasha and may be that you've previously had an incarnation or an incident with one of these cultures and that is why you're being shown the dialect. As we are engaged in this soul level reconnaissance work our results are subject to comparison by others in the field who may be getting the same or similar styles of writings. The style of writings may vary from person to person even as a person opens to great bodies of a certain writing style. At this point you may look at a body of writing and be able to get a vibration from it, whether angelic, alien, ancient or Akashic. It is All streaming through the Akashic Records and this is one reason the Akashic is so vast.

As you look at some of the symbols, whether here with examples, or as you do your inner inquiry work of allowing and listening for the story, messages, ideas and words as they flow to you. Build on it and let it unfold for you. This is a subtle area where the imagination and the intuition are overlapped. As you build the story it is speaking to you.

The symbols and language have a certain style that you will come to recognize when you see it from certain channelled writings, your own inquiries or in channelled art forms such as paintings. It can also be uniquely specific to you with it's own special style as you learn to connect with it and it unfolds for you and speaks to you in it's meaningful story based messages. We will go into more depth and detail in the Work Book but for now, let's look at a few symbols and their stories of transfigurative meanings:

Symbol 1

Man Stepping Forward or Standing, Foundations, Moving Forward, masculine energies symbolized by upright pyramid,/ triangle moving forward - pyramid/ triangle pointing to the right. Foundation symbolized by the base.

Symbol 2

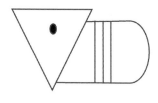

In recognizing Feminine Energy balance there are 3 steps. Downward triangle - vessel or female energy. line passing from and back to the triangle represents a continuing or moving to and from triangle. 3 vertical lines = 3 steps to balance, conscious focus and the dot equals focus or point of reference.

Symbol 3

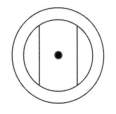

Creating a stable and balanced expression of Unity with a central focus.

Symbol 4

The expression of two which are uniquely different or even opposing. The enjoinment could symbolize challenge or working together. Two different aspects or outlooks of the same nature.

Symbol 5

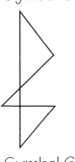

Power of the light moving through all things. Synergy

Symbol 6

A fountain giving or pouring forth. A vessel receiving or catching as it moves down to settle or level

Symbol 7

A snake or serpent of transformation moving into new territories. The 3 mounds represent new territory.

Symbol 8

At the surface level and below the surface level, evenly expanded over moments there are balanced levels of being.

Symbol 9

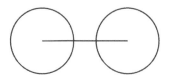

Travel. Two destinations connected by a straight line.

Symbol 10

Relationships are feminine in nature and crosses through all things.

Symbol 11

Crossing over we start climbing again, learning, remembering again through the many mountains of time.

Symbol 12

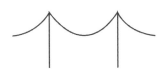

Water or waves of consciousness are moving as the depth is realized.

Symbol 13

Space - Time. The more natural state of it's movement.

Symbol 14

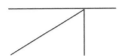

Coming up to the surface and balance.

Symbol 15

Eclipse of the Self. The light body self and the shadow body self as you look out and focus on the light source over the event horizon or the external world and coming events. Recognition of the selves by the reference of viewing.

Symbol 16

From Oneness to duality. From the source light of Creator God down to earth.

Symbol 17

The Duality within the Oness.

Symbol 18

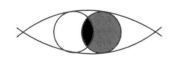

The dark and light of perception. Elipse of 2 worlds within the eye of the beholder.

Some of these symbols might seem astonishingly simple. The interesting energy behind them as they were seen from within the inner vision or mind's eye into the Akashic Records is that they are glowing with energy which indicated movement, synergy and a translative message or energy of knowing what they mean as they communicate a story to the viewer. The symbols came from a central archtypal base though can also be stylistic to the individual viewer.

As I sat down to bring through and translate a few symbols for the book, I might add that when you are in the space of connecting with the symbols, they will have much more meaning, energy and feeling when you are 'in there' and connected with them. They will speak to you in ways that might be challenging to re-communicate. They are communicating energetic information to you in that moment which may have much knowledge translated by ways of simple knowings and feelings. That's why it is important to write down what you see and keep a journal of it. As you continue the practice it will continue to unfold and bring through more profound messages and information. So continue your creative mystical visual journeys into the Akashic Records!

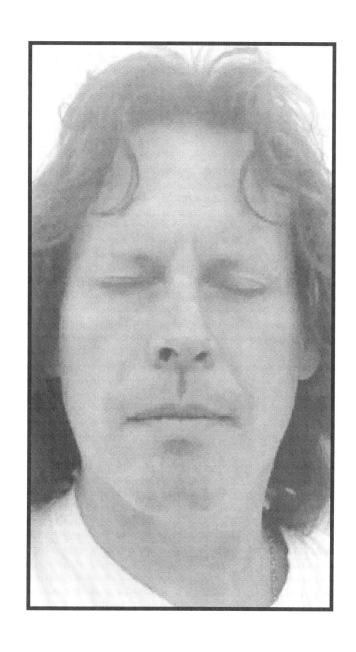

Learn to practice
Meditation & Prayer as a way
to continually contact the Divine.

The earthbound Gate Keepers are important players in this story because they relay the knowledge and understanding of the Records to the world as well as use the Records to intuit information for others who seek to know themselves.

Chapter 6

Keepers of the Records

There are beings within the higher realms and in physical form who have agreed to be watchers, keepers and guardians of the Akashic Records. As the Records are a way station for the Souls either visiting the planet earth for the first time or checking in between reincarnations, there are spiritual guides who lead us to the Records even if we are not familiar with them. For many of us we have been to the Records so many times between lifetimes that we start to develop a subconscious memory or knowing of the energy signature of the Records.

During times when there are life altering situations such as a near death experience, a deep coma or illness or other events of great change, guardian angels or arc angels may intervene as they are watchful and interactive over the light and dark situations and happenings with humans. They were made by Creator God with instructions to guide, heal and interact with humans from the higher dimensions. As they cross over from the angelic realm into other dimensions much in a way we would consider time travel or the folding of space, they can protectively and watchfully guide the way for a person's soul, mind and consciousness to enter into an interpretation of the Akashic Records which speaks to them, sometimes familiar, common or very different in order to translate the knowledge, wisdom or messages that need to be communicated to an individual which helps them to have an experience and to understand what their agreements might be. What were their karmas or connections to a life changing illness? The signature of their soul allows them to integrate with messages of who they are, who they have been and possibly why a current situation is happening. This is truly divinely guided work. As they look into the Records and experience the other side, they may see the possibility of crossing over and leaving the earth plane or they may feel the need to return for some unfinished business (karma) and the natural unfolding of their life and the events presented to them for a response which brings wisdom to the soul of that person.

True location of the Records remains hidden within the higher dimensions, much like other ancient and sacred places such as **Shamballa,** which was known to have existed between dimensions like the Akashic Records. You may think of the hidden qualities as a natural self protection mode of that which is pure knowledge. A special place that has a vibration that welcomes the Ascended Masters, the Souls of humanity and many other spiritual beings.

There is a more easily or locally accessed version of the Records available as an astral experience. To have any Akashic experience at all, even with the astral version of the Records, will have the signature and information of the Akasha. The astral version is a simplified working model of the Records which many have an experience of. Much like the advanced version or 'upper chamber' of the Records much information can be accessed and there are many experiences to be had. Your Soul, mind and consciousness will be naturally guided to have the experience which is perfect for you. Energy can be translated there from the higher dimensions to us on the inner plane and also down into our mental planes and physical reality.

When visiting the Akashic Hall of Records you may meet the actual Keeper of the Records. A very astute and friendly guardian and gate keeper of the Knowledge of All that Is. This Keeper may have an other worldly appearance streaming with pure energy as a very tall angelic-like figure or may even appear in 'human form'. There are some of us who have worked in the Records between lives to be of service, study the Records and to assist others who are coming to seek understanding of their earthbound journeys or to instruct new souls on what to look forward to in the colorful movie of the 3 dimensional world as well as being 'way showers' for those coming to and from different dimensions and star systems.

The **Ascended Masters** are also Keepers of the Records in that they have complete access to these great banks of knowledge in order to assist others by showing them the way and coming to the Hall of Wisdom frequently. The Ascended Masters have meeting places which are located between dimensions, much like the Akashic Records and Shamballa.

There are certain people who have incarnated upon the earth who are entrusted with the knowledge of the Akashic system. These people are often referred to as Gate Keepers. They are gate keepers because they understand the dynamics of the higher realms. They also understand the divinity and the special quality which the Akashic holds unique to all others. Some keepers after many spiritual lifetimes have come to understand the special unique vibrational quality of the Records and have a strength of will for right usage and service to others with the unique gifts of looking into the Akasha and the individual Books of Life.

Can you imagine coming to Earth and living a life and

then passing into the higher dimensions of the afterlife with your intellect still intact and experiencing an amazing hall filled with books and scrolls containing all knowledge and record of any soul who has ever visited the earth plane? You might be so enthused that you would want to stay and help out, learning, studying and filing away records as they are written. I hope they put in a coffee shop soon...and snack bar! What's that you say? Oh yes, that's why we're here on earth, of course. Currently over 6 billion people on the planet all writing an experience in their own Book of Life with every thought, word and deed. Billions even trillions more souls surrounding the Earth waiting for the chance of incarnation and yet here we are having our multi-lifetime experiences. To be living a life in human form as a soul is in and of itself the true miracle and one of grace.

The earthbound Gate Keepers are important players in this story because they relay the knowledge and understanding of the Records to the world as well as use the Records to intuit information for others who seek to know themselves. Without these 'way showers' we would have only mysteries and myths from ancient cultures to research our currently fragmented earth history.

This is in part why the Akashic Records exist. So that we all may know ourselves at the greatest possible capacity. In the clearest moments of understanding we can get knowledge from another time and place or lifetime that helps us expand our view of ourself in relation to others and the world around us. When we find the Records while still in human form during our earthbound life we can have the wonderful and powerful knowing experience of completing spiritual, emotional and intellectual work which before we would only have the experience of between lifetimes as we would naturally visit the Records. We can also retrieve clearer information regarding Earth's history and historical events as we become more spiritually tuned through our personal healing work including the work done in the Records.

A family member or an ancestor may come for us at our time of passing and lead us into the Records. Now on the other side, if they are still available to us in the astral plane they may have knowledge of the Records from their own visits or helping others, and again assist us the way they would have while still in human form.

We may even have the experience of meeting Creator God Himself at our Book of Life as THE Keeper of the Records. It really depends on our personal experiences here and beyond and even our preference as to how everything is shown to us.

Our Guardian Angels and the Arc Angels, Ascended Masters, The Keeper of the Records, Ancestors, Creator God and the earthly human Gate Keepers can all be keepers or guardians of the Akashic Records as they hold sacred space for us as way showers into the multidimensional movie, pictures, feelings and experiences that make our journey across time and space to earth and beyond.

© 2012 Bill Foss

Copper Christ

30" x 40" acrylic on etched copper

Guided Visualization Prayer

Grand Invocation

*D*ear Creator God, Planetary Logos, Mother Earth Spirit, Divine Celestial Holy Spirit, Realms of Pan, Angels and Arc Angels of the Light of God, Ascended Masters Kuthumi, El Morya, Quin Yin, Djwal Kuhl, Sanat Kumara, Deserkara, St. Germain and the Holy I Am Presence, Serapis Bay, Buddha, Sananda, Jeshua, Mary of Magdala, Mary of Sephoris, Great Spirit, Native American Spirit Guides, Animal Familiars, Holy Tao, Babaji, Merlin, Sai Baba, 144,000 Bodhisattvas incarnate. The Green Tara, the White Tara and the 22 Tara (including the hidden Tara), Ganesha, Lakshmi, Saraswati, Divine Personal Spirit Guides and Keepers of the Akashic Records. Divine Healers Teachers, Spirits and Friends be with us as we connect into the Akashic Records to fulfill the greatest instruction from Creator, "Know Thyself" We call all of the Great, Great Ones to stand around us in this Sacred Circle as we now call forth our Family Members and Ancestors, Relatives and Bloodline to join the circle. We call forth the Council of 12, the Elohim, we call forth the Star Elders, Pleadian, Andromidan, Arcturian, and Sirian Leagues and High Councils of Light, we call forth our own Soul, our Soul Group, Our Over Soul and Monad. We call forth the Atlantian High Priests, the Earth Keepers and the Shamans of the world. And Now with Creator God's Hands reaching down into our energy body we ask for his direct compassionate healing powers to transform our life as we sit quietly for a moment and receive Healing, Blessings and Clearing. Negative energies are released from our fields in gentle layers as we sit quietly and allow the release to happen. Karmas, any psychic chords or entities are all cleared, healed, released and forgiven. As we continue to allow the healing process to take place. One or more of the masters or your spirit guides including family members may step forward and bring messages or a dialogue about the healing that's taking place now. As we're connect by a golden thread to the Akashic Records we ask the Keeper of the Records to bring down any information that's beneficial from our Book of Life to the Sacred Circle we continue to receive. As we let the transmissions continue for as long as we have allotted for our healing to take place at this time from within the Sacred Circle of the Grand Invocation, we continue until we feel complete or the healing and clearing energy has slowed to a close. You will know when the process is complete. Thank You Divine Healers, Spirits, Teachers and Friends for your powerful Healing, Clearing and Blessing this day. I ask that you continue to hold sacred space for my healing, In Gratitude and Full Faith, It Is Done, Blessings, Om, Peace, Amen.

If you have extended time you can use to experience this method of connection and healing you may feel a draw to do this prayer and healing procedure more than once. You may feel a bit altered as you finish and move around because energies that have been with you for a very long time have been removed as you have just experienced a powerful clearing from Creator God and the masters. Drink some water, eat something for grounding, fresh air and going for a walk may be in order.

Blessings to You in your Personal Sacred Healing.

Mary of Magdala

© 2012 Bill Foss

36" x 48" acrylic on etched copper

Akashic Healing Angels CD & Download

As you bring this energy into your mind field and project it back out around the body, you are manifesting your physical reality as you perceive it with your senses.

Guided Journey 1

The Akashic Healing Angels

*R*elax and just start to take some deep breaths. Breathing in slowly and out, as you sit straight up in a chair with your feet on the floor in front of you. You spine straight, your neck and head straight. Relaxed and at ease. Palms are on your thighs or knees facing up and open. And as you continue to breathe in and out slowly, picture the pineal gland in the center of your head, in the center of your brain. And as you breath in, see the pineal gland glowing with golden energy.

As you breath in....and as you breath out, it's pulsating with this golden energy. As you continue to breath deeply and relax see now the colors of pink, white and gold. These are the colors of healing. See them pulsating around the pineal gland in the center of the head in the center of your brain. And as it gets brighter and brighter this soft glow of pink, white and gold energies expands out around your head to form a healing halo of pink, white and gold energy.

Picture now a golden thread coming from the pineal gland as it comes up through the top of your head and straight up through the ceiling. And this golden thread of energy, follow it up as it goes straight up. Up, up & away. Up into the night sky. Into the heavens as you follow it straight up. See the stars glowing and twinkling and the heavenly bodies of the celestial cosmos with all of the clouds. Following it up, up, up & away, up, up & away. As you continue to follow this golden thread up and you come into the stratosphere. Following the golden thread up through the white cloud banks. Up, up & away.

And as you gently feel a pressure on the top of your head you find yourself coming through the floor of the Grand Hall of the Akashic Records. This beautiful grand temple, the storehouse of the consciousness of all humanity. Before you now see the Keeper of the Records, a very tall being glowing and emanating energy. To his left and right are two smaller beings. These are the Akashic Healing Angels. They are white light beings with rainbow colored wings and rainbow colored auras or energy fields with a very joyful demeanor.

As you notice them, they step forward and they step over to you and as they're just about to come close to you, they slip through the floor and follow the golden thread down, down, down. Down through the clouds, down through the celestial bodies, down through the cosmic night skies. The two healing angels of the Akasha, these white light energy beings with their golden rainbow wings and their rainbow auras following the golden thread down, down, down back down to earth. And they come through the ceiling following the golden thread and they hover as they land very softly and gently one on each side of your physical body. The male on the right and the female on the left.

And as they put their hands out in front of you over the head and your crown chakra, their hands become a blur of energy as they are rewiring your neural net and the neural pathways in the mind, in the brain, in the mental field, in the mind field. You may feel the energy sensations around your head. as their hands are doing the work and they're healing your neural pathways, the old decision making processes that no longer serve you, the old emotional triggers, the old habits and habitual thinking, the old laborious ways of thinking. These are being diminished. The wiring pathways are being disconnected. And as they are reaching into the mental mind field they are placing new cosmic elemental building blocks of energy from the cosmic Universal down into the subtle bodies, into the mind field. There are new elements to utilize, cosmic building blocks of pure brand new cosmic energy, available there for your mind field and your thought process.

As you bring this energy into your mind field and project it back out around the body manifesting your physical reality as you perceive it with your senses. The Akashic Healing Angels, their hands are working very quickly as a white blur of light and as they reach around the body, they may make connections down into the heart, into the lungs, and back up to the brain, into different areas, different muscle areas, the back, the structure, the nervous system, the organs, the glands of the body, the legs, the feet, the hands, the arms.

Wherever healing is needed in the nervous system, the circulatory system, the muscular system, the skeletal system, and the epidermis. They are healing the neural pathways of the mind. And as they have placed these new cosmic elemental building blocks of universal chi into the mind field and rewiring the neural pathways, the neural net, creating new pathways for:

HOPE, PEACE, LOVE, UNDERSTANDING, TRUST, DIVINE LOVE, PURE JOY, BALANCED HUMAN LOVE, CREATIVITY, HUMOR, LAUGHTER, INTIMACY, MEDITATION, EXERCISE, REST, FAMILY TIME, CONSCIOUS AWARENESS, KNOWING, HEALING, ABUNDANCE, PROSPERITY, FORTITUDE, RIGHT ACTION OF THOUGHT, WORD & DEED.

And as the Akashic Healing Angels are rewiring the neural

pathways and you're feeling the energy around your head and in your mental field. As they have been doing a grand amount of work, their hands now slow down, they come to a slow pace and they both take a step back from your physical body. And as their feet become light, these white light Akashic Angels with their rainbow wings and rainbow auras start to float back up. They float back up following the golden thread up through the ceiling, up, up & away, back up, up & away through the night sky following the golden thread through the cosmic stars. See the stars twinkling and glimmering with soft white light. Following the golden thread back up through the clouds. As they come through the floor of the Grand Hall of the Akashic Records. They walk back to take their place on each side of this grand being emanating energy, the Keeper of the Records. They all three give you a subtle smile, a peaceful gaze as they gently bow letting you know that you are welcome here for healing anytime you wish as often as you wish. You give thanks and wave back. You take a step forward as you slip through the floor and follow this golden thread back down to earth following the golden thread down, down, down through the clouds, through the celestial bodies, the twinkling glimmering stars. Through the night sky as you follow it back down, down, down. Back down, down, down to earth all the way back. Back down to the room that you're in, back down into your physical body. Feel yourself, your mind, your super conscious and your subconscious minds all blending back in together as one as your neural pathways have now been healed. Think about different things and test out the thought process. Wiggle your fingers and toes, take a deep breath. Give thanks for the healing time with the Akashic Records and Thank You so dearly and divinely for doing the work, may you be healed.

Om, Peace, Amen.

Arc Angel Uriel

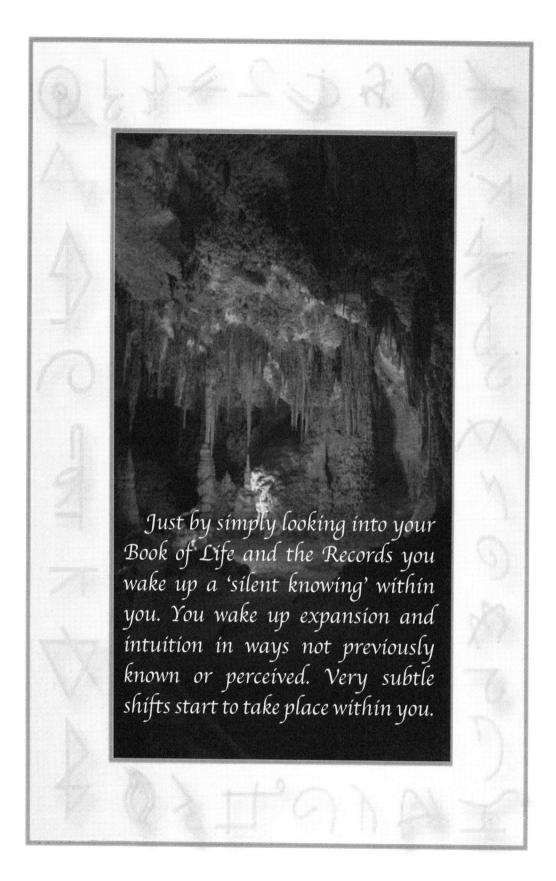

Just by simply looking into your Book of Life and the Records you wake up a 'silent knowing' within you. You wake up expansion and intuition in ways not previously known or perceived. Very subtle shifts start to take place within you.

Chapter 7
Knowledge
Wisdom &
Philosophy

Knowledge - Facts, information, and skills acquired by a person through experience or education; the theoretical or practical understanding of a subject. Awareness or familiarity gained by experience of a fact or situation.

Wisdom - The quality of having experience, knowledge, and good judgment; the quality of being wise. The soundness of an action or decision with regard to the application of such experience, knowledge, and good judgment. The body of knowledge and principles that develops within a specified society or period.

Philosophy - The study of the fundamental nature of knowledge, reality, and existence, especially when considered as an academic discipline. A set of views and theories of a particular philosopher concerning such study or an aspect of it. The study of the theoretical basis of a particular branch of knowledge or experience: the philosophy of science. A theory or attitude held by a person or organization that acts as a guiding principle for behavior.

The Akashic Records, Akashic Library, Hall of Records, Book of Life or Sky Library are some of the names that have been given to this great store house of knowledge in the etheric energy field of the Earth, Which contains a record of all past, present, future events and all probable or optional future events along the event horizon. If you could have any information about any person, place, or thing in any past, present or future moment what would you do with it? We are all connected to the earth & sky through our energy fields, magnetically and physically and have access to visions at the level that we can move conflict, fear and stress out of the way and be able to journey or view with our full senses to experience events from past lives, insight into the reasons we have a current set of circumstances, insight for future events, and how to navigate more clearly and easily through life. We may want to look at historical events for storytelling or artistic reference. It is helpful to use an advanced balancing, harmonizing and relaxing meditation to get into the Records. This is a wonderful multidimensional guided journey of expanding up into the Akasha through guided symbols and imagery.

We go in and then we come out. This gives the mind a sense of order or a tangible pathway in order to deal with the etheric and expanded oneness of the process and once you learn to go there it will continually happen more easily and quickly for you.

The Akashic Records is a like the world wide web. You can find any information about any topic. We are all depositing information of thoughts, words and deeds into this 'Sky Library' constantly. Some of us have been exporting information from these great banks of knowledge, though, as everything collapses into unity or simplifies itself in the ethers and dimensions, we will all start having a natural simplified version of extra sensory perceptions or **E.S.P.**

Often you will get information that you can't do anything with. I say this because as you continue to practice reading the Akashic your psychic (mental) and intuitive (soul) abilities will continue to increase naturally also. You may get intuitive or psychic knowing about someone you know or anyone else in a moment of passing them on the street instantaneously just as easily as riding a bike. The challenge is that if you share with them things not known to them yet at the current time or share your knowledge of something they might secretly be involved with, you could be introducing conflict for them and for you. This 'conflict', for you, may interpret itself as a subconscious or subtle block that keeps you from fully accessing information in future moments. Not to mention different levels of karma (cause & effect) that could befall both parties.

For the other person it may involve fear, anger and a whole litany of thoughts that aren't really true including worry about someone else being able to know their every thought. This is why it's important to use good judgement and wording when getting information for others or about others and sharing it with them. Again remember the saying: 'With great power comes great responsibility.' You have the opportunity to see beyond the veil of physical reality into the ethers and access not only your own soul but all thoughts, words and actions of all lifetimes, as well as any events in history and possibilities for the future.

So again, I ask, If you could have any information about any person, place, or thing in any past, present or future moment what would you do with it? For what reasons would you use the knowledge? Could it be to know yourself at the deepest level by accessing your own past lives and viewing, feeling and accepting these previously hidden parts of you? This is a natural process of remembering and knowing the Self. There is nothing to get rid of or deny and only acceptance available to you. The acceptance of deeper levels of your True Self will come by viewing into these hidden parts of yourself while staying in an uninvested state of mind. By being present in the moment and viewing as personal experience or looking in from the outside to watch without conflict, you are silently acknowledging these hidden parts of yourself. What is needed to know yourself at a deeper level? What is needed to understand yourself or to heal yourself at a deeper level? The act of perception by way of the mind through inner vision on a soul level with zero emotional investment brings pure acceptance, acknowledgement, understanding and healing.

When these moments take place with these simple personal truths, past life moments, and even in-between lives or childhood memories are viewed, we can fully accept and understand them. As the moments come up to the surface, like any other healing or deep intuitive process, the key is to not become emotionally activated by what we see or experience.

This is the Healing Moment* It's that simple. You can experience the emotions, and that's an important sentient part of it. Though I say, be removed from it so that you are looking into the situations and emotions and you are experiencing and able to balance between looking remotely at the moments that the emotions were part of, and then being in that remote moment simultaneously experiencing the emotions first hand so you are in both places at once. The director and the actor.

However, in a typical modern response, we may react or respond emotionally, therefore placing a label or judgement on this part of ourself or the remote movie moments. In doing so we localize the energy bringing it into a suspended state of animation within ourselves. This now has the potential and capability to influence our goals, dreams and visions, our every day lives, our every moment from hidden subtle levels. It may stay hidden until we bring it up to the surface to respond or react to it in a situation during our day or life colored with inner and / or outer conflicts. This can really hold a person back in life from operating at their full potential.

This all points to what the great masters have been referring to over time - **Know Thyself**. We know our selves by understanding ourselves and we understand by observing ourselves at different levels and in different ways. This brings us self awareness. It help us to get in touch with who we really are. As simple as it may seem, it's these invisible things that may be so silent in life or harder to see. Looking into our own lives, whether past, present or future. The masters and great philosophers of our world have contemplated and come to find words and methods which they could communicate, demonstrate and share with others in hopes that we as a race would have the opportunity to experience pure simple Truth at a greater, deeper, clearer level. This Truth contains pure knowledge and information as pure clarity. It also is a bridge to often sought after happiness, simplicity, joy, love and prosperity.

To Thine Own Self be True. What's the interpretation of this statement? The true definition is the same as 'Know Thyself'. To be true or have a clear view of yourself. Notice how the perception of the statement changes.

So why is all this relevant to the Akashic Records? When we go into the Akashic Records we are literally also are going into our own Soul simultaneously. Akashic guided journey meditations will bring you directly into the center of the **wheel of life** to the hub or center which is the Soul. From this perspective you are now experiencing oneness as you start to look timelessly at other lifetimes without the partitions of the current life or the input of the waking senses.

This is the gift: As you look into the Akashic Records and your own Book of Life you are stepping into the Soul simultaneously and looking, perceiving and operating from it. You are in a super relaxed state to do this. Just by simply looking into your Book of Life and the Records you wake up a 'silent knowing' within you. You wake up expansion and intuition in ways not previously known or perceived. Very subtle shifts start to take place within you. You have opened the gateway to your Soul and for it's clear communication and streaming through the physical body into the 3 dimensional world.

The process and action of looking into the Akashic Records can clear out karma, heal your body, and heal your soul. That's quite a profound claim and it's the truth! We might say that after accessing such information that wisdom is gathered and shifts are made to happen for us. This is true as well. I'm talking about the actual act of viewing into the Records with the mind's eye, the senses and the soul. The actual act of looking will shift you. These are esoteric or hidden truths which have never been shared quite in this way. If you go to a guru or yogi, they will usually tell you to just do the exercise without asking why. This is common because they want the student to experience the full effect and find it for themselves. I believe in that way of teaching, though, I also believe that you will be quickened in your study of this material by 'knowing' the true inner workings and subtle dynamics that will be achieved in the outcomes of what is possible.

The dynamic of connecting to the portal to the Akashic, the act itself of viewing into the Records simultaneously pulls you into the Soul perspective which has the power and radiance to heal and lift you up in every way.

Quan Yin
Divine Mother of Compassion, Healing and Prosperity
24" x 36" Acrylic on Metal

As we go into the Records our stream and connection by way of natural, practiced or known means is bolstered or added to in subtle ways. That connection is remembered even more so if you can consciously direct yourself back to that momentary stream or experience.

Chapter 8

Psychic, Intuitive & the Akashic Records

Pyschic - Relating to or denoting faculties or phenomena that are apparently inexplicable by natural laws, especially involving **telepathy** or **clairvoyance**: psychic powers. A person appearing or considered to have powers of telepathy or clairvoyance. Of or relating to the mind. Bridge denoting a bid that deliberately misrepresents the bidder's hand, in order to mislead the opponents.

Intuitive - Using or based on what one feels to be true even without conscious reasoning; instinctive. Easy to use and understand. A person who is intuitive. Knowing which comes from the Soul.

Akashic Records - Higher forms of the psychic and intuitive processes. An etheric record of all things past present and future which gives a true source of information in relation to a Soul, person and their tendencies in order to know the self, transform, accept or heal. A repository of a person's lifetime which is accessed in the afterlife as a life review.

The Akashic Records can really be looked at in a **multidimensional** way. As we have stated previously, the actual act of aquiring Akashic information can be similar to gathering information from or through the astral realm psychically. It operates as a field, a non-location location or localized energetic destination. Psychic work is often compared to Akashic reading. In a general format where multiple modalities are shared, such as a metaphysical fair or conference featuring multiple practitioners, the Akashic may be just another modality, or mode of inquiry. In this view it is put into a box in the mind and limited to a finite expression. It is localized. The true nature, for those who care to know, is that everything is linked to the Akasha. The tables, chairs, crystals, incense, the fair, and all the readers and healers. All the clients and their life experiences, and the psychic activity and healing energy itself are all part of the Akasha. Literally everything. Psychic activity, astral, or 5th dimensional in nature, is only a sliver of what is actually available for us from the Akashic on a comparative level.

One might say that psychic activity is part of the Akasha and the Akashic supersedes psychic activity. The two have a unique relationship because to a degree one doesn't exist without the other, though not on a 50/50 basis. The psychic activity itself is being documented in the Records, and recollection or confirmation of the Akashic may be available on a psychic level. For psychic readers, they will have to be clear and possibly a little more silent in order to really look into the Akashic and get the clear, clean messages as to why something is happening in comparison to an 'in the moment' reading or quick look confirming something to happen or something about an individual.

This is where the main difference lies between psychic reading and Akashic reading. Again the psychic reading comes ultimately from the Akashic. In turn, the Akasha, by way of it's transcended nature is usually limited as to what vibrational info will naturally be allowed to come through in a normal astral-based psychic reading. This may sound a bit heady for some, though, vibrationally sound and true. As these are the normal expression of Universal Laws at work and play, we are not judging or 'playing favorites' here for the nature of one way to be better than the other. One is more 'in the moment' and may be a result of a person's actions and the other 'is the moment' and the reasons behind a person's actions. This reminds us of the comparison to western medicine in comparison to holistic medicine. One treats the symptom and one treats the cause.

Intuition is pure knowing and comes to us by way of the Soul. It is a purer and finer version of what has been in the past, what will happen next, or information about anything else under the sun. Because intuition is guided by the pure energy of Soul on the 'other side' and it's oneness connection to the rest of creation, it can be a finer, quicker and clearer version of what's actually happening as one thinks of receiving information in these ways. Intuition seems to be much more naturally close to the Souls's connection into the Akashic Records as the Akasha is here for the purpose of the Souls. When one goes into the Akashic they experience a presence of stepping more fully into their own soul. It may well be surmised here that the same must be true as we experience full intuition which takes us into the Soul more fully that we are simultaneously taken into the Records. As we go into the Records our stream and connection by way of natural, practiced or known means is bolstered or added to in subtle ways. That connection is remembered even more so if you can consciously direct yourself back to that momentary stream or experience. There you can find re-entry into the experience and a natural knowing of the process will start to unfold.

Intuition itself or the act of being intuitive is more like the allowing of a flow, rather than fishing for answers. As you allow the intuition to open and flow within the stillness, the ego moves out of the way and becomes silent or inactive. Judgements are not formulated within the mind about the information coming through to you. You will find the silence of the intuition to be much like that of the Soul. You can find the energy of the intuition silently streaming through your mind field by way of your heart or directly into the heart as a knowing.

The Tibetan Buddhists called this the 'Heart-Mind'. If you ever have the opportunity of an actual full blown heart-mind experience it can be quite an amazing example of how the intuition flows into and streams through the energy fields and physical body giving you an instant or continual streaming download of knowledge or knowing. In this dynamic you experience thoughts as they are occurring and they are coming through the heart although there is also a slightly fainter signal coming simultaneously from the brain and mind as the thoughts are witnessed.

The mantra 'Om Mani Padme Hum' is known for combining a stream of energy between one's heart and mind. Below are the **Sanscrit** syllables and the centers they represent:

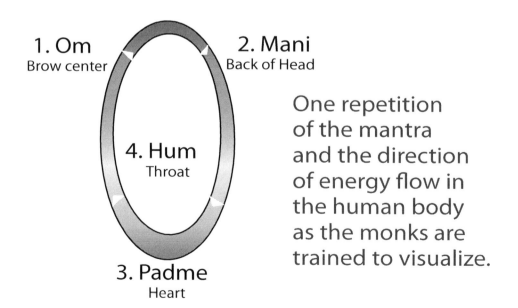

1. Om
Brow center

2. Mani
Back of Head

4. Hum
Throat

3. Padme
Heart

One repetition of the mantra and the direction of energy flow in the human body as the monks are trained to visualize.

Om - Third Eye - energy center between the eye brows coinciding with the pituitary and pineal glands in the brain.

Mani - Coinciding with the Soul chakra in the back of the head. Also home of the neo - cortex and energy vision centers of the brain.

Padme - Coinciding with the Heart center or chakra.

Hum - Coinciding with the Throat center or chakra.

As the prayer mantra is chanted the energies of the sanscrit syllables are circulated through the energy centers of the brow, back of the head, down to the heart and back up to the throat, causing the flow of energy to bring the heart and heart field together with the brain and mind field.

This is one mantra that has a lot of magical gifts and blessings and if you have been thinking of exploring mantras, what better way to start than with a general classic mantra that has many uses. This one mantra will give you a good 'hands on' experience of mantras and help open your intuition by way of balancing your heart, mind and life naturally.

There is also a channel of nerves that runs from the heart up past the thymus gland and through an important set of nerves that run along each side of the neck vertebrae. The energy center or chakra coinciding where the neck joins the brain stem is called the **Alta Major**. The Ancients also called this the *Mouth of God*. This nerve then runs up through the brain and surrounds the pineal gland. This nerve channel coming from the heart up to the brain actually sends impulses of energy stimulating thoughts, levels of vibration within the mind and therefore telling the brain what to think.If you don't believe it try a simple test for yourself:

Sit and focus on some old thought patterns driven by the **ego** (*which is hiding in the heart*) while being aware of this nerve channel. Notice the thoughts that follow...angry? hurt? depressed? out of sorts?

Now focus on opening this nerve channel by receiving Divine Energy of God's Love or Universal Cosmic Light Energy into the heart as you breathe, bring it up along this nerve channel and open it.

From the heart, to the Thymus gland between the heart and throat and then continuing to open up to this Alta Major in the back of the neck, then to the 3rd eye (brow center), and up to the crown. Feel Better? Better thought patterns? Yes!

The Alta Major is a coinciding and secondary chakra whose reservoir runs up from this nerve branch area at the back of the neck and runs up through the brain stem or **medula oblagata** through the pineal and pituitary glands and to the 3rd eye chakra or brow center between the eyes. Opening this channel continually can slowly or periodically move you towards moments of Enlightenment or even an ultimate moment of Self realization.

The true nature of learning to use our intuition more clearly involves becoming more clear by balancing, releasing and allowing or opening to it. And that's just what this amazing mantra accomplishes and more. Karma is healed or cleared, the heart is opened, negativity is cleared and transmuted.

Let us look at now the Akashic Records as a destination for our intuition to visit. We can have intuition or intuitive moments just fine without the knowing of, destination or focus upon the Akashic Records. The act of intuition or the practiced experience of intuition is in and of itself, a good and very useful tool and in different ways will give you different levels of information.

The Akashic Records and the act of visiting it whether with sight, sound, or any and all of the other senses up to a full body visionary experience, is a transitory destination. A system and a mystical spiritual set of tools geared for higher knowing of the Soul, the afterlife, past lives, and the 'in-between'. In many ways as we've stated before there is quite more than one could understand in any one setting and yet it's a great pathway and mystical road map into ways of knowing governed by Creator and the special angels and masters who reside there, and the souls who donate their time between lifetimes to be of service to those visiting in order to understand their Karma and look at their Soul Schedule of Lifetimes.

So we have Psychic, Intuitive, and Akashic awareness. Each one bringing a progressively deeper level of knowing, understanding and the wisdom of what to do with the information. For many people in today's world with the fast paced social system of society based on survival, psychic readings are quite popular to be able to provide for the divining of quick informative reference material about a person's immediate and long range future. There are some really amazing psychics out there who are truly gifted.

Sometimes naturally gifted psychics can give colored information because their ego is quite sure of itself. This can be a self diffusing mechanism that could hamper any deeper levels of information from flowing through. Often anyone who has natural psychic gifts becomes sure of the psychic process itself. The ego can equate this as being an advantage in their own life movie, and could create a silent competition to seek continual self -validation of the psychic information itself. There are very balanced psychics out there as well with a good sense of service. The idea here is that we're all just real and normal people with our own 'stuff'. So how do we move past the life issues in relation to clear intuition?

By challenging the ego's grasp and looking into deeper levels of intuition that is streaming through the Heart & Soul bringing understanding and wisdom with it, while accessing the Akashic Records. When you're ready you'll have the opportunity to really go as deep as you want to with your visionary enquiries. At this level you'll have the tools and facilities being presented to you to know yourself and to heal, transmute karma, and to change & energize your life. What's needed to reach these new heights? Patience, Trust and Perseverance.

Kalachakra

The Kālachakra tradition revolves around the concept of time (kāla) and cycles (chakra) from the cycles of the planets, to the cycles of human breathing, it teaches the practice of working with the most subtle energies within one's body on the path to enlightenment. Looking into the Kalachakra slowly is an excellent way to stimulate your inner vision for Akashic Reading.

Within the experience of finding the existence of the Akasha you will start to unravel the knowings and mysteries of the Universe, yourself, the world & everyone in it.

Chapter 9

Why Experience the Existence of the Akasha?

As we share new perspectives about the Akashic Records we build within our mind's eye a story of knowing with descriptions, mental ideas and imagery. We build a foundation for a much larger or wider view. We use multiple points of view to open the subconscious, conscious and super-concious parts of the mind into a stream of access. The naturally occurring dream state of R.E.M. (rapid eye movement) that happens in the subtle moment between wake and sleep. As the mind hovers momentarily between the Beta and Delta states, the R.E.M. occurs bringing visions and dreams of what can be introduced here as a direct stream into the Akashic Records.

As this stream occurs we begin to have sensory input from the Akashic Records as a hub or network of experiences and also directly from the Soul as the walls of normal sensory perception are lowered and we look into the experiences of other lifetimes. This may happen as moments in dreams. For example: We are in a setting with people we are comfortable with and know within a dream. In that moment we're sure we know them and comfortable in that dream moment with their presence, and then upon waking we do not have any relevant connection to them or the movie at all. Or do we?

The next time this occurs as you're coming up from sleep, try to catch a glimpse long enough to remember the characters or players even if you have to jot it down on paper. We may look deeper into these moments through meditation and ask the question, is this a previous lifetime?

Ask yourself: "What is the knowledge or wisdom to be gained from the connections in the dream for me to know at this time?" As we look into these past, future or other worldly moments of dreams, we are experiencing the non-ordinary reality of the Eternal Now Moment streaming *beyond* linear time and yet *as* linear time in a string of moments or sequences of events.

Let's look at the Brain Waves: *Beta, Alpha, Theta, Delta*, What do they mean, and when do we have them? When you're awake and totally active, your brain waves operate at a level called **Beta** where they mainly oscillate between 14 to 30 cycles per second.

As your mind relaxes and disconnects somehow from the external material world such as when you're daydreaming or meditating, or watching a movie, you enter a more focused, expanded state of awareness where brain wave patterns are mainly composed of **Alpha** brain waves oscillating at between 8 and 13 cycles per second.

When relaxing even more, your mind enters a region that correlates with a large relative quantity of brain wave patterns of 4 to 7 cycles per second. This is the **Theta** zone of the mind.

The **Beta** level corresponds to a focus of concentration by the mind upon the outside or perceptually separated world, and the Alpha and Theta levels correspond to a more internally focused, self-reflective state.

Each human being experiences the **Theta** level for a fleeting moment every night before the mind dips down from the **Beta** level of awareness (awake state), to the Delta state (brain waves of less than 4 cycles per second equal deep sleep), and passes rapidly through the Alpha and Theta states to enter the profound sleep level, where consciousness of self is totally lost, and where even dreams do not occur. When dreaming, a sense of self is necessary and the mind has to go back up to the Theta or Alpha state.

Delta is the level of the mysterious Universal Mind. It is the level at which the differentiated self or ego expands to become the undifferentiated I Am, and/or the Higher Self and operates outside of the confines of linear time/space in the Infinite Eternal Moment.

Alpha, **Theta and Delta** (sleep) are defined as altered states of consciousness, as opposed to **Beta**, which is considered to be a fully conscious state. They are called this because it is necessary to alter one's state of consciousness from the fully awake state (Beta), to either Alpha, Theta or Delta (sleep), which are all progressive states of expanded awareness and thus are subject to less vibratory interference from the biological brain.

Beta is the so-called conscious level of mind. Alpha and Theta form the subconscious regions of the mind's operation, and Delta is the super conscious region of thought activity. These states form the spectrum of mind operation.

Small children function mainly at the Theta, Alpha and Delta states of mind, as do animals. Human adults operate mostly at Beta.

We input energetic information into the Akasha at all of the cycles even Delta or the deepest state of Universal Oneness where the Self is lost or beyond Self. As you read about the different states of mind Alpha, Beta, Delta and Theta, think about how you can have a conscious experience of accessing the Akashic Records at each one of these states and even as you shift between these states, from one state to another.

So we are now indicating a looking at 'looking' from within and into the mind at these states of visionary, mystical and simple sensory experiences and how they occur. We can let go of over identifying with these four states of mind. I say this because I don't want you to become side tracked in another analysis while working on entry to access the Records. Though if you're a scientist, numbers analysis person, engineer, etc. then this informational approach might help you. You will know best how to be natural with it. If it doesn't help you and overwhelms you let go of it, whatever it is, and move to a perception or exercise that helps you access more easily.

Within the experience of finding the existence of the Akasha you will start to unravel the knowings and mysteries of the Universe, your self, the world & everyone in it. It truly can be a humbling experience. This system of reading the Records can bring enlightenment to us naturally by taking us continually and directly deeper into our own Soul energy, which is connected to our Soul Group of 12 Souls, the Over Soul which is connected to 12 Soul groups and the Monad which is connected to 12 Over Souls. Beyond this we have higher dimensions including the Akasha as the vibrations continually rise all the way back to the Source of Creation, First Moment, home of Creator God. So as we start to expand, relax and intuit information, we first get information concerning our own path, immediate karmas to be worked through in order to know more, expand and have more joyful moments in the life of our earthly experiences.

As we simply and clearly understand or 'get it', we are

shown clearer pictures as we may have been incarnate many times over and there are a lot of experiences to possibly heal, observe, or access for knowledge, wisdom and talents paid forward.

Here's a little known secret or truth of doing this work: As you look into your Book of Life within the Akashic Records you look directly at moments which one may normally emotionally react to or have accompanying thoughts of needing to heal these moments. Once you get to a place within yourself where you can view these moments without any reaction whatsoever, the simple act of viewing, looking or gazing into the event or moment being presented to your inner vision, is healed, released, let go of, brought forward, strengthened, or whatever else needs to occur in order to return you to a perfect state of divine balance.

Whatever needs to occur will occur. You are operating from the pure grace, divinity and the platform of observation of the Soul. This is where 'magic' happens. Seeing something that has been bothering us for years or even lifetimes in different ways, whether emotional, mental, physical or spiritual, seeing it in a pure moment of true light with no judgement what so ever truly allows it to release. We can do this in practiced super relaxed states of inner guided journey work into the Akashic Records.

This is the highest benefit from experiencing entry into the Records. This answers the greatest instruction to all souls, 'Know Thyself' and for this reason these moments are paramount to our complete and continual lives and existence. The other reason is to be of service to others by reading and accessing information in order to give them information about not only the symptoms but additionally the cause of their soul's healing journey.

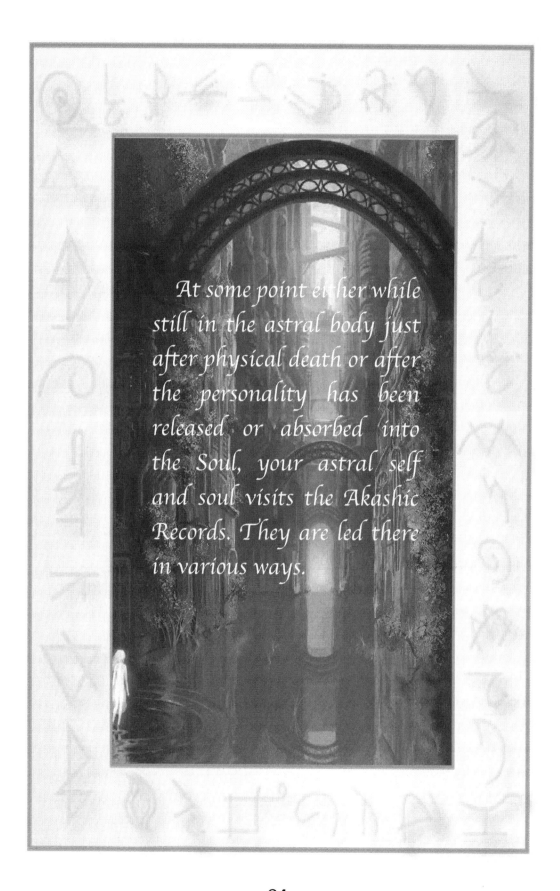

At some point either while still in the astral body just after physical death or after the personality has been released or absorbed into the Soul, your astral self and soul visits the Akashic Records. They are led there in various ways.

Chapter 10

Way Station
of the
Souls

Soul's created in the First Moment of the Universe from the center of creation moving out from that moment across space and time to experience life times. Incarnating in different star systems, different worlds with very unique qualities and bodies, minds and energy fields. Worlds so different we might not even be able to perceive. Other worlds we may recognize as very similar to our own current existence, with human and/or humanoid incarnations among the stars as well as many other species variations.

Souls also created from within the conception of stars and star clusters with the help of certain guiding angelics and high councils and even special chambers where certain souls were created on behalf of Creator with the help of these councils.

The other worldly presence of the Angelic realm, a very different world which exists within the 6th Dimension as home for the legions of angelics including the Arc Angels as they approach the Throne of the Light of God.

The many worlds of the Astral Plane (5th dimension) with

worlds upon worlds created by thoughts interjected into it by the 4th dimensional minds and mind fields of humans. Additional energies, singular thoughts and thought patterns are also being generated from within the 5th dimension or astral plane and coming down from higher dimensions. And then we have all of the Souls coming, going, living and visiting there. The astral plane or 5th Dimension is a very busy place. It has been referred to as the Grand Central Station of the spirit worlds because there are so many spiritual beings crossing through to the earth plane and leaving the earth plane. It also plays home to all psychic activity and mental thought projections as well as angelic, demonic and alien activity.

Many Souls visit the higher dimensions as they become ascended. As they move away from earthly life having finished karmic lesson programs and/or self imposed karmic projections. The release from duality and a naturally occurring dynamic of enlightenment or illumination for some Souls causes a state to occur where as they can transcend physical reality while still keeping their personality in tact. There is no right or wrong way to ascend, become ascended or experience ascension. There are a few known general ways of ascending, though it can happen uniquely for different souls.

Other versions of moving out of earthly incarnation would entail dropping the physical body while experiencing the identical astral body with mental and emotional capabilities while the Soul stays with the astral 'You' for a time to be determined as your personality remembrance and emotional and astral bodies are absorbed completely by the soul, as the soul moves up into the ethers to await it's turn for the harmonic moment when it is called back down to reincarnate through the human birth process.

At some point either while still in the astral body just after physical death or after the personality has been released or absorbed into the Soul, your astral self and soul visits the Akashic Records. They are led there in various ways. Often times by the angels as they are the messengers and assistants of God. You can also be taken there by a family member on the other side, an ascended master or your spirit guides. You may even already know the way yourself and naturally go there for the first time or in the midst of an out-of-body or near-death experience by finding yourself at the crossroads of either going home or returning to your life. In this crucial moment you may find yourself holding council within the Records at your Book of Life. Your life templates, purposes, accomplishments, missed opportunities, regrets, failures and triumphs all laid out here for you to study with the help of those on the 'other side' to show you how to understand what's going on. What are the lessons for your specific soul to study, observe and learn? Were you pulled out of body and brought here through an event just to have this experience of looking at your Records?

In a divinely guided single moment of 'weighing the scales' within one's own personal checks and balances of soul progress you may receive a large amount of information that you process in that moment as a simple knowing. Has enough been accomplished to go on into the light? Is there a special soul you're taking care of or connected with that you have to go back to be with for a while? Are there still lessons to be learned from this life and/or even previous lives? All of these questions are answered for you harmonically as you step before the Book of Life and look into your own Akashic Records.

It acts as a way station for all of the Souls coming to the earth plane and those who have or will ever incarnate here. In this way it can be a very busy place and as you visit the Records you can experience it as busy with others present or as an isolated solitary meditation event. The latter is usually the case so as you can really observe the information more easily. There are other moments when you might visit with groups of souls or groupings of people such as a group of inventors, a group of spiritual masters, or maybe a group of souls who all passed tragically in an accident together. So as special and tucked away as it is, the Records can be very busy in many different ways. This is why there are souls who volunteer between lifetimes and Keepers of the Records with angelics and other special beings keeping close watch over this special place.

As souls finish there lifetimes here on planet earth they check in at the Akashic Records where they are approved for take off to other star systems, other worlds, for other lives or to graduate to higher dimensions. Remember you are eternal and you will continue your existences as you continue to evolve. For this reason many in the spiritual community think or feel that ascension is the best opportunity of a long range life projection beyond the incarnations of the earth plane.

"My Fathers House Has Many Mansions"
John 14 (King James version)
"Let not your heart be troubled: ye believe in God, believe also in me. In my Father's house are many mansions: if it were not so, I would have told you. I go to prepare a place for you. And if I go and prepare a place for you, I will come again, and receive you unto myself; that where I am, there ye may be also. And whither I go ye know, and the way ye know."

My intention in pointing to this verse is that it gives us a direct message of the myriads of worlds which are available on the other side, particularly, this sensual reference would be to the astral realm or 5th dimension. 'I go to prepare a place for you', indicates travelling there in mind, body and spirit in order to create a working stream into the heavens including the sacred Akashic Records. Christ also shares, 'Where I go you know (such as in spirit, meditation or astral travel) and 'the way' you know (to go).

The challenge with literal Bible interpretation is that it was never meant to be interpreted literally, that is why the actual words, sentences and messages need to be examined more closely before making a face value assumption. It was meant to be able to speak to the individual reading it. Originally the parables of Christ had hidden meanings and messages as there were some things he just didn't come right out and say for fear of being killed prematurely. The writings and wording were changed over time and important parts grossly omitted and misinterpreted, such as the role, supposed promiscuity and integrity of Mary Magdalena originally known as Mary of Magdala. You can thank syndicated religion for that as well as the genocide of the Cathars. The Cathars practiced the original teachings of Christ and of Mary and lived throughout the world in communities. They were systematically exterminated under false pretence over time in a silent struggle for power by changing the original story and beliefs in history. If they were all dead then no one would know the true history or be practicing the original teachings...the Way. (*The Knowing Way of Truth and Light*)

Modern day misinterpretations happen continually in everyday life just as much or more so than with Biblical translation and interpretation. In today's international community we have may people speaking other languages and often times the interpretations can lost in the communications of limited vocabularies. As the world is more connected nowadays through the information super highway. Can you see in relation to this, how Aramaic (the language of Christ's lifetime) could be misinterpreted after being re-written in old English during medieval times by multiple people who omitted and changed parts of the writings sometimes even under direct orders from their superiors to do so?

There is hope though! (*Rays of light bursting through clouds*) Through deep states of meditation you can access the Akashic Records of the true life of Christ and the Disciples and you can find the real history of what happened. As you develop your skills, look into historical events and look at the inner workings, the individuals involved and the reasons why things played out the way they did. You may be surprised to find that the main stream story could be a little bit or a lot different in report than what we might find. Go within, like the early 20th century mystic, Edgar Cayce. He was often referred to as the 'sleeping prophet' who went into deep states of trance and brought back amazing information about, Christ, healing remedies and the ancient civilization of Atlantis.

You may find that if you go into the Akashic Records in a meditation you can connect with the Master Jesus Christ and have a discussion directly with Him. He can give you direct information about your life or past lives, your healing, your karma, and the best way to proceed in life. The results of such an experience are almost sure to be exciting and very inspirational. Tune into the voice, heart, mind and soul of this Teacher as you see Him in the Akashic Records. Bring back wisdom which you can feel and know at a deep level.

Violet Light Clearing Meditation

While sitting or lying down in a relaxed position start to take a few long slow deep breaths. And as you continue to breathe, picture a field, stream, pool or blanket of violet energy above your head. As this deep purple of the **I Am**

Presence and **Violet Flame** moves down through your aura, inhale and pull it down through the subtle, causal, mental, emotional, astral, and etheric bodies. Clearing them, healing them restoring to balance your chakras, glands and organs as it passes through them. Clearing out any and all negative residuals, emotional and psychic chords or tethers from others, all energies which are not of your highest good.

Healing balancing and energizing you as it passes down through your body and out the bottoms of your feet into the earth as the earth gladly and willingly absorbs and transmutes the negative energies back to pure positive elemental energy.

This exercise will leave you feeling clear and light. As you continue to breathe, bringing the violet light down through the body, bring it throughout the brain, and the **pineal**, and **thalamus** glands in the brain, through the eyes, the ears, nose and mouth, the throat and throat chakra. Clearing you as it moves through the shoulders, the heart and the front and back heart chakras. Continuing down through the solar plexus and all the organs and tissues of the torso and abdomen, clearing the intestines, and sexual organs and these lower chakras, as the violet energy moves down through your hips, waste and pelvis, down through your legs and out through the bottoms of the feet. As you continue this violet breathing process you may want to picture St. Germain, the Ascended Master associated with the violet energy and the **Violet Flame of the Holy I Am Presence**. It is not required if you do not know who St. Germain is, though by calling him you will summon his presence and his help, as with all the Ascended Masters. Simply continue working with the violet energy.

As you continue to breathe in now clearing the 7 main chakras and also the all the extended 12 chakras, including the higher centers above the crown chakra and the lower chakras at the kness, feet and below. Breathing in & out as this violet flame energy clears down through your Higher Self chakras. As it continues now healing, clearing, balancing and energizing all of your DNA strands, both in the body and outside the body in the energy fields. Clearing the Skeletal system, the muscular system, muscles, tendons and ligaments, the veins, arteries and capillaries of the circulatory system. The digestive system, the nervous system with the extensive network of nerves throughout the body. Clearing the meridians and zones of the body where the emotional energy visits and sits or deposits in these meridian points causing our external world and life path to materialize. And exhaling down the body and the two lower chakra centers at the knees and below the feet and out the bottoms of the feet into the earth and away from us. Use this exercise to keep yourself continually clear as you feel a need and also in conjunction with the following Christ Light Visualization.

Christ Light Clearing Meditation

As you continue to relax after the Violet Light clearing, now become aware of a tube of cylinder of Christ Light in the very core center of your being. Between the spine the front of your solar plexus. This Universal Cosmic Christ Light is shining and glowing very brightly as you now focus your mind on it, continuing to breathe in and out slowly and comfortably.

You may even see or visualize the presence of Master Jesus in the room with you during this exercise. As you continue to breathe in & out visualize now that this Christ Light in your core center is growing So bright that it lights up the entire inside of your physical shell. Filling up the 99.99% empty space inside your body with this powerful loving, healing and clearing Universal Christ Light Energy. It clears out everything that is not of your making or your highest good.

Clearing and healing karmas, and healing your body to perfection! As it continues to grow brighter and brighter, the Christ Light within You, now operating as your core energy, is so brilliant that it can longer be contained by your body, as it starts shining out through every pore of your skin.

Shining a great field of Christ Light energy around your body. You are shining like a star as the Christ Light emanates from within you. As you continue to breathe in and out, now as the Universal Christ Light Energy exudes from you, it again becomes even brighter and expanding the brilliant blazing field clears out your whole room, your home and the surrounding neighborhoods where you are. Clearing, healing, balancing and energizing the surrounding areas back to it's original state of perfection.

Christ is with You here now in the room and the Christ Light is continuing to shine from you as you hear the words "This and greater things shall you do" and "If thine eye be single (focus the 3rd eye) let thy whole body be filled with Light".

Meet Christ Within the Akashic Records Meditation

As you relax and continue to breathe gently, see now with you in the room and in your mind Christ Jesus, Jeshua. As you visualize Christ with you, start to see Him more closely feeling His presence as you listen to His words speak to you. What are the messages in his words that you hear in your heart, mind & soul? Listen to the vibration of His healing Love energy as it moves through you. You are now in the great midst of the power of God's Universal Christ Light Healing Vibrations through messenger Master Jesus. As you continue to listen to him you now ask to journey with him into the Akashic Records to view his life, as your feet start to become light you both move together up through a portal of light which has appeared in the room where you are. As the golden beam of light becomes bright surrounding the both of you everything else in the room fades back.

As you continue to rise through the beam of golden light being lifted upwards, you hear His voice bringing you personal healing messages as you are together with Him. Listen gently to the kind words He is bringing to you. What are the messages?

Pause for a moment to listen.

You instantly find yourself in a beautiful outdoor setting with Jesus as he shows you his homeland, the area where he grew up. It is so peaceful and clear, very pretty with trees and blue skies. This place speaks to you about your own life bringing you comfort. Christ shows us that in many ways human life was the same there in the past as it is here now in our present day, in that whatever the mind has to focus on creatively it moves through it's challenges and interactions with the emotions, life's experiences and others in our lives.

Mary Magdalene and Mother Mary come to join Christ standing on each side of Him together with you. They are showing to you the healing energy of family and the vibrations of male and female energy together in it's expressions.

Mary and Mary begin to speak to you messages from within. What are the messages that they have for you as they lovingly support you in this moment with their healing and nurturing energy. They move through you as Christ does, moving through your heart and your hands, healing your life and all others in your life including You.

Listen to their gentle soft voices as they connect with You.

Pause for a moment to listen.

They are bringing you messages that touch your heart & soul. That they will touch many, many lives through you during your life. Always listen and open your heart to their messages and you will be lifted in Love, protected, cleared and healed. As you listen to their words, the love, the healing vibration through the messages of Christ, Mary Magdalene and Mother Mary you are lifted up into the 'Kingdom of Heaven' on the inner planes.

Giving gratitude for this experience to Them and to Yourself, ask now for their messages and healing to continually pour through you as you listen continually with your Heart, Mind, Body & Soul. As you open to receive their messages, guidance, healing and blessings, the 12 disciples now materialize around you for a final blessing and confirmation that you are in the Holy midst of Divine family.

As you look to your right you see now joining the circle the Holy Arc Angels of the Light of Creator God of Love letting you know that they will be standing guard, blessing, healing and lifting you up, during your meetings with Christ, Mary and Mary. Divine Blessings to You in this moment as you are lifted up, cleared, healed, and loved! Now given thanks in gratitude for this special meeting. Having connected and received the information and healing that was given to you, start your journey with Christ back down the portal of Light, back down, down, down.

Coming back to the earth, back to your country, your state, your town. Coming back down into the room and into your physical body. Take a deep breath and wiggle your fingers and toes as you blink your eyes. Welcome Home to the New Loving You! Remember your time with Christ, Mother Mary, Mary Magdalene and the Disciples. Remember your conversations and their words. Healing and Blessings to you. Divine Blessings of Peaceful Strength and Comfort to You.

Om, Peace, Amen.

Visit with Mother Mary,
the Holy Family
and all the Ascended Masters
As you go within during your meditations
into the Akashic Records.
As you listen for the Answers,
they will surely come.

Mary Of Sephoris
18" x 24" acrylic on aluminum

It will all be waiting for you there once you connect in with it through reflecting moments of remembrance, dream analysis and interpretations from yourself, family and friends, past life regressions through the Akashic Records.

Chapter 11

Dreams, Past Lives & Alternate Realities

One of the most immediate way that Spirit talks to us is in the dream state. We have some of our most memorable experiences with the spirit world here behind the wall of sleep. As we relax at night and move into softer and quieter vibrations at peace where our body gathers chi or cosmic energy in the natural cycle of sleep, the soul is also naturally allowed to expand in the quietude. We journey up into the ethers of the Astral plane and even sometimes farther, deeper, higher to other planes of existence. Simultaneously we journey within as we are connected at many varying levels to these planes to have experiences of mental visions, pictures, dreams and participate in movies inspired by these connections. While this is occurring and the visions are being shown to us, our soul is experiencing the dynamic of connecting with our true essence on deeper levels. At this place and in these moments we have the opportunity to step into other movies of incarnations we have lived. Have you ever had a dream in which you were part of a movie and in that setting you knew everything and everyone in the movie, and yet upon waking you have no recollection of the relevance of it in relation to your current life? You have just experienced a past life *or* a parallel life reality within the dream state via your Soul and the Akashic Records.

As you view into the dream again looking at the actors including yourself, the setting and surroundings, and let the message come through to you about what the message behind everything represents. You will come to find the meaning behind the meaning. This is paramount to the deeper dream interpretations process because you are looking past the ordinary symbolisms from dreams.

Never discount these symbolisms as they happen. The dream state can be peppered with these simple or sometimes trivial symbolisms as they try to wake us up or attempt to bring our attention into an aware or lucid state. So if you have simple, pure and clear symbolisms in your dreams by all means pay attention to these, yet look for deeper meanings and ask from within as you meditate on it. The answers from within you or from your guides will surely come. You may have simple visions pertaining to practical matters concerning tomorrow or the next days ahead that could include a car repair or something else that needs attention in your everyday life.

I'm also indicating to you here that there are other moments of the dream state that are more involved and you may see things which are not simple indicators such as movies you are part of which you have no recollection of. These movies have messages and represent other lives you are living simultaneously which are usually referred to as past lives. They could also be future moments or parallel realities of which you are part of. Not to worry. In these elusive visions in which you may not understand at the moment you are always protected and guided by Creator God, Universal

Laws and your Spirit Guides, which is also to say that Spirit never gives us more than we can handle. If we're seeing something strangely new or with increasing regularity we are naturally being asked to expand our view and know more about ourselves. How many people are continually receiving deep states of input and messages in the dream state who haven't paid attention to it or simply may not have had the knowledge or training in meditation or journeying within, dream or symbolic analysis and/or deep states of perception in order to do so? Learn to watch or act upon the multidimensional reality which is the Real You. You have the opportunity to explore, think, view, ponder and traverse these vast regions of the subconscious, conscious and super conscious minds as they speak to you.

A footnote for you here; It may all seem overwhelming as the process is ongoing and/or that you possibly may be missing things in these continuing movies of symbolisms and dreams. They are only waiting for you to recognize yourself within them as a **lucid dream** which means being awake within the dream or consciously aware that you are dreaming.

It will all be waiting for you there once you connect in with it through reflecting moments of remembrance, dream analysis and interpretations from yourself, family and friends, and past life regressions through the Akashic Records. Some of us are naturally more aware of these deeper levels and even practice lucid dreaming. For others it is a new idea. As we have the experience more and more we have the access point of lucidity to really remember these moments and have the experience of knowing ourselves as part of them. There are indigenous tribes who teach each other to lucid dream or to be fully aware of their roles and actions within their dreams. They even train themselves to control the dream itself by allowing themselves to have control and power over situations in the dreams. This is a very powerful practice. Think back to a nightmare you may have had. It may have seemed so real as things went wrong that if you could have woken yourself up in the dream state and took control of it, you would have therefore changed the outcome and in so doing, created an immediate comfort and strength within yourself. The power of this is that the 'real world' power of attraction is all based on thoughts super-charged with emotions or feelings. This creates your reality. So lucidly taking control of the movie in the dream state can bring you great successes and healing! What would you dream? You may even learn to use supernatural or superhuman abilities to protect, heal, change yourself or others in these dreams. This can be very transformative for you because as you are able to overcome your fears in the dream state you are able to overcome and dissipate fears in the waking state as well and even change possible outcomes.

We can practice the lucid experiences of being in control of our dreams just as we would be in control in our normal waking state reality. The difference in the dream state is that you get to participate in it with special abilities and powers if you so choose. You can do anything in the dream state right? This again is paramount to dream experiences because when you get to this place where you say within yourself what will happen next within the unfolding moments, you are creating your reality in the truest and deepest essence possible to you at that time. This will also take shape even if it's only subtle in your waking state.

You may have moments of conquering dark spirits or entities simply by recognizing mundane movie moments within the dream and change it by responding to it, through the Divine Universal Law of Free Will. This will, time and again, give you personal and silent knowing within yourself at the soul level that you are protected naturally by your true soul radiance of the Light that is You.

Once you have seen this you cannot be told otherwise. You cannot be vampirized or energetically lied to. These subtle workings of the dream state are huge. The yogis have said that we are dreaming with our eyes open which indicates that the dream state, sleep and spirit world are just as active and real as the waking state if not more so. The waking state is somewhat of a movie set for the senses that is not entirely true or real.

Many scientists and great thinkers have indicated to us that the human body and all physical mass is 99.99 percent empty space. It is real to us through our senses, though all other dimensions exist here simultaneously, and when we step beyond the waking state we have access to more of the real essence of existence itself in a Universal Truth Light Way. This is the dance between linear time and the Eternal Now. Between **Gregorian** clock time (linear past, present, future) and **Quantum** Universal Space Time Reality (eternal now moment).

Linear time is only a sliver or part of the greater truly occurring continuum. As you experience this or 'know' it, the rules of the game will start to change in life for you on all levels. You will not be lost to yourself or to the world. You are asked from within and beyond to open up to greater levels of being, perception and reality. This may occur momentarily, in frequenting moments or open up to you more as a continuing experience that changes your outlook of life from the inside out of reality.

You have keys at your fingertips to unlock hidden doors. Doors of perception that have been continually tucked away by you yourself and the continuing mundane effects of the 3rd dimensional reality of the physical world. There are conditions of reality and levels of society associated with external experiences who are seeking to creatively express parameters of control through their own versions of the world they are dreaming and we have agreed or allowed ourselves to participate at whatever levels within it. A colleague once said 'You are either living in your own dream or you are living in someone elses.' Remember the illustration of an elephant who has been trained to walk around in a circle with a rope tied from it's ankle to a stake and it hasn't known that it had the power to simply snap the rope like a string with it's mighty strength and run free?

You are now being given your own opportunities to creatively express your own self control and freedom by true perception which shifts everything in and of itself. This has the potential of shifting the 'matrix' of your reality by revealing your True Divine Essence, something which has been waiting to find you forever within a moment. You can use your dreaming and lucid dreaming process to rid yourself of fears, heal yourself at deep levels and create great and new experiences for your life all from within yourself while you sleep.

Many healers visit others who need physical or energetic protection and healing by way of travelling to them in the dream state and working with them. We may also visit family members who are in need of council or healing and work with them in this way. At times this can often be effective as they may not be open to receiving messages or healing in the waking state. We may also have visitations from family members, relatives and ancestors during sleep who bring us messages and guidance for our life's journey and path. There may even be unfinished situations that can be healed and released giving them and you comfort. Another amazing thing that can happen is the visitation of spirit guides, angels, masters and teachers bringing you symbolic or actual discourses to help guide your life. This can truly be an inspirational experience. There are so many people and beings we can connect with on the other side and that we have been connected to in past lives.

Past Lives are lifetimes which are actually playing out simultaneously from within the Mind of God. So as we consider past lives from even thousands of years ago, these are actually occurring simultaneously in the Universal Now Moment of the Mind of God. As you look at Infinity from a distance and you look at the length of a few thousand incarnations of one soul in relation or in comparison to the expansiveness of the Multi-verse, it is relatively instantaneous in comparison to the vast grandeur and reality of the Super Universes.

Past Lives are other expressions of You that you may find within the Akashic and your Book of Life. You may access your past lives via the Akasha and view or participate in these lives in meditative vision work or during sleep. These other versions of You are lifetimes when your soul was/ is experiencing, processing and creating other cumulative information and observation that it uses as You in other lifetimes to live even more meaningful sentient lives here in the Now and beyond.

As you look back into the past and fill in the chairs of a visionary Akashic gathering of all your other incarnations. You call them forth with your visionary intuitive perception, you will spell out to yourself more of your history and nature by filling another chair and yet another chair, and so on.

These other versions of you may have only been available to you within your current life moments and experiences as your personality traits, tendencies, thoughts, words and actions. When you start to realize yourself at this subtle level you are making good progress at Knowing Yourself as the True You.

Again stated here: that the *pure act of perceiving without judgement of* the other incarnations and lifetimes of You, even if there are questionable or dark things you may see or have been involved with in other lifetimes, will release you from it and gather you back more fully with a deep acceptance and understanding of it all. When you look at all of these past and current life thoughts, words and deeds without any conflict, they come up to the surface and dissipate, release, and at the same time come home as you truly and more fully accept yourself and the experiential life lessons and karma you have acted out in the movies of past lifetimes.

The simple act of perception without judging, just the the act of viewing can release and heal, lifting you to a clear more fully integrated living perfection of everything in life. You might envision that these parts of you are released and yet brought home at the same time as still reflections bringing non-judgemental understanding as to why you are the way you are. This can bring deep healing and acceptance. You and these other parts of you are brought to peace like a still lake.

You may ask 'How can the pure act of 'looking' or viewing while watching with no conflict heal on such a profound level? The precursor and answer to this question is that by coming to the classes, reading this book, experiencing the journeys into the Akashic Records themselves, you have energetically sent the Universe, Creator and the Keepers of the Records a silent message that you are now becoming ready to know yourself at a deeper level or in the purest, clearest way. To 'Know Thyself'.

We move from the current state of senses in this reality whether in waking state, dreams, sleep, meditation or parallel reality to experience what is happening in past lives through the Akashic Records. We move into the Records through meditation and we can even ask to access our Akashic Book of Life in the dream state during sleep and receive information, meetings with spirit guides, masters and family members, past life moments and movies that speak messages to us and even parallel realities playing out that we may be connected to and/or are unaware of with our normal senses through the combined mental and astral plane reflections of thoughts themselves. Other dimensional selves connected to you on higher planes of existence. Many texts and teachers often refer to this commonly as the Higher Self, the God Self, the Higher Mind, the Inner Teacher and so on.

There could also be parallel parts of us not yet realized in reality or parts which are playing out in non-ordinary states of reality as mental movie projections which are not of our higher calling or in harmony with our paths yet and are simply different versions of what could be. These mental movies and versions of us are often balanced, reserved and/or transmuted, transfigured or dispersed by our spirit guides, guardian angels and even Creator God. Spirit knows the best course of action to help guide us, protect us and for us to take. Creator, our Higher Mind and Self and our Guardian Spirit Guides see our lives much differently on the other side of linear sequences of events in our lives. We can move parts of our lives which are not beneficial for us to live out or for our highest calling and best interests into these parallel realities. Sometimes we try to force the hands of fate by focusing on something continually and causing it to become manifest. This can create conflict in our lives. There are also parts of us waiting there to come forward here into our earthly dimensional life movie to manifest as our greatness. It is possible for some individuals to be processing karma or even be connected to portals in one or more parallel realities which could be stimulating or influencing their current reality.

When limiting or challenging patterns of this dynamic are known by the individual, shown to them by way of their own intuition or that of an intuitive/healer they may want to seek the guidance, council and healing powers of a local shaman for clearing. This is *your* body in the 'here and now' and nothing else has the right to connect with you by deception. Hidden or dark portals of energies from parallel realities can be lifted, closed and released from a person that might be having physical, mental or energetic unrest.

So continue your work regarding dreams, past lives and parallel realties or other dimensions by using the Akashic Records for some of your greatest levels of self inquiry. You will expand your deeper personal knowing by practicing guided journey meditations into the Records and also perceiving visionary information from dreams, waking remembrances and observations of your life and the world around You. Remember that as you are doing your Akashic journey work concerning anything mentioned in this chapter you are divinely protected and guided. Have a Great Journey!

A Spiritual Dream of Comfort

I'm sharing this as an example of what can happen for you in the dream state when you need insight, guidance or help. Several years ago, I was living in Phoenix and working in my art studio at a local gallery. I had created a large mural painting called the 'Masters of Light' which was 8 feet tall by 20 feet long in 5 stretched canvas sections. I had taken the mural to Mt. Shasta, CA to the Wesak festival the previous 2 years and it was used as a backdrop for the main stage. (page 326) A spiritual festival that people came to from around the world and truly inspiring to be part of. One year I was not able to go. I had challenges which were really only myself holding me back from going. As it came closer to the time of the event, I became more and more depressed. I felt like I was slipping away from what I was supposed to be doing in life. I went to sleep that night and in the morning had one of the most memorable lucid dreams I've ever experienced.

In the dream as it began I was walking into my art studio as I noticed that all the walls were moving with living energy and paint. It was amazing and it looked like the after life that Robin Williams visited in the movie "What Dreams May Come". As I walked in, I immediately knew that this was the art work of Sathya Sai Baba. I don't know how I knew, I just knew, I could feel it. I then told patrons walking through the studios and fellow artists that this was Sai Baba's artwork!

After a while a little toy car came moving across the floor and it bumped into my foot. All of a sudden Sai Baba came rising up as a small boy. As he rose he was wearing white and he became older in age as he started a conversation with me. As He spoke he grew to adult in appearance he was now wearing the usual safron Indian robes of a saint we are used to seeing him in. He walked over to my desk and sat down and had a supportive conversation with me. I knew he was mentoring me though upon waking I had no recollection of what was said. As he talked for a while he then got up and walked around the desk and looked closely into my eyes with a rainbow colored light that was shining from a robotic being behind Him into my pupils. "We just want to make sure that you're alright" He said. So as I stayed in that position looking ahead He then walked around to my right side and transformed into Babaji. As parts of me were sad and depressed he was then holding me and cradling me with a divine loving look in His eyes. His arms were around me as he sat close rocking me gently and bringing compassionate comfort. After a few moments he then got up changed back to Sai Baba and morphed to the boy. As he continued talking he walked to the door as I saw New York in the distance He said "I have other work to do" as he walked off into the distance. I awoke with the inspiration of having had a true lucid dream of the masters. Sai Baba does not visit people in dreams unless he wills it, let alone the theatrics of Babaji!

Special Edition Chapter

Psychic Healing

And How To Use It

Psychic - relating to or denoting faculties or phenomena that are apparently inexplicable by natural laws, especially involving telepathy or clairvoyance: *psychic powers.*

Healing - the process of making or becoming sound or healthy again: *the gift of healing.*

Psychic Healing is an ancient spiritual practice. Many gifted clairvoyants throughout history have employed their abilities and gifts to help others, both knowingly and unknowingly. That many more of us have silently healed others naturally with the presence of the Divine or by silently willing healing towards a person unbeknownst to them.

Often times when someone is working with psychic energy they may be directed to the natural progression of working with other different variations of energy. Once you are sensitive to energy you will find that energies will find you again and again. In different vibrations and sensitivity levels these energies may be more present from time to time, or may be a cascading or continuing experience for some of us who are naturally gifted or have found their way into being opened to a higher sensitivity rate of energy.

121

Though it seems that the energy finds us, this energy is everywhere and all around us just waiting for us to recognize it's presence. Once we start to become aware of energy in general, we naturally become more sensitive to it's presence as sentient beings. We naturally realize energy or the absence of it. When we exercise and experience heightened circulation in a cardiovascular workout or from physical moving and working we are energized. After we have exhausted a certain amount of chi energy our body becomes tired and we need to rest. Meditation also helps us to restore the core energy levels which are used during an active life.

Pranic Life Force Energy

The ancient siddhas investigated and found the dynamics or mechanics of universal energy and how it interacts with the physical human body. They developed ways of living longer life spans in order to continue their studies of energy and how it dances with the human life force. Some have even achieved immortality or an ageless animate state of existence. When this occurs a persons vibration rises and they usually experience special phenomena such as bi-location, teleportation, instantaneous manifestation, levitation, psychic powers, instant recall of the Akashic Records, and the ability to heal others including psychic healing.

Prana in vedic studies or chi in Asian studies refers to the life force energy that animates the human form and existence. This energy is also everywhere present as the cosmic primordial energy that all things are made of, and that we and all things originate from.

As we breathe we take in oxygen as it's conventionally carried from the nose and mouth into the lungs where it mixes with our blood and is carried out to every cell of our tissue. For us here on planet Earth breath is life and we naturally breath in the atmosphere to survive. Studies of

122

the ancients show us that there are pranic energy particles of light energy attached to the molecules of oxygen. These light particles are actually what we are made of and what we need to sustain physical existence as well as operate on all dimensional levels. We are made of energy. Everything here on this planet including us is made from primordial cosmic star energy as it shines down into our world. As we breathe in the light with the oxygen we become charged with energy. Conventional texts teach us that oxygen is drawn in through the mouth and nose. This is true though not isolated to only these openings. With a great surrounding pull and flow of Air and Light the lungs via the muscular diaphragm in the solar plexus pulls in air charged with oxygen and pranic light through all of the pores of the surrounding skin. The whole face, the eyes, and the torso in front and back of the body. In this way we are breathing more with our body than just through our mouths and noses. Take a few strong slow deep breaths and see if you can feel the flow moving in through your whole being, more so around the lungs and face. We also need a healthy amount of pure water to run our hydro-electric bio-dymanic multi-dimensional beings in a balanced, healthy, joyful and prosperous state. Feeling low? Make sure you're getting plenty of water, fresh air and sunshine!

As the cosmic energy comes into the body, the recognition of this process can start a whole plethora of energetic sensations and dynamics for you. As you slowly breath in practicing meditation or a yogic breathing style such as the 20:20 yogic breath found on page 125 in the next chapter. There are other helpful techniques to activate energy for you so that you can start having an interactive experience with energy itself. You will develop a friendship with it and it will recognize you and find you more easily as you continue. It will also start to build and you may have available to you extra energy as you need it for creative endeavors, helping others with energy and psychic healing.

As you continue to practice different energy exercises learning to experience and feel the different subtle ways that energy works in, around and through you. The energy will build and you may feel it's ebb and flow in waves. As you call it to you, now you may start using the energy for different applications. As you work with energy one of the most foundational practices you will want to do is moving the new energy in and the old energy out. We call this clearing. There are many ways to clear. You may practice with nature or the trees by receiving energy in through the left hand and projecting old unwanted energies out through the right hand. This is a great way to clear, heal and charge yourself with fresh new energy. When we are naturally psychic or starting to become more activated psychically, We sense, see, feel, and come into contact with many psychic impressions.

Mental Clearing Technique

Here's a clearing technique for removing unwanted psychic debris from others, and also psychic protection during psychic and healing work:

Visualize a large pyramid of White Light around you. The geometric shape of the pyramid coincides with mental energy and also is an antenna for Divine Intelligence. You can put a white light pyramid around your self, your home or your work space. Feel the difference of how this can work for you. Practice it when dealing with challenging people and situations and take mental note of how it works.

Connecting with the Cosmic Energy

As you breathe in the cosmic energy your brain and senses are ignited with it. Your multi-dimensional self and your multi-layered energy fields are filled with it. Take some long slow deep breaths and consciously focus your mind on the process of breathing itself. As you continue to breathe the energy is slowly and naturally building. Now as you have been focusing on the breath move your mental awareness out from your brain into your surrounding energy fields.

Visualize the cosmic energy in your fields with your eyes open and with your eyes closed. Try it both ways. Now also expand your etheric field and see if you can sense the energy empathically all around you in your energy field. As you do this, the energy has a consciousness and it becomes aware that it is being looked at. So as your awareness of it expands out in this exercise, it now turns towards you as it is in the millions of particles in your field and coming to be around you and your field. The cosmic energy in a quantum way can be attracted from close proximity and very far away such as the stars.

While you and the energy are simultaneously aware of each other also continue to sense the emanations of waves of conscious thought energy as you send brain waves into your field to connect with this energy.

As you continue to practice this and other techniques you will become more aware of the physical and etheric properties of energy on many levels and how you can influence it and work with it to help yourself and others.

Vital Life Force Energy

Another portion of your energy and associated with this Pranic Cosmic Chi Energy is your Vital Life Force Energy. This energy is the phantom power that keeps all the batteries and backup systems in your body charged. So when your Vital Force becomes too low you may feel drained and unable to comfortably exert yourself. With proper rest, nutrients and water you can be back at your optimal operating energy level in a relatively short time. If a person has ignored the warning signs and continued to push themselves way past the point of moderate recovery, then they may experience this uncomfortable and sometimes hard to recover from state of complete drain.

There can be nothing more uncomfortable for the achiever whose used to getting things accomplished than to lose their base operating energy. The key to understanding the vital life force dynamic is that when it is present and operating at full strength you feel normal and so it is usually more unnoticed. When it is running low to depleted you will definitely feel it's absence. This can be a very alarming state to be in. The hyper-alertness and hyper-acuity that brought a person to this state of depletion can often continue after the depletion occurs making for a push pull of trying to rest fully and not being able to because of the egos survival tendency to jump back into action. The adrenal glands which sit on top of the kidneys become inflamed and overworked. The back may start aching or burning as a result of this.

In order to rebuild there are many helpful nutrients out there such as B-12 and B vitamin supplements and adrenal support. The main thing will be to stay down and rest. Often as soon as we feel the least bit better we jump into action. This is an energetic situation in which you want to fully nurture yourself and rekindle your inner force because it's absence can lead to a litany of other disorders. You may want to cut out all caffeine for a few days. And maybe even ask 'Would I do better without any caffeine in the long run?'

There are minerals and crystals that can help you sense and rebuild your subtle energy. I find orange, green and blue calcite very soothing to hold and helpful for extreme exhaustion. Red and orange calcite will help you rebuild lower chakra energies.

There are also mudras (hand yoga gestures) and mantras (sound energy toning). Both of these you will feel quite an effect from when your vital chi has run too low. They can bring relief, balance and help you rebuild more quickly while you're taking some Extra time to REST. You can learn much about energy if your life force does run low and while you are rebuilding it.

Rub your palms together until they are hot and then reach around and place them on your kidneys and adrenal glands. Aaahhh! Yes, it feels great! This will also help you to feel better.

You will become more sensitive and consciously aware of energy around you in your fields. You will also become more aware of the energy inside you as your vital life force and also bringing in extra energies for healing and meditation or spiritual practices. As you become more aware of ever so subtle frequency vibrations around you, and sometimes not so subtle, you will be another step closer to working with spiritual and psychic healing.

Psychic Awareness

As we continue our journey in human life, one thing is for sure we are all thinkers. From the time we are born until we pass we never stop processing mental imagery, voluntary and involuntary messages to and from our body, subconscious thought forms, personal values, dreams, goals, wants, needs, relationships with others and many other things. The human mind is a very busy place! So any amount of meditation that we can engage ourselves in is a very good thing. This quiets the mind if even only slightly, it's helpful and to bring in extra energy for us to start processing.

As we start to study metaphysics or the spiritual world, we find that one of the first personal references that we may gain is that psychic awareness is one of our natural inborn gifts. For whatever reasons with many people it is undeveloped. This could be due to poor diet, stress, too much television, cell phone and computer exposure, or simply not believing in it. As you learn to trust your own gut feelings, intuitions, dreams as consciously aware moments you come to a new plateau or a quickening of the mental senses. Beyond belief and trust is knowing, and knowing can also come from your Soul. Knowing will simplify everything you've been mentally dabbling with and sifting through for however long you've been sampling it all.

When you are around someone who is psychic you may notice that they have a certain frequency or vibrational field around them that has a heightened feel in the air. This is their psychic mental field as it vibrates with the ethers. Many psychic people are born that way naturally and may have had no instruction or very little of it. This does not make a person a better or good person. Just like physical beauty does not make someone a better person. Though in our world of checks and balances we often equate these comparisons together. If you have natural gifts hopefully you are using them for your highest benefit and to help others. If you suspect or realize that you have psychic abilities then keep reading. If you're not sure and you want to open your abilities then also keep reading, you're in the right place, with the right book!

One deterrent from gaining more clarity on the psychic path is silent levels of the ego. When someone is psychic and they are constantly getting information at whatever level, sometimes it can be a crutch. It can also show up as a silent comparison to others. Sometimes it may give a person an edge in business and personal matters. Make sure that you're operating at a level of goodness. You don't want to be using your natural gifts to create more karmas of resolving life conflicts which can divert our mental attention and clarity.

If you are stepping into all of this as a new student, continue to do your clearing as indicated in this book and the meditation processes. It will all help you to filter out the unwanted and unneeded thoughts and emotions that the ego likes to entertain and the lower level astral information that you might be picking up from others. We don't want to be a spiritual or astral catch-all.

Psychic awareness primarily operates from the 4th dimension which is in tune with your brain, your mind, your mind field and also tuning into the 5th dimension which is the astral world. The astral world is huge and a very busy place. More so than planet Earth or the human mind. Worlds upon worlds of thought forms, beings and manifestations reside there as well as it being the Grand Central Station between other realms and the 3rd Dimension of our physical reality.

Psychic activity involves energy transmission between the physical brains of two humans directly. It can also be accessing from one person's brain, mind field or Soul to another person's brain, mind field and Soul. This energy transmission may be direct or it may move up into the astral and back to the physical simultaneously.

Focus your mind on your mind itself and ask to become more psychic and to open your psychic gifts. Your spirit guides will help to protect and filter your process so that you can have a healthy and safe expansion process. As you focus on your mind itself, this is an internal energy exercise. This can also bring mental clarity for many thoughts, feelings and situations in life. Doing meditation and energy work as described in this book will also help with the mental psychic unfolding process. Be patient with yourself and present. Document your thoughts, feelings and ideas about it all by writing it down in a journal. There is a special "Journey to the Akashic Records Workbook" available that can help you. No subtle thought, feeling or idea is too small to document. With this work sometimes small subtle moments can equal big realizations.

The Dynamics of Healing

There are many ways of healing the Mind, Body and Spirit. We have numerous modalities available to us today. Some from ancient times or developed over centuries of study and many new ways of healing developed by people who want to help others. One example of this would be Reiki. While it's roots are from ancient times, it has been popularized in recent years and has taken off like wildfire. It's benefits in comparison with other forms of healing can be subtle yet gives the practitioner a base of working with energy. The results like many other forms of healing can vary from person to person. This is natural. One of the main gifts of this technique is that it has reached a wide audience and has become accepted by the medical industry.

Reconnection Healing, Theta Healing, and Matrix Energetics are just a few of the newer modalities that have cropped up from gifted individuals working with healing energy through new creative ways.

Chi Gong is an ancient form of working with energy, practiced by the Shaolin and Shinto monks and priests, as well as much of Asian culture, that has many benefits from subtle benefits to very pronounced sensations and activations within a person's body and energy fields. This practice much like many of the other ancient practices has one unique quality. The same practices that can be used for simple energy benefits are also the same practices that can open a person into more masterful levels of existence. The same principles are true of Kriya Yoga which offers subtle ritualistic practices for the common householder as well as master level energetic techniques used by the ancient masters and siddhas. The same techniques used for mastership are also used by meditation practicing householders as a more subtle everyday ritual. Often time the higher truths are held, hidden and maintained within the simplicity and ideas of the practices.

Healing energies can operate with the same principles. There are many ways for the healing energy to find you. The most common is through prayer for yourself and others. A continued focus of healing energy can yield sustained results. At other times a recognition and then a release of the situation or affliction which is in need of healing without further focusing on it can have dynamic results. There is no right or wrong way, only better ways for each situation. What may work for one person as a healer or person in need of healing may not work as well for another, though both approaches are valid. You will learn to find what works best for you as a healer and for the person receiving the healing over the course of utilizing different creative approaches and/or variations based on a central theme. This is where your intuitive abilities start receiving information to help another person in the way which is best for them at that moment.

We humans tend to want to feel good. Feeling normal or balanced sometimes has no feeling to it, so it can be hard to recognize. Much like the vital force energy is more noticeable when it's not present in comparison to when it is. Mentally, spiritually, emotionally and with our diet often times we will challenge ourselves with situations which create a dramatic response for us. Remember normal often has no drama, so if we are craving sensory experiences then we often create it in our experiences, surroundings and lives. This can bring colorful varied results in lives not always to our liking or for our highest good. Personal observation of these patterns is key for change to occur.

This is one reason why it works to have the benefit of another person (*aka* Divine Soul in human form) working with the person in need of healing even if you know and trust your own abilities to heal. It bolsters the dynamic of the healing energy. Remember '***Wherever two or more are gathered in my name (God) so shall I be'***. This is true of all spiritual practices and certainly applies also to healing. This doesn't mean that Creator and the many healing agencies are not present when you are alone, just that it is amplified when together as two or more. So the energy of 2 people together is not simply doubled...it is squared! This is good to know because it brings more power to the healing.

Healing energy can come through different channels and directions as we work with it.

A. It can come directly from one person to another.

B. It can come through one person to another.

C. It can be directed remotely from one person to
   another in the same place or over a distance.

D. It can be directed remotely from an outside source
   by one person to reach another person over a distance.

Sometimes the person who is emitting the healing energy may not even feel that there is a healing taking place for another person. This is when God, Spirit, the Angels and Spirit guides are attending to another's healing through osmosis or simply by being in contact with someone who has made agreements with Spirit to be a healer. On this level the person with the healing energy may not even yet know that they are being called to be a healer, though they may discover through reports from others with stories of relief and healing taking place. If you've been working with healing energy or energy in general to open and expand your own horizons, you may experience plateaus of normalcy with the increased energy seated in your body and fields to the point of not continually being present to it. You may also recognize it naturally at all times just fine.

Some of the ways in which you might feel or sense energy are:

A. You may feel or sense a field of energy coming from another person from a short to moderate distance.

B. You may feel or sense a field of energy by talking to someone on the phone, seeing them in your mind, or looking at a photograph of them.

C. You may feel or sense energy coming from the ethers, a spiritual master or another source during a meditation process.

D. You may feel or sense energy coming through your heart, 3rd eye, crown or another part of your body.

E. You may feel or sense energy coming from the Earth, sky, the ocean, the trees and other elements of nature.

F. There are many more ways to sense energy as you become present to it in the present moment. A-E should give you a good idea of feeling and sensing energy in different ways.

If you do not notice the increased potency of your energy and you fall back into old emotional or lifestyle patterns the extra energy you are now carrying can bring amplified with varied results. Your spirit guides will help you to balance and filter these situations so you don't become lost in it, slowed or karmically challenged. Simply noticing what's going on and taking action to correct or improve matters will release and clear karma for you. You are in the midst of a creatively unfolding and ever changing universe, cosmos, planet, race of people, not to mention social, economic, and personal situations. So take good care in moving forward with your own self development process when starting to work with increased energy. For many of us change will be your best friend on many levels.

As your practice with using healing energy continues so will your personal levels of trust, knowing and proficiency. You will learn what works and in what situations to use different techniques. For instance someone may come to you for a reading when they really need an energetic clearing. A person may think they need physical healing when they really need to recover from a childhood trauma that can be released in various ways.

You will know the best way to approach what they need and will find ways to communicate with them so that they are comfortable in your approach. This insures that the person will remain open to receive healing.

One person may intervene in conversation with you as you're talking about healing another person and state that it is not you but God doing the work. Ultimately this is true as all things are God. You are a Divine Expression of God in human form. So it is best to continue your own process and simply agree with the other person. Do not let conflicts of hamper your path. Often times we are subject to hypnotic suggestions from others that seek to dis-empower us in the moment by redirecting conversation and energy.

We're all human, let it be and move on. The key is take what you need and leave what you don't need. Do not become confused by another's reflection of the way it should be. Trust your own intuition, especially if you are a sensitive person and are used to taking in information given from your own personal platform of observation. Don't let others inhibit your ability to grow. The intricacies of the healing energies are simple and yet vast as you continue to become more sensitive to them. There is a point of reference for each of us as healers that is important for us to experience in that we are part of the healing process, whether giving or receiving. It is important for you to know that you are part of the process. It is also important to know that God, Spirit and the Cosmic Healing Energy flows through you to reach the other person.

You Can Heal From Different Perspectives:

A. You may heal by a voice command, mantra or prayer creating a quantum healing effect as You, the Divine Soul have been given the power to influence the ethers through your voice.

B. You may heal through touch or 'hands on healing' as You and Spirit have the power to be a conduit for the healing energy to directly flow through and instantaneously heal or affect healing gradually over time.

C. You may direct the healing energy through a field of energy while being in the room with another person without touching them.

D. You may direct healing energies with your mind as all things are connected through the Universal Mind of God with distance healing, medical intuitive healing or clairvoyant healing.

D. You may also heal through silent meditation as you direct your mind to heal another. You may also employ the Holy Spirit, The Arc Angels and Angels of the Light of God, Spirit Guides and the Ascended Masters.

The main thing is to get in and start somewhere. So read the books, practice the techniques, take the classes, though do not be lost to being the eternal student. The world needs your healing abilities so at some point you've got to give it a try, move forward and get out there.

You may be pleasantly surprised at your level of involvement with helping another and that can be inspiration enough to catapult you forward on the path of becoming a healer. When the moment is right Spirit will present a situation or person to you that is in need of healing. Truly their healing is between them and God, Great Spirit and the Universe via their own learning, healing, self development and Soul contracts. We'll discuss in other chapters in this book Healing the Inner Child, the dynamics of the Soul and Ancestral and Family Healing through the DNA.

Healing energy can be visualized in many forms:

It can be the release of a childhood memory from the cellular tissue of the body, as thoughts and memories are stored throughout our bodies over the course of our lives. Colors may vary of old energies leaving: Black, grey, brown, or any color that works to complete the healing for the individual.

It may be a golden light, a white light or any other color which you as a healer and the person receiving can respond to.

It may be a sphere of light, a stream or a field that you bathe them in.

It may be light that is expanded or directed from inside of them.

It may also be an energy transference coming directly from your hands into their energy fields, DNA or the physical body.

You may start by visualizing with them a beautiful emerald green (the color frequency of the heart chakra) or a pink, white or gold light within their heart and then direct it out to other areas of the body or to engulf the whole body and fields.

You may visualize with them the colors of the 7 main

chakras and go through each chakra, announcing the properties associated with that chakra and vocally clear, heal, balance, harmonize and open the chakras through a guided meditation. Usually from chakra 1-7 or 7-1 in the direction of up or down along the spine.

You may use ancient healing techniques that are channelled to you from the Akashic Records from past lives in other civilizations of which that person has been part of.

You can heal by clearing, balancing and harmonizing the DNA of the person either all at once as a whole or by addressing each pair of strands and what it's connection is.

You may use the Mother Earth energies and the energy of nature such as the trees to project healing to a person and also to absorb and transmute unwanted, dis-harmonic or negative energies. The Earth is a great being that we are connected with and will gently and willingly participate in any healing process for the greater good.

You may conjure the power of the elements for healing. Bring down the primordial energy of the starlight into your hands or directly to the other person returning them to wholeness and wellness. You may use the living consciousness of water by charging it with the imprint of healing energy. The other person may drink the charged water or bathe in it. You can also have a bowl of water possibly with sea salt, essential oils such as lavender for clearing and absorbing unwanted energies close by or between you. Dispose of the bowl of water after the healing and clearing. You may also spray them with a water misting bottle of sea salt and lavender as you announce healing and clearing.

You may also conjure from the ethers of the air itself quantum healing energies to heal, transform, energize and transmute unwanted energies and sickness for a person. You learn to direct this energy with your mind as you call on it.

Energy is just energy. All energy seeks expression. Sometimes when people are starting to experience energy for the first times their not really sure what they are getting as long as they feel a charge. This can have an addictive quality for some people. As you open yourself up for healing to flow through you, be sure that you are announcing the presence of God, Healing Light, The Masters, The Christ Light, Universal Cosmic Healing Energy, The Arc Angels by name, or any references to the Good of the Light that sets the frequencies for healing to occur. This insures you are always getting the best! Also noted: Spirit Guides and Angels can also heal. There may be a family member now on the other side which wishes to participate in the healing as they are now on the other side and have a birds eye view of how to help and can help to direct the healing to take place with ease. As you open for the healing energy to flow through you, this also insures that you will not drain your own personal energy and that you are not absorbing the other persons unwanted energies which need to leave. As you perform any healing be sure to send the old energy into the Light of Source to be disintegrated and turned back into pure positive energy. Though Light or Universal energy has a noticeable charge or quality to it, you will also notice that when healing is called upon, the Healing Energy will have a certain or specifically noticeable soft vibration to it. Supportive and soothing and you will come you know when it is present.

Arc Angel Gabriel

18" x 24" acrylic on aluminum

© 2012 Bill Foss

Arc Angel Raphael

© 2012 Bill Foss

18" x 24" acrylic on aluminum

Arc Angel Michael
18" x 24" acrylic on aluminum

© 2012 Bill Foss

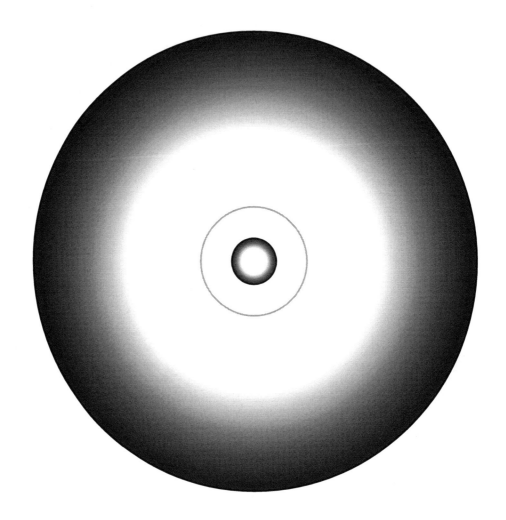

The Power of Psychic Healing

As you direct your visual energy from your eyes into the geometry, let the energy build as you focus on the center point. Continuing to focus you will notice that the external circle will start to vibrate and radiate with energy patterns from your peripheral vision. Focusing both eyes now activate your 3rd Eye or brow chakra center to also focus on the center point. As the image reflects energy back to your eyes like a mirror you are supercharging your psychic energy for healing. Now hold in your mind something within yourself, your life or another person or situation which you intend to project healing energy to. Once you have a sufficiently energized focus in your mind of that which you intend to heal, look out through the whole larger ball or outer circle all at once softening your gaze. Feel your mind expanding out with invisible emanations or rings of energy. This is the power of your eyes together with your 3rd eye, the pineal gland, your brain and your mind field emitting a high frequency of powerful psychic healing energy.

As you continue to practice with the geometry you can then practice without the geometry while looking at a picture of someone or something you want to heal. Gazing into an object or place in your thoughts to feel the expansion and direction of your optic projections and brain waves. You can also practice the procedure with eyes closed focusing on the inner sensations of the mind and brain and then picturing the person, place or thing you want to send energy to and affect healing for.

Receive a download of the process by visiting:
www.billfossworld.com/psychichealing.html

The power of the mind is immense. We are shown through studies that the human brain has enough energy to light up a whole city. Is it any wonder that in Atlantis they did just that and much more. By working with the mind together in groups and individually they sent out great waves of energy to create from the very ethers many things they needed including healing, more energy to power their cities, blessings to all of the earth, the waters, and the elements for their use and even structures and art forms!

Psychic Healing has it's roots in many ancient cultures. Ancient Greece had many healers who worked with the power of the mind to directly affect healing for the people. Ancient Egypt had it's priesthood of schools where they indoctrinated the royal families into the practices of psychic healing by teaching them to send out or broadcast a signal to those who were brought before them to be healed and also out across the land to all the people. They harnessed the power of the sun by using golden oracles to collect it's energy which was used for many applications. Solar gazing was used in Egypt to achieve higher levels of enlightenment and healing.

Solar gazing is a key element in many ancient cultures including Tibet. It has been reported that Christ solar gazed as well as the Siddhas and Yogis of India. Just by bringing the cosmic energy of the sun into the eyes at daybreak and sunset for a few minutes this process has had transformative effects and gifts for many, many people throughout history, including expanded psychic activity, and the power to send out healing energy via the brain and the mind field. Also personal sustained well being and even in some cases a shift into higher consciousness and on into ascension.

In Brazil and South America Spiritism is a form of psychic healing that has many varied techniques as the healing gifts that come through different individuals can be stylistically unique, such as Mauricio Panisset often referred to as the Man of Light. He would project a brilliant light from his body that would light up the room and bring many amazing healings to his patients. There are many psychic surgeons who pulled diseased tissue from human bodies by using their hands and some by using only their minds.

As we look at the image on the preceding page and read the exercise for learning to project psychic healing energy, we can start to feel the energy moving through our eyes, our brain and our mind field. The ancient siddhas of India discovered the properties of thoughts. The eyes, the 3rd eye or brow energy center between the eyes, brain and the mind field are all connected and work together.

They found that thoughts actually enter into the brain through the eyes from the mind field. The mind field is one of the multi-layered fields around the human body that is anchored with the 3rd eye chakra. As thoughts enter into the eyes from the mind field they are sent into the brain where they are processed simultaneously for a multitude of functions including the human body, the emotional body and all the other chakras, their coinciding fields and the glands and organs associated with each chakra. This is an amazing dynamic. The internal external flow of thought energy into the eyes and brain from the mind field and from the brain through the eyes and back out into the mind field simultaneously. This is a synchronous flow and exchange of multi-dimensional energy.

The mind field is in turn in the midst of many layered bands of vibrations surrounding the planet. As you have a vibrational response you are tuning into a certain field or frequency which in turn moves thoughts and ideas in through the eyes and to the brain where more processing is done based on input from the surroundings via the senses, childhood and lifetime experiences, learned and stored knowledge and events, wisdom and more.

As we tune into meditation techniques we utilize the 3rd eye and the crown chakra. Energy practices and meditations may be involved around any or all of the chakra centers. When activating the crown and 3rd eye centers the coinciding glands in the brain are activated which are the Thalumus and the Pineal glands. These glands become activated with cosmic energy and start broadcasting a frequency or emitting carrier waves. The energy can be focused in a directed beam. It can also radiate in more of circular waves or radiate as a sphere coming out around the body.

At this point you are in touch with energy of the higher dimensions and Divine connections with Spiritual beings including Creator God Source. You may consciously invite them to be present in the transmission of energy taking place. So as you practice the technique of psychic healing you are becoming consciously aware of the feeling of the conjuring of energy from within the brain as it creates a vortex there while flowing in from your mind field and then directing it out to that which you intend to affect.

For instance you may be working with someone who has a sprained ankle or pulled muscle. As you look at the area on the body you will instantaneously focus on the power from within your mind and send it out through your eyes and your brain as a beam or an emanating field of healing energy. Once you start working with this process it will find itself through you more quickly and strengthen the healing qualities of the healing work that you are doing. You may also find that in using this technique you will naturally become more psychic or empathic. If you are already psychic this is a great way to use your natural gift in a new way to help others. If you are a working psychic and give readings for people in person or over the phone you can use this extra added technique to amplify the messages coming through your words and affect change for an individual on new levels. How exciting for you! Creator, the Spirit Guides and the Universal Energy of Healing working in conjunction with you will know best in finding the ways to help the person you are reading for. They may even experience emotional or physical healing in the moment.

If you are an energy healer or practitioner this is also a new added way you can affect healing change for the individual and will not challenge any of the modalities you are currently using. It will simply add to your repertoire.

You can use the technique of psychic healing to project colors as well if this helps you in your work. Keep a mental focus as you start practicing the process on the sensations of the energy moving through your brain and eyes. This will help you to become fluent with it more quickly. Also focusing on the mind field, the pineal gland and thalumus glands is helpful too. It can bring added gifts to your mental abilities and strengthen your mind.

As you continue the work and practice this procedure you may also find that you can start to look into the body of the person that you are healing. You may go into the tissue and see what is in dis-ease. This can be like remote viewing on a micro level. You can focus in as much as is needed and start to project healing energy through your mind's eye to correct the situation. Take as much time as you feel needed, though do not limit the healing energy to a certain time value as this energy is working on a quantum level through you. This may also be done in a long distance healing session.

You may also use the technique of broadcasting energy to help manifest something you want to create in your life or bring into your experience or something for another person. If it resonates with your life path and your greater truth, it will manifest that much more easily for you.

Congratulations to You in learning to explore a new way

of healing. Psychic Healing can work for yourself as well as others. It is inspirational to find more keys to the secrets of spirit. Every time we expand we find that we are standing at the threshold of a new frontier where we will all learn that we are interconnected through the Universal and the great gathering of Souls experiencing human existence at the truest and purest level that we can perceive, both individually and as a race. Pure Love and Joy. Blessings to You.

Chakra Music CD & Download

As we enter the Records we are connected within a multitude of ways including thoughts, feelings, actions, notions, gut instincts, dreams, waking state thoughts and aha moments of problem solving, creative ideas and even inventions.

Chapter 12

Entering the
Akashic Records

$\mathcal{M}$editation and Tantra or Tantric techniques are excellent ways to ready yourself to move into the Akashic Records.

Meditation - a broad variety of practices that includes techniques designed to promote relaxation, build internal energy or life force (chi, ki, ka, prana, etc.) and develop compassion, love, patience, generosity and forgiveness. More ambitious forms of meditation aim at an effortlessly sustained single-pointed concentration or single-pointed analysis, meant to enable its practitioner to enjoy an indestructible sense of well-being while engaging in any life activity.

Tantra - Or 'Technique' - A body of beliefs and practices which, working from the principle that the Universe we experience is nothing other than the concrete manifestation of the Divine Energy of the Godhead that creates and maintains that Universe, seeks to ritually appropriate and channel that energy, within the human microcosm, in creative and emancipatory ways.

$\mathcal{M}$editation is a great way to relax in general with it's many ways to benefit our bodies, minds and spirits. The positive effects of meditation are multitudinous. Everything from physical healing to better moods and emotions during the day. Better sleep, continued relaxation, enhanced creativity, the ability to experience love on a deeper level in the body, the thoughts and the mind are all gifts of meditation.

I strongly recommend meditation not just as something to dabble with from time to time, but as a way of lifestyle to practice continually day by day, night by night, morning by morning, and moment by moment. It will bring good health and peace of mind to the rest of the moments, hours and days of your life.

Here we will use meditation to relax our minds, bodies and energy fields in order to become still enough to have an experience within the Akashic Records. It is beneficial to use any type of meditation which helps you personally to relax and get into a more quiet and/or an expanded state. As you relax you can begin to move into the visionary practices of accessing the Akashic Records, whether you go *up and out* into it, merge with it, bring it to you, transport there through your body & heart or through the earth. There are many pathways we can creatively take and you will probably be drawn to one or two techniques though you may try them all.

Meditation helps to prepare the way for you and it also relaxes the energy around you and your natural connections into the Records, though, the stream of these portals will continue writing whatever your state is even at great levels of tension or stress. The more you relax through meditation the more you have access to these great banks of knowledge. We will recommend a few ways of meditation here for you, though, if you're already involved in a great way of meditating that you're comfortable with, by all means keep doing what you're doing.

You may use a way you know that already works for

you to relax before entering the Records. Though current meditations may be working wonderfully for you, new processes you learn can help your **psyche** to have a profound experience just because it is different.

As you prepare to enter into the Records or your own **Book of Life** within the Records, it is important to use some meditation and relaxation techniques or tantras because you will be moving into areas of energy that are continuing to become more subtle as you continue to travel through portals to these places and visions from within yourself while in the Akashic Records.

As you continue your practices of sensing, viewing, travelling and opening, you will become more aware of subtle layers of what I call 'conflicts'. These conflicts are layers of denial in the mind as the ego tries to continually pull at you in the relaxed state to try directing or controlling the experience. Subtle layers of conflict can also be in the energy fields of the eyes or in the eyes as you try to relax them even deeper into a purposely stimulated R.E.M. (rapid eye movement) state. R.E.M. state is a very good and stable state to engage the visionary process during, though not always present in these states of viewing. As we enter the Records we are connected within a multitude of ways including thoughts, feelings, actions, notions, gut instincts, dreams, waking state thoughts and aha moments of problem solving, creative ideas and even inventions. The moments of R.E.M. that we are simultaneously experiencing as we enter or slip into a place just between wake and sleep are, for now, what we want to focus on ever so gently.

This place will give us voluntary and involuntary responses corresponding to the vision and sensory process which are precursors to a much deeper level of visionary seeing, intuition and 'in the moment' sensory experiences. As you relax the eyes and the muscles of the face, you will become subtly aware of the essence of silence and more of a clarity. As you step down within conscious/unconscious moments of perception to the sensations within the eyes and the energy we may feel on the face, the crown chakra or the 3rd eye (brow center), these sensations become more minute, smaller even precise, as you allow the flow of the relaxation to continue. These moments are why meditation may prove to be helpful in order to relax even deeper and start to have a lucid experience. As these sensations are happening you will be using your imagination or creative mind to envision the process of the Akashic journey, whether you are listening to a recorded Akashic guided meditation, or you are creatively envisioning your own journey with your mind and senses as you view your unfolding new Akashic journey process.

This is actually the way you will probably continue to journey. With a mental road map you creatively view the guided journey process. The imagination starts the process and the intuition takes over and starts playing the movie on it's own as the creative mind relaxes and just watches. This is when you will have a reference point of knowing that you are making some visionary progress with the process and will start trusting, knowing, naturally accepting and integrating the mechanics of energetics with the process. In these subtle moments, this is where the magic occurs.

Let's talk about meditation exercises:

Meditation processes include:
- **Kriya Yoga: Kundalini Pranayam Breathing**
- **Tai Chi/ Chi Gong**
- **Still Focus Breathing**
- **Hatha Yoga**

From the ancient Kriya yoga tradition Babaji and the Master Siddhas bring us the 20:20 breath.

20:20 breathing meditation exercise. Sitting in full or half lotus or in a chair in a relaxed and upright position. Breathe in and out at a long continuing and even rate. Count to 20 as you breathe in slowly and the same count of 20 as you exhale out slowly. This creates a breathing rhythm that is slow and long and brings much relaxing chi or pranic energy into the body via the light particles attached to oxygen molecules as it enters in through the nostrils and simultaneously through the rest of the body.

We actually breathe with more than just our nostrils. The oxygen is inhaled directly through the pores of the skin. Enjoy the healing and relaxing effects of this meditation as you sit for 10, or 15 minutes of breathing. As the lungs are usually used to a 20:10 ratio of breathing it may take a few minutes of relaxing the lungs enough to breathe slowly and evenly.

If you have to take a catch up breath in between, not to worry, the key is to not inspire or create any conflicts of mind or emotion, our key here is to relax, let go and practice the process. There can be many other insights that will come with this breathing technique, though we will discuss those more in depth in the workbook. For now we will practice this meditation to become more expert with the process itself.

The mind and body tissue will become oxygenated and you will relax as your mind becomes more creative. Thoughts may come and go, though the yogis will focus on a white or blank screen, signifying to them, no thoughts. First get the breathing process down and then be concerned with the thoughts. Just notice when the thoughts are over active or when they seem to stop and the mind becomes still. Enjoy this beneficial, simple and powerful meditation.

Tai Chi & Chi Gong

If you know one of the Tai Chi forms or know some of the postures this is a very good moving meditation to do. The subtleness of the movements as you flow with this 'internal martial art' will bring a flowing peace and much soft earth and sky chi as it moves through you. This stimulates the senses as well. I remember back to an initial Tai Chi class held in an art gallery with my original instructor. As we looked at the paintings while doing the postures, the images became more vividly colorful to our sight. While practicing one day in a park with him, I asked him to demonstrate more closely a particlular stance. He looked at me and very subtly announced *"The idea of the form is to become formless"*. You can do the form or postures anywhere indoors or outdoors. Check out a local Tai Chi class or look online for examples of the forms and postures. I recommend the Tai Chi Chuan 24 posture form. If you have used any Chi Gong still pose meditation and energy exercises this will also be very helpful and beneficial. This is also a good way to access the calm stillness and energy of the Universal or Tao before an Akashic journey. There are many postures, so let's learn a simple and powerful stationary Chi Gong exercise:

The Foundation, Standing like a Tree

As you stand indoors or outdoors stand up straight though relaxed so none of your joints are locked and knees are slightly bent. Standing outdoors barefoot on the earth is the best way if possible. With back straight and eyes closed gently, open your armpits as if you are holding an egg under each one, but not tensed. Lean slightly forward on the balls of the feet and envision a rod of energy going all the way down to the earth's core from the balls of the feet. Bring your palms facing up to rest at the creases of the legs or just under the belly. Now just simply stand and breathe while being peaceful. Envision your crown connected to the sky as your feet are connected to the earth. Envision your inner smile. Now just keep standing and breathing for a while... Do you feel the energy? Good! Relax and shake it out. For more see 'Patting Down the Meridians' in the next section of this chapter.

Still Focus Breathing

Vippassana is the original process that **Guatama Sidhartha** (the Buddha) learned as he taught himself to become enlightened. This breathing technique is one of the introductory practices and has many benefits. The breath is very simple and will bring deep release and insight if practiced correctly. The process: Simply sit in a relaxed position and breathe in and out of the nostrils normally.

As you breathe become aware of the subtle and gentle wind on the rims of the nostrils as the breath touches the nostrils on it's exit and entry. While you are doing this direct your mind to this sensation and keep it there. Do this for 10-15 minutes or more. If your mind wanders away in thought bring it back to the focus on the nostrils. This is a powerful and unique process which brings you to a state of connection through this subtle wind of the breath being connected to everything external as it now enters and exits your nostrils. It is all connected and you are connected to it through this breath. In that moment there is no conflict just being.

No right or wrong, just you, the breath, and the world. Shifts take place elsewhere in the mind as you practice this for short or longer periods of time. No thoughts just focus on the wind entering and exiting the rims of the nostrils. Still Focus Breathing is a consciousness-opener and a good precursor for accessing the Akashic Records.

Hatha Yoga

Hatha Yoga is also a great moving exercise which is also a tantric technique in that we are physically working with and manipulating the muscle tissue and energy of the body and skin. The **asanas** or postures are great ways to get in touch with the Universal as we stretch in the poses, we are unlocking the meridians of the body as they connect with source energy and also release negativity out of the body at the same time. So there is an exchange and an eb & flow. This stretching of the tissue in the pose and the relaxation in between the poses is a wonderful moving expression of meditation. You are also opening the zones, meridians and channels of energy in the physical body used by the emotions, and your body soul to store experiences and charges of energy. This will bring you the peace of a still lake so that you can access the Akashic Records after your moving yogic meditation.

The **Tantras** or Techniques will be interesting to you as they activate and stimulate the energy in various associated ways making our Akashic visionary experiences that much more colorful and vivid.

Tantic Techniques include:
- **Patting Down the Meridians**
- **Stimulating the Senses**
- **Mantra Sounds to Activate the Chakras**

Patting Down the Meridians

Take your hand placing it on the opposite shoulder and start patting down the top of your arm to the hand and then the palm and up the under side to your armpit and down the side of the body to your waist. The sides of the rib cage contain the largest cluster of surface nerve endings in the body. Now in the other direction back up the side down the underside of arm over the fingers and backup the arm to the shoulder. Repeat the same process on the other side. Take some long relaxed deep breaths while patting.

Next place your hands at your hips or waist and start patting down the legs on both sides all the way to the ankles and then the insides of the ankles and back up the insides of the legs ending at the crease in the legs where the **lymph glands** reside. Give them a few extra pats. You should now feel fully stimulated with energy. Take a moment to experience the peaceful balance and heightened energy sensations. How do you feel? Good!

Buffing the Nails Together to Create an Energy Field

While in a relaxed position start to breathe consciously and slowly as you take both hands and place them together facing the fingernails of each hand together. Start briskly rubbing the fingernails together of each hand in an up and down motion. Here the clicking sound of the nails as they buff the nails of the other hand. Continue to focus on the breath, breathing consciously deep and slow. Continue the buffing for approximately five minutes. Now open your hands in front of your solar plexus or stomach area as if you are holding something. Feel the ball of energy that you have created, just continue to experience the sensation of this energy for a few moments. Next bring your hands up to your mouth and blow out energy from your breath across your fingers. Feel the surges of cosmic energy as it glows around your hands. This gives you recognition of the divine energy existing in the breath and the amplified energy (chi) glowing around the hands that you've just stimulated.

Stimulate the Senses of the Face

Again consciously focus your mind on the breath, coming from your exhale as we discussed earlier. Now take your hands and start massaging your face. Rub the forehead, the jaws, the mouth, the nose, your eye sockets and with eyes closed, the eyelids. Rub your ears as if you are cleaning them stimulating all the thousands of meridian points there. Continue to breathe in and out slowly and deeply.

Rub the throat, massaging the thyroid glands, the sides and back of the neck. Now tap moderately or briskly rub your scalp as if washing your hair. Feel the energy tingling as it ignites and flows up around the head, scalp and shoulders.

Massage the Glandular Systems

Next, massage the thymus gland in the sternum area halfway between the throat and the heart behind the upper breast plate. You may tap it gently or rub it with a soothing sensation.

Next reach around to the kidney area and place your hands over the adrenal glands which sit on top of the kidneys. As you continue to breath in energy, gently rub them and now hold your hands still as you breath energy into the adrenal glands through your hands, revitalizing them and soothing them with healing and supportive energy. These little glands regulate all sugars and all energy flow in the body. It is important to give them some extra healing and soothing attention especially when feeling fatigued. We have opened all the meridians, massaged the glandular system throughout the body which regulates energy and controls the organs. We have also stimulated the senses, upper openings of the body, face, crown chakra, and the epidermis or surface tissue of the body with the patting. Take a moment to experience the peaceful balance and heightened energy sensations. How do you feel? Good!

Sound Syllables to Activate the Chakras

Sanscrit mantra sounds also called seed syllables because they are known to vibrate certain areas of the body whether meridians, pressure points, chakras (spinal energy center), organs, glands, etc. Sound activates vibrations as it permeates the body, mind & energy fields of the person chanting the tones. These tones have long since been used as special healing tools to clear energy, open, and restore balance to the spinal energy centers known as the chakras which correspond to aspects of our lives, energy fields, organs, physical surroundings and so on. By activating the chakras with the seed syllables we are clearing, healing, vibrating, and balancing the energies of the whole being therefore restoring, changing or transfiguring the life of the individual. We will use it here to stimulate the natural flow of kundalini in the base chakra as it flows up into and through all of the chakras to the crown.

The syllables are:
LAH, BAH, RAH, YAM, HAH, AHA, AUM

The basic chakra centers (lower to higher) are:
Base of the Spine, Navel, Solar Plexus, Heart, Throat, 3rd Eye (brow center) and Crown.

The syllables are chanted in monotone in this sequence:
LAH, BAH, RAH, YAM, HAH, AHA, AUM

To Open & Bring up the Kundalini Energy

As you chant these tones in a monotone of your choosing that feels good to you, start to rub the tummy brushing away the energy and flicking it off as you move up to the heart, brushing the energy out from the heart and flicking it off the hands and then up over the back of the head and crown as the energy moves. You should start to feel some real energy stirring around in the areas where you're rubbing as the energy is pulled up the spine through the body and playfully circulates in and around the body. You may feel goose bumps, tingling on the skin or other sensations.

From the base of the spine to the top of the head,
  Here's a diagram:
LAH - Root Chakra - Survival, Connection, Primal,
      Foundation
BAH - Navel Chakra - Creative Energy, Sex, Flow
RAH - Solar Plexus - Action, Emotions, Core Energy
YAM - Heart Chakra - Love, Healing, Joy
HAH - Throat Chakra - Sound, Voice commands,
      Expression, Wisdom
AHA - 3rd Eye (brow) - Connection to world, others,
      psychic, creative
AUM - Crown Chakra - Connection to God, Soul, Spirit

As you use these exercises they will stimulate energies within the body, mind and energy fields you will stimulate a more vivid Akashic Journey. Practice all the techniques of this chapter to get a feel for which ones you really resonate with. You can do a whole sequence in 20-30 minutes and then take another 30 minutes for your Akashic Records guided experience. As you use the meditation techniques you may find 1, 2, a few or all of the meditation and energy techniques beneficial for your use primarily as a relaxing and energizing agent before you begin your visionary inquiry work into the Records.

The Tantra of Touch
Gather together a few objects as you sit down after doing

your energizing or meditation techniques. This exercise can be done together with the meditations or separately on it's own. These objects can be detailed, colorful, geometric, or inspirational. Do the objects you choose have certain textures? As you sit quietly examine each object closely, the size, the shape, the colors and the details. Now touch it. Feel the texture, the shape and the weight. Really get 'in touch' with each object. Now as you sit quietly with eyes closed, put down the object and see it in your mind. As you have looked at it with your eyes open drinking in all the details and visual essence of the object look now with your mind's eye at the object and see it clearly in your mind. Next with eyes closed pick up or touch the object and feel the texture and shape as you continue to see it in your mind. Practice this with a few objects. You are turning on or stimulating your inner vision to come alive. You can use this practice before your guided meditation journey to experience clear and vivid visions and images. Enjoy!

The Tantra of Art

Now with the same idea as with the objects, stand in front of some art forms, sculptures or paintings and try the same technique. Check out all the interesting colors, brush strokes, and styles of the paintings. Drink in the vibrations and tones of the pictures. Maybe there is a carved piece of wood or a decorative mandala or sculpture which you can observe the detail of. As you look at each piece allow your eyes to move very slowly around each piece. Close your eyes from moment to moment seeing with your mind what you have just seen with your eyes. And then walk slowly to the next piece of art allowing yourself to really be fully present and sentiently alive with feeling. This exercise opens the mind and the senses. You might find yourself slowing down in the moment and having a true child-like moment of appreciation for the art forms you may have not experienced otherwise. You may even see or find the world of Spirit expressing energetically through the art pieces. This will open your inner vision and energetically enhance and clear your regular vision and levels of perception with the mind. This exercise will stimulate and enhance your inner vision as you look into the Akashic Records and you may even have much clearer and vividly life-like dreams during sleep.

The Tantra of Music and Sound

Try listening to some classical music, your favorite meditations or new age music. This is very relaxing to the mind. Just be aware of yourself listening to the tones of the music as you enjoy the relaxing vibrations of sound. Maybe you have a special series of mind enhancing or expanding tracks you enjoy listening to. Native American flute and drumming can be very inspirational. Solfeggio tones in music and the pure tones themselves can be healing and stimulating throughout your whole being. Classical music is known to have harmonically dynamic effects on the body mind and spirit. Allow yourself to relax as you listen to music that opens the heart, mind, body & soul lifting you up, soothing and relaxing you as you prepare for your Akashic Journey experience.

Note: In this chapter we have discussed multiple meditation and energy techniques for preparation of going into the Records or your Book of Life. Do not for like you have to do all of these together every time. Practicing these techniques can be helpful before a journey. Find the techniques that work best for you and utilize those as your core practice, trying a new one every so often. You don't want to become overwhelmed with conflict prior to an Akashic meditation.

Super Divine 2 CD Set & Downloads

Use the Akashic Records
to enter your Book of Life
and heal your karmas by
allowing yourself to look
at the events of your life
without judgement and
watch for the silent grace of
transformation to unfold.
Create good karma and live
your darma.

Chapter 13

Using the Akashic Records to Heal Karma

Karma - (in Hinduism and Buddhism) the sum of a person's actions in this and previous states of existence, viewed as deciding their fate in future existences. Destiny or fate, following as effect from cause.

Karma has long since been an intriguing subject of spiritual seekers the world over. So much that even common folks usually know the meaning of this term. Although often because of our fear based tendencies of society and duality, it is often used in a context referring to negative or bad karma. Karma or effect from cause can also be good in nature.

There are many different kinds of karma. There are karmas for eating meat. There are karmas for lying, cheating, stealing or taking a life. There are karmas for not taking good care of one's health. There are even karmas for incarnating into physical form. We may also think of karma as every action has an equal and opposite reaction. As you think of karmas as a connection to your life's actions, thoughts and words, you may think of or write down a list of these checks and balances in your life. Look at how certain actions balanced other actions. You may look at how certain actions caused other actions to happen even if they weren't seemingly connected. This can be a powerful thing to do because of the actions and reactions we are able to see about our life and what we have lived, experienced and achieved so far in life.

The recognition or realization that karmas are present within one's life as a series of events that happen over time or even closer to other causes or events, can be at times undetectable by a person. We often as souls incarnate in human form tend to want to do the next good thing. We tend to continually work with creative energy as souls experiencing 3 dimensional reality and creating through interactions, situations and known materials of this planet.

As we do this we want to move from one event, good or bad in perceived nature, to the next perceived good or bad event. This creates perceived cause and effect over the course of our lifetime's coming events. As we move forward we are hoping for the next best event in life. We may also be blind to the ways in which the coming events will manifest based on the blind faith and lingering hope that the future might be better. The ego is heavily involved in these thoughts words and deeds.

Now there are moments, actions, benefits, gifts and blessings we have coming as good karma. When things are going good for us we usually don't think along the lines of karma. We tend to think of being in the flow of life, and as we're in this flow we are experiencing our **dharma** or life path.

Karmas can be easy to see when thinking about one's life or they can also be more silent and undetectable while playing out in a series of seemingly unconnected events as the energy balances are paid and repaid. We may have endured times of great need or pain, searching or sickness. In these times of great opening and drama we may be directed to a guru or living spiritual master. A living master has the power to transmute karma by taking it from a person if the person agrees to follow the instructions or teachings of the master which may include the righteous path of learning and study of spiritual practices. Great peace may find a troubled Soul in this way. We also call this **Grace**.

Grace may find a person in their hour of need as they are asking for help and in turn protected by their spirit guides and God. Grace is also sometimes interpreted as undeserved gifts or blessings from Spirit. By nature this is why sometimes Grace is needed. Grace can be a blessing bestowed upon someone before that blessing has been cultivated by them and often given in times of need. Grace doesn't have to be born out of struggle or need, it can simply be coming to someone gracefully on the wings of the angels or in the peacefulness of the Tao.

The Angels over at Grace Bank have a special savings account set up so that when someone gets a ticket from the Karma Police, they can intervene with a Divine Dispensation of Grace. It's always a good idea to help others by paying it forward.

Karma can be a little tricky. There can be karma between two people in that one person has karma with the other only. The other person has no karma with that person. The situations that arise between them will still seem like there is karma for both parties, whether it is good or bad karma. If it is good, it is usually not questioned unless of coarse it appears as great gifts mysteriously appearing out of nowhere.

However, if there is a situation that develops between two parties such as a disagreement where emotions are involved and perhaps assets or money, it could seem like there is karma for the party that actually has no karma in the situation. If the person or party in question looks into the situation or interaction they may think they have karmic involvement because of all the negative energy and emotional charges being exchanged. The real trick in this case would be not to create karma where there is none. Often times a person with conflicts will try to involve another person in their emotionally conflicted movie and karma can be generated by actions and reactions. Also for the person or party who views the situation and has considered or asked 'What is my karma in this situation?' As you look deeply into it you can receive messages that it's not at all what you thought it was. Perhaps both people do have karmas but not with each other, and they are playing out their responses to other karmas generated with other people.

Often we have hidden karma which we have generated in other lifetimes. We can access this by using the Akashic Records to look into our own Book of Life. As you look into the events of past lives you will see many people or personalities you have been. Male and female and usually a variety of different life paths and job descriptions. We may see ourselves involved in some questionable situations. Maybe you were a bank or train robber in a past life. Maybe there was a traumatic injury or a loss of a loved one that left a scar on your emotional body.

Whatever the case may be, the key is to look into the Records and view them silently without emotional judgement or reactions, even though you may be feeling the emotional responses or reactions in the past life visions while you are looking in. This is paramount to having a successful Akashic experience. Remember the only thing that will keep you from having a successful journey or vision into the Records is conflict. These can also be emotional conflicts.

You may come to know what I'm referring to here by actually having an experience of it. That is one way to know the emotional conflicts or judgements. We make emotional judgements based from our ego's version of right and wrong continually in all of our affairs. Examples: 'Was that a good experience or a bad one?' 'Good relationship or bad?' If you're looking to clear your karmas from other lifetimes you will need to look into it with no judgement in order to do it. Looking into the Akashic Records at karmic events can be much like looking into traumas which have been buried from earlier in this life that we haven't released by allowing them up to the surface. When they do come up to the surface we have two options. We can relive the emotions as a filter in the immediate moments as a reactionary response in which often we may tend to hold on to the emotional baggage... or... we can, at any moment, when these buried emotions rise to the surface choose to see it for what it is and let it go.

In these moments we get pieces of our Soul back. So there is a releasing and a coming home at the same time. This can be achieved through viewing the events from within the Akashic. As we look at the events straight on as they originally occurred and hold space by simply viewing them with no conflict or emotional investment of right or wrong, the events or traumas which we once experienced can be immediately released in that moment. Just know that in the simple seeing and looking at it for what it is, it is known without judgement to our Soul perceiving it through the senses. When there is no reaction to it from us we are free from it. This can clear up a lot of karma or even trauma that has been generated from the initial event. As we've endured these events earlier in life, possibly from an illness or maybe emotional or physical abuse, through our reactions then and over time since the event, we may have created a lot of reactions or emotional karma that now can be cleared through healing and releasing due to simply viewing the event and not reacting to it. We are allowing. As we allow we have insights and understanding as to the true causes of the original traumas or karmas and now we gather compassion to heal within the peaceful grace of the Akashic Records. As we go into the Records and we're looking without emotional response we do have the knowing that we are doing reconnaissance work, so there is a purpose, focus or mission, that is enough to steady the release if we can just simply be with the visions as we watch. As we watch the visions we do so from the seat of the soul, this is another reason why the allowing heals the dysfunctions. The Soul is powerfully radiant and when you're in the Records you're squarely in the middle of the Soul and the Soul is more present with you. This simple dynamic alone clears and heals you to perfection. The key with the Soul presence is no emotional response. The emotional contraction or reaction holds the event within the subconscious, the emotional body and/or the physical body tissues. Remember we're dealing with subtle layers of awareness when looking into the Records, so we learn to tune in our vision and watch the visions and messages for the clear truth as we allow it all to unfold with no judgement. When you have no judgements the viewing process continues smoothly. When judgement occurs the visionary process may be interrupted or skewed. The information can be colored by the emotional judgements as to what is actually occurring. So you will have the opportunity to see things on a physical real time level, a soul level, and you may also have symbolic messages given by guides, angels or teachers.

As you may be a practitioner reading this book to get insight for deepening your healing abilities with others, you can definitely affect a person's path by giving them info you may see while reading for them. You may also get your information as a series of pictures while doing body work, or feelings from the person that translate as an inner dialogue from them or their guides. In whatever way that comes naturally to you, your awareness of the Akasha and how to use it can bring more finely tuned information to accompany what you 're already 'getting'. In truth it all comes from the Akasha anyway, though with just a slight bit of conscious asking, looking, and receiving you can really help someone change their life. You may be able to receive a message for them that gives them the inspiration to become alive again and get fully involved in life. If someone has been disconnected this can be an absolute magical experience for them and bring you great joy in being an instrument in helping to facilitate their process.

As you come to know yourself at more intimate levels, you will heal much karma for yourself and with others. You will come to know when karma is cleared and you are free to live and love in joy. One thing is sure, whatever the case with karma, we usually know if we listen deep enough as to whether we've got some work to do and what the nature of it is. Use the Akashic Records to enter your Book of Life and heal your karmas by allowing yourself to look at the events of your life without judgement and watch for the silent grace of transformation to unfold. Create good karma and live your dharma.

Mantra for Clearing Karma
Thiru Neela Kantum Markala Shivaya Nama
Tee roo nee lah kantum mar ka lah She vi ah nama

Karma is primarily stored on the throat area of the body where the soul makes commands out into creation through words and tonal vibrations often paired with an emotional charge. This mantra can clear out your karma and/or start to transform it. Focus on the throat and the color blue. The presiding diety is Shiva often referred to as the Destroyer. This is one reason why.

173

Journey to the Akasha CD & Download

The Akashic Records, the presence of God, our Divine Spirit Guides are all helping us now directing our vision, looking into a past moment, as the pages stop. What does the book say? What is the message?

Journey 2

Journey to the Healing Temples of Atlantis

ivine Akashic Masters, Angels and Arc Angels of the Light of God, Divine Ascended Masters, Spirit of the Four Directions, Great Spirit, Bodhisattvas, Avatars, Divine Spirit Guides of Everyone present, come with us, accompany us on this Journey into the Akashic Records. Reveal to us Divine Akasha that which is most helpful on our journey out into creation from the First Moment. To Know Thyself and to Heal. Reveal to us that which is most beneficial for our journey and completion. Thank You.

Sit in a comfortable position or lay down, covering up with a light blanket to make the body feel safe. Start taking some long slow deep breaths breathing in and out evenly. Just relaxing the physical body. Feel the relaxing power of energy, of Spirit, nuturing, soothing, comforting, lifting you up, expanding, merging.

As you're breathing in energy, breathing energy in now through the back of the neck, the medula oblagata. The

Ancients called this the Mouth of God, the Gateway. See the energy coming in through the back of the neck. And as you exhale, send the bright and colorful energy, up into the back of the head, the cerebral cortex where the vision centers are located. And as you breathe in energy through the back of the neck, and send it up to the visual centers in the back of the head, just continue to relax.

Relax your feet and your toes, relax the soles of your feet. Feel the relaxation coming up your shins relaxing your calves, washing over you like a warm sunny water, bathing your body in this relaxing energy. Relaxing your knees and your kneecaps, relaxing your thighs, your groin muscles and your buttocks, your stomach, lower back, solar plexus all completely relaxed. Relaxing your chest, relaxing all the internal organs, relaxing the lungs and heart, and relaxing now even deeper.

Soothing, healing, this relaxing energy of Spirit, moves out and down your arms relaxing your hands, fingernails, your palms, arms, elbows, forearms, biceps and triceps completely relaxed. Relaxing the neck muscles and jaw muscles. Relax your teeth. Relaxing your gums, feel the energy now moving up the back of your neck, surrounding the head, relaxing your hair, relaxing your scalp, relaxing all the muscles in the face, relaxing the eyes and the eye sockets, relaxing your facial expressions into timeless nothingness. Continuing to breathe in and out evenly and slowly.

And now use the kundalini activation mantra to open the channels of energy for Akashic Soul intuition:

LAH, BAH, RAH, YAM, HAH, AHAA, AUM.

See all the chakras and energy centers blending and working as one rainbow expression. One rainbow as colors of light.

LAH, BAH, RAH, YAM, HAH, AHAA, AUM.
LAH, BAH, RAH, YAM, HAH, AHAA, AUM.

As you continue to relax and go deeper, now picture a rainbow colored light ball of energy, bright as the sun over your solar plexus and stomach. Floating there just growing brighter and brighter. This energy completely lights the room. Moving out until the light is so bright it moves through the walls. Continuing to expand out to encompass the whole house, building or dwelling in which you are now relaxing.

Expanding out down into the earth, up into the sky. Expanding even farther to include the whole neighborhood. The whole neighborhood is shining very brightly in your light. As the light, your light, continues to grow brighter and expand out, encompassing now the whole town or city in which you are residing. Expanding out into the whole region. The whole region is shining very brightly in your light.

Continuing to expand until your whole country is shining very brightly in your light. Continuing to expand this rainbow colored energy is now moving around the planet earth. The whole world is shining very brightly in your light. You may have noticed you have ascended up over the earth, up over the planet.

And as you're looking down from the stillness and the silence from space, you may notice that there are many bright crystalline pin points of light. Different colors and some are brighter than others. Some are glowing , some are grouped together, some are farther apart. These are all of your many lifetimes on planet earth existing simultaneously in the Mind of God.

Look at the countries and the continents where these points of light are shining. Feel the connection to these places, to these lives. As we're floating up over the planet turn away from the earth and look directly into the sun, past the moon right off to our left shoulder. Looking past the moon into the brightness of the sun, let it take your site away blinding you temporarily. Trusting, feel this cosmic energy coming through your eyes, coming through your crown chakra, down into all of your energy centers, and meridians of your body, healing balancing, nurturing, charging you with cosmic energy. Raising your vibration as the soles of your feet connect with the earth energy. You are suspended between cosmic energy of the sun and the earth energy.

A living conduit, a living circuit, and as your energy slowly, rises in vibration you feel your Soul body expanding out, becoming greater and greater in size, relaxing you're floating in the warmth of the sun. Turning now away from the sun, look back down at the planet, notice the cloud patterns and the blueness of the oceans, we will now start our journey to the Akasha.

As we're floating in space, spread your arms out and start to sail, start to soar, gently down towards the atmosphere. Into the etheric field of the planet, soaring now over the oceans over the mountains and terrain, over the deserts over the cities, flying, sailing, soaring, down, circling in, we now see Europe, and the continent of Africa, we see the Mediterranean Sea and area. Continue to journey and as we journey down.

As we travel beyond time and space, we're going to a very, very special and sacred location. We're flying now we start to see pink energy patterns and gold through the air and through the clouds and the mist. As we soar down into the clouds, we see nothing but the clouds. Coming down out of the clouds continuing to spiral down, down, down, we now see the main city of Atlantis. Concentric islands lush and green, surround the central city, as we continue to spiral down, we will visit the Healing Temples of Atlantis and the Akashic Records, continue to spiral down. Spiralling, soaring, sailing on the wind, we see pink, white and gold energies. Turquoise blue of the water, the water is so blue and clear. And as we come closer to the architecture, beautiful buildings, glass arches, crystalline sculptures, glowing with light, ancient technologies.

Coming closer, we will go to the main healing temple in the center of the city. See it coming closer, as we sail down, down, down, closer. Flying right into the temple, this huge round hall. Beautiful marble, stairs coming up from the north, south east and west. This circular temple has no walls only pillars, as we look out in every direction we see the ocean past the concentric islands surrounding the main healing center.

It's very calm we see nothing for miles just the calmness of the ocean. The sky, see the turquoise blue of the water and the pink, white and gold healing energies in the air arising. The wind is gently breathing, the wind is gently blowing. Feel the wind on your skin and in your hair, it's very soft and the perfect temperature here.

And as we turn towards the center of the temple, we see huge crystals, lighted on a circular altar, there is a candle burning, a single flame, and as we walk over to the circular stone altar decorated by these huge glowing crystals, you notice that there is a book on the table in front of the candle. There are two large crystals wrapped with gold healing wands. Pick up the crystals from the table as energy starts streaming out of the Akashic Crystals on the healing altar into your hands and into your 3rd eye. Your whole body is activated with healing. We are now connected into the Akashic Records. Look into the Book on the table, it is set to the present time and moment. As we see the pictures in the Book, the pages magically start to turn from left to right. The crystals in our hands are glowing as the pages are turning themselves.

The Akashic Records, the presence of God, our Divine Spirit Guides are helping us now directing our vision, looking into a past moment, as the pages stop. What does the book say? What is the message? The pictures in the book may be moving with energy. What do you see? Through the connection with the Akashic Records the glowing energy of this healing place, look deeply into yourself. Look deeply into yourself as you see energy shapes coming into form in your mind's eye, you may see the ancient technology of the Akashic language, glowing and streaming with energy patterns. You may see symbols, you may see pictures. What is the message here for you?

Pause for as long as you want to look or study.

The pages magically start to turn once again in this ancient manual, this Book of Life, to a future page, as the crystals in our hands are magically glowing. The pages stop on a future time, a future place. Looking into the book once more, what are the writings that you see? What are the symbols? The pictures are moving with energy. You can feel the glowing light from this healing altar entering in to your whole body. The crown chakra, the 3rd eye, energizing and directly connecting all of your energy fields into the Akashic Records. Into the Source and the Mind of God. What do you see?

What are the symbols, the visions? As you see shapes coming into form, different colors, in this highly creative energy field, what does your imagination connect with? Your imagination is stimulating your intuition. Create the forms and go into them as they continue to create themselves streaming through your mind's eye taking form, focus in and look around. Where are you? There is a message on the page for us. What is this message written out specifically for us?

Pause for as long as you want to look or study.

As we step back from the altar now, As we step back from the altar now and lay the wands on each side of the book. The energy of the crystals starts to dim going back to the soft, soft low light. We look up from the altar and look out at the nurturing energy of the ocean, the pure consciousness of water. Noticing the most beautiful sunset we've ever seen, looking into the sky, walk over to the edge, through the pillars, and as the wind comes up and starts to blow more and more, we will fly up into the clouds. So take off now and fly up, journeying back up into the clouds into the sky over this vast ocean.

Giving thanks to the Akashic Records, for this joyous moment, the excitement, the inspiration, the imagination, the and the intuition that we have just accessed   through this divinely spiritual energy center. Timeless. As we continue to fly up, flying up, flying through the pink and the gold energies, seeing the turquoise and the bright blue of the ocean leaving us.

Going up through the clouds, we're flying back to our present location, back to the country in which we reside. See the country side, see the surrounding countries. Flying now, starting to descend through the clouds, through the clear air space, see the surrounding cities, and see your city as you continue to move closer to home. See your place, your surroundings your countryside coming closer now to your neighborhood coming closer gently descending back down into your house into your home. Gently descending back into your physical body. Into the physical moment, Thanking God for all we've experienced, take a deep breath, wiggle your toes, move your arms and open your eyes.

Thank You Divine Akashic Records, Amen.

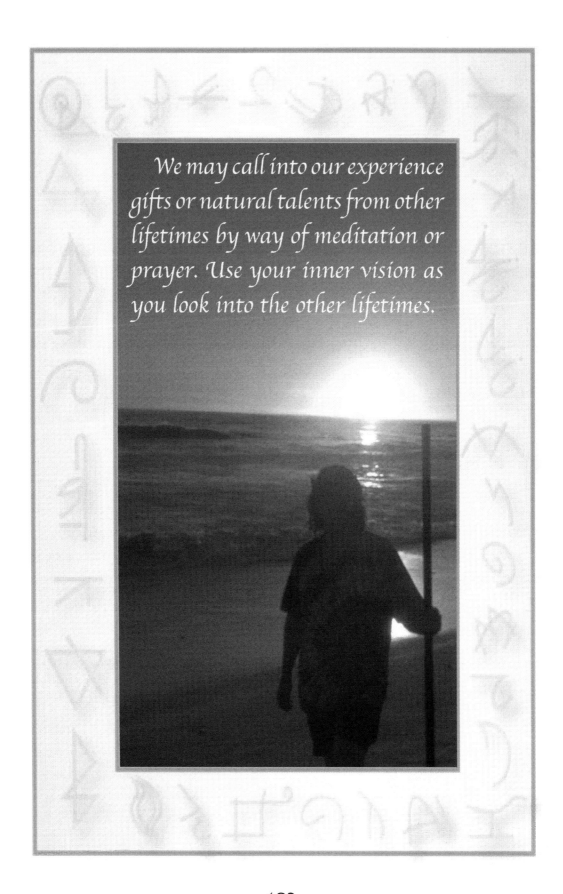

We may call into our experience gifts or natural talents from other lifetimes by way of meditation or prayer. Use your inner vision as you look into the other lifetimes.

Chapter 14

Accessing Abilities & Gifts

There are many ways to access natural gifts and talents. Have you ever had a time when you were with someone doing something and it just seemed like you were naturally excelling at it? They may have noticed that you were exceptionally good at horseback riding. Or "You're a real natural at playing tennis", or running track and so on. Some of us are just born to excel at sports in a very natural way. Others are gifted in art or music. Maybe your gift is working with people and social communication skills. Maybe you just have a knack for making people laugh! Are you a writer? Do you excel at loving your family and really strengthening the family bond with love. All of these things are natural talents or learned skills which might somehow be connected with natural tendencies or talents you hadn't considered. These skills naturally come to us and come through us because we have the natural creative flow of energy coming through us from Source. So we may look at it in a classic way: "What do you want to be when you grow up?" Choosing a profession or direction in life and just going for it. Taking the training or schooling to become certified and excelling at your natural gifts and talents through a vocation.

Or we may look at it in more of an esoteric way. Maybe

these natural gifts that we all have and the types of jobs that we go after are skills and tendencies that we have used in other lifetimes. So as we look into the Akashic Records we may see that someone's Soul Purpose is to really be a communicator with people throughout society. And in experiencing all the many different aspects of being a good communicator with others, the lives that person could have lived in order to study all of the various aspects could be diverse. From being a postal delivery rider, to the leader of a tribe or village, perhaps working in theatre as a playwright. A shaman often communicates messages to many people individually and the tribe as a whole. An actor or a musician experiences the acts of communication out to large groups. So you see there are many different roles that can be played around a central theme.

This is the way the Soul expresses, learns and even heals. These roles can be experienced by the same soul or incarnating person attached to that soul expressing and experiencing a myriad of other colorful attributes and sensations from these roles played. Other incarnating souls and enjoined humans can experience these same jobs or kind of roles, traditions or vocations for completely different reasons with completely different experiences gained or participated in and have a completely different movie to play out while the same aspects are present and may mean different things to different people.

We can find these similarities and Life Path Soul Purposes when we look into the Akashic Records and our Book of Life. We find the reasons behind the reasons we may have been a sailor, hunter or inventor. We may find a recurring theme or central lesson that these different lives bring. And they don't necessarily have to be in order, there may be a chaotic synchronicity to it. So as we find more and more of the different lifetimes, we fill in more of the seats in our circle of our personal **Wheel of Life**. The Tibetans refer to the Wheel of Life as the great wheel of all incarnations in a circle while the central hub is our Soul. The spokes moving out from the central hub of the Soul represent the connection of all lifetimes to the Soul while all are simultaneously connected throughout the center and on the wheel next to each other.

Here is an example for you to consider:

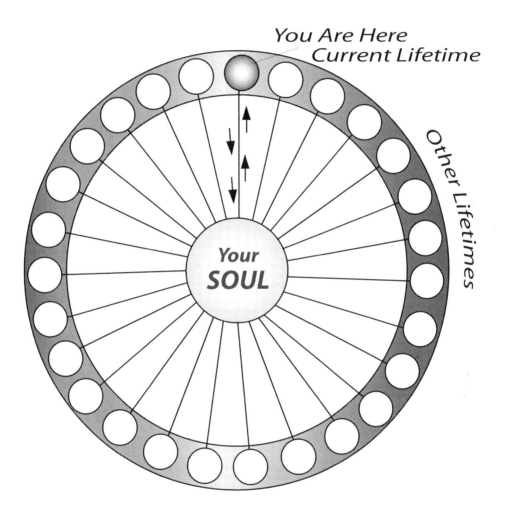

You live each life connected to the hub of the Soul. We could also say that while you live this life your soul has the knowing and experience of all of the other lifetimes or incarnations that you've lived. This gives us the keys to access other lifetimes of experiential information including emotions, natural gifts, relationships and responsibilities. Advancements in business, finance, progress or success. We have already had successes in other lives with many things we are tending ourselves towards in this life. It could also be that we did experience lack or scarcity in other lives or even at a time in this life that has prompted us to learn about success and experience it as our healing birthright. Perhaps you were very successful though used the power of success in ways that affected others or many others in a negative manner creating karma. Now it's time to use the understanding of success and get it right. To have prosperity and use it wisely by giving joy to others in support of their dreams. To lift others up by being involved in ways that benefit and help society. In this way the karma is cleared, healed and forgiven.

We may call into our experience gifts or natural talents from other lifetimes by way of meditation or prayer. Use your inner vision as you look into the other lifetimes. As you connect with yourself through the soul in these other lifetimes you will see yourself doing different things, maybe things you've always wanted to do. In the here & now you now know the reason why: You've done it before and you know it. It feels right and will give you joy to experience it again. Maybe it is a new thing you never considered or another way to make money. You can be creative and this information when it flows through to you can be exciting, uplifting and inspirational. To now see another piece of life's puzzle, as it all comes together.

We may also want to heal past life karmas and lesser versions of life paths by entering our Book of Life and simply viewing what happened. What were the choices made? Who else was involved? Is there a knowing or indication that anyone in your current life is in that past life movie as well? Does it bring light to current situations happening between you and family, a lover or another person? As we see, assimilate and begin to again know the details of these former lives and moments we can gain compassion and understanding which will truly show us how to heal the events or those parts of ourselves that may still be shining through or lingering in this lifetime.

As we look at these events we may also want to close the Records of pathways to undesirable events and incarnations. Especially if you are a healer or **empath** and tend to absorb things from others. You could be absorbing the energy of these other lifetimes and naturally by trying to balance and heal them unknowingly, and inadvertently creating unrest or imbalance in your current life. It could be that your natural tendency as a healer is to take on physical and energetic challenges from others and as you tend to do this you may also indirectly absorb things from other lifetimes you're living and balancing simultaneously beyond linear time.

These dynamics are subtle though can really throw a curve into our lives if we don't know what's going on. If you've done a lot of healing and life path work to become a more whole and prosperous person and certain things keep reverting back to an older or less comfortable expression, you may want to look deeper. Looking into your Akashic Book of Life is a perfect way to start the process. As you uncover your clues with your detective work, remember that just by knowing the dynamic present without judgement of it allows the visions to open and the knowing and healing to begin. As you now know what's going on you can simply be disconnected from the energy of it while you still now have the memory of it. So it's no longer affecting you on some deep unforeseen level. This can be truly freeing and help you to understand more deeply as a person and a healer or reader by having had these experiences. You will know the feelings when they are buried or when they are present by the certain kinds of thoughts you may continually have. The ideas or creativity that led you in a certain direction so that you would now uncover it's intricacies and details bringing great self understanding and appreciation forward to you. Great things abound as you enter into to these levels of knowing yourself. You will be able to welcome new aspects which are helpful and leave behind old aspects which no longer serve you, or we may say, the older unwanted and unneeded aspects have done a great service by bringing you here now as you come to the moment of releasing them with love.

So your technique is to look into your past lives by way of the other techniques given in this book or that you use naturally, and first see the events of what you want to heal and release or bring forward as a gift. Let your inner vision with it's 'no conflict' perspective see, feel and experience the situations. Then after you have seen these attributes, bring them back and write it all down.

Always keep a journal or use the accompanying workbook that comes with this book. As you journal in it, be present with your thoughts and feelings and express it from your heart. Both the gifts you want to bring forward and the things you want to release. Your heart is a very powerful battery and generator and will integrate these by way of love and gratitude coming through the heart. Great Blessings of Personal Self Knowing are upon You as You Continue Your Journey! Enjoy.

King Tut Profile
18" x 24" acrylic on etched brass

Save the Planet CD & Download

In this ever changing, self perpetuating, continuing and simultaneously symbiotic relationship that the Akashic Records has with all the souls, there are myriads of creative streams available to us.

Chapter 15

Using the Akashic Records for Creative Endeavors

The nature of the Universe is pure creational energy. The cosmic energy emanating and coming down from the stars reaching the earth, is what sustains our life here. This cosmic energy or **prana** reaches us as light particles attached to the oxygen molecules that we breathe. And as the energy continues to rise and change we are now experiencing this energy in more quantum ways. As we are doing energy work for others and with ourselves, and as we experience meditation, prayer and healing energy, we access this pure cosmic light energy. All things on the earth are composed of the elements of elemental cosmic star energy. Tables, chairs, the earth, cars, animals, you and me. We are all made of this creational energy.

In our tendency as Souls coming to the earth and incarnating here in human form or enjoining our soul with a physical body, we are involved with experiencing creation and observing through the senses of the physical body as we create continually here on the earth plane through thoughts, words and deeds. So we literally cannot not create. It's what we do. We are literally all about the business of creating. This is one reason why world systems just keep on changing. We're creating through all streams and in all ways. We focus pure cosmic energy into projects, creations, living our lives, raising families, building villages, towns and cities, painting, playing music and making all other forms of art. We procreate into families and tribes. This is our nature. As this is our nature we sometimes forget or become lost to witnessing our own actual creativity. This can happen for a number of reasons. In truth we could never become lost to it because all things we do in life are creative. When we do feel disconnected there are many things we can do to get back in touch with creative energy. Sometimes we grow up and we forget how to play. This is one reason why art forms are so therapeutic in life and in such seeming cases of discontentment, stress or severe trauma. Creativity soothes our souls and brings us joy.

As we now look at creativity in relation to the Akashic Records we are in for some amazing creative gifts and blessings. I will share here predominantly from the perspective of being an artist who has connected into the Records on this level for creative purposes. The Akashic Records is a store house of ever continuing, ever unfolding, ever creative and transforming light synthesis vibrational activations and encodings. In this ever changing, self perpetuating, continuing and simultaneously symbiotic relationship that the Akashic Records has with all the souls, there are myriads of creative streams available to us. Look at the worlds of fractals and mandalas that continue to change through animation and reanimation. Much in the same way you can find an astonishing library of pure creative energy in the Records. You may see it as 3 dimensional mandalas or sacred geometries ever changing and evolving. You may see or tap into the most amazing collections of classic art pieces in the world! It would be like having all the galleries and historic art museums under one roof and at your fingertips or available to you through your senses. You can also access all the great artists of the world and their lives, styles and energy. You can access the great inventors and their inventions. You may see the energy of inventions much in the same way, ever evolving and speaking to you in creatively changing patterns. When you see these patterns of creation or pure creational energies, you can lucidly look into it and watch it evolve into different and changing forms before your very eyes. As you watch the templates being shown to you, you may notice that the patterns are living and breathing with pure cosmic energy. The art forms can appear in much the same way. Paintings, statues, glass work, architectures from different civilizations, etc. are all there in stored visual imagery files or in streaming energy forms that change, create and recreate themselves before your very 3rd eyes!

So if you want to look up an artist's work and the artist you can do this. You may receive all kinds of energetic information that helps you connect with their classical style of art. There are other ways of looking into the creative stream of energy which you will locate once you enter into the Akashic Hall of Records. You will be drawn to it's location as you look into it. You may look into a large dark mirror or a huge crystal sphere, or even be guided to a certain room where the energy is stationed and spinning or changing as it shows you it's variations.

As you're in the presence of these energy variations of creational energy, you are directly receiving pure energy on the inner plane to your Soul and from your soul to you via the senses. You may come back from such an intuitive Akashic journey and find that you are super charged with energy. This is because you are looking into pure energy itself. Also the stream of the energy as you are looking into the Akasha is pure energy vision. This is why it has such a crisp and bright picture when you really tune into it. Akashic vision can be dreamy, stationary pictures or as lucidly clear and bright like streaming high definition television movies. When you access this level of Akashic vision, you will be receiving a transmission of energy as you are looking directly into the Akashic Records themselves from within your Soul energy. Both of these perspectives will bring you energy. When you are in the Records you are directly placing yourself in your Soul energy.

Now as you sit down to draw or sketch your next full feature artistic creation, whether it's a film, painting, sculpture, abstract, mandala or whatever art form you work with. You're placing an intuitive call to the Universe for this energy of creation. As you now have some ideas about what you want to create or maybe you don't know what you want to do yet so you leave it open for creative and imaginative input, you get ready to do an Akashic Journey.

As you become still and start your meditation and energy techniques for entry to the Records, use your protocol techniques for entry and then begin your sensory inquiry. As you are guided into the areas of the Records where the creational energy connects with you via your senses, you now start streaming the information that is alive and energetically speaking to you creatively and harmonically. This will bring you powerful inspiration and intuition for your projects. You can use this not only for art forms, but also for inventions or any other projects in life. As for art forms, projects and inventions, the energy continually communicates through a stream as you connect with it to intuit it's ever unfolding interpretations to you and bring back the energy into the waking state to realize it into your projects. As you are doing this you may notice that as you work on your project it starts to take on a life of it's own. It now speaks to you in ways you might not have been aware of before. You may now receive continual evolving ideas on the central theme. Interactive variations that continue to stream to you as your art form or project is in progress. You may have to be the one to know when to say stop or bring a project to a completion point as the art has taken on a life of it's own. An old saying from the classical masters hint to this: *'No painting is ever truly finished'*. Maybe there is one piece that develops into several or has new supplemental additions. Maybe a whole new series is born! The possibilities are truly endless. Your newly found pathways into advanced portals of creative energy are ever sustaining and continual and will always be there for you. Enjoy this inspired new way of working with the Akashic Records to share your new and improved creations with the world.

Many times the spirits of family are held here close to the earth plane in order for completion to occur. We can meet them in the Akashic Records and help to facilitate healing by holding space and sending them energy and even help the whole family linage by sending healing energy through the bloodline back through time.

Chapter 16

Connecting with Ancestors & Family Members

$\mathcal{W}$hen I hear the word ancestors I always think of the Native American tribes. The American Native lineages are powerful because they are so elemental in nature. They pray to the Mother Earth, the Father Sky and to the Ancestors. The ancestral lineage would stay with the earth, the sky and with the tribes. Their focus was simply honoring nature and honoring their ancestors. Their power and strength is in their simplicity.

We may often find that when working with the earth or in coming to find the voices of our spirit guides present with us that the Native ancestors can be very talkative, helpful and easy to connect with. When we visit sacred sites such as the Southwestern United States, places like the Grand Canyon, Sedona, the Four Corners or Ship Rock we might find the Earth energy to be very powerful for our initiation into healing. the Native American traditions and spirituality of the indigenous tribes still intact.

There have been areas of the country where the tribes were either originally more focused on survival of the weather or warring with other tribes and in some of these areas we find disconnections with the original spiritual traditions of the tribes. When this happens the tribes become more homogenized with society. The elders of the tribe aren't sharing the traditional medicine and teachings of the tribe with the young for whatever reasons. Not to judge this as bad, simply a dynamic of evolution that has occurred. Native tribes are wonderfully elemental in nature and will exist with strength within any conditions or terrain.

The spiritual traditions of the Native Southwestern tribes such as the **Pueblo** and **Hopi** are continuously preserving their spiritual traditions as are the **Lakota** and **Sioux** of the north and many other tribes.

Traditionally the native shamans and elders worked with the animal spirits or familiars. The animal spirits are very connected to the earth because they live in the Eternal Now or the continuous 'now moment', as they are pure and clear energetically untethered like the linear reasoning mind of man. Their presence is often used as protection against invading forces or dark spirits and entities, because they hold the natural elemental power of nature. They are pure and connected with the earth and the elements.

The shamans would often call the familiars as they travel through what is now known as **shamanic states of consciousness** or **S.S.C.** as they would journey to retrieve missing pieces of a persons soul in the upper, middle and lower worlds and sometimes even to the land of the dead. These are considered to be paranormal other worldly dimensions, though, very real for the shamans. You may have followed the teachings of Duan Juan's books in which the author Carlos Castaneda talks of the powerful shamanic magic of the mexican medicine men & women, healers and animal spirits. Often the shamans use herbs and tinctures that they've learned to work with in their cultures. We can also use the energy of meditation and the sound of a drum, shaker or rattle to get into a naturally relaxed guided journey.

Forcing the mind's eye open with the stimulation of natural psychedelic herbs is another traditional way and sacred practice. While this can be a traditional ritual we will visit these realms naturally without the use of 3rd eye stimulants in order to have a completely natural experience as the great masters, yogis and adepts have done. We will be combining the sacred art of meditation and science of **kriya** yogic breathing while accessing the Akashic Records and then visiting the Shamanic worlds.

Let's talk more about the ancestors, family members and bloodlines. We can work with family members in their soul body while they are still in physical form or on the other side of the veil with their consent. There may be immediate family members or distant relatives that we have unfinished business with. Maybe there are things on an emotional level that still need to be resolved for healing and for a release of the astral body or soul to occur. Many times the spirits of family are held here close to the earth plane in order for completion to occur.

We can meet them in the Akashic Records and help to facilitate healing by holding space and sending them energy and even help the whole family linage by sending healing energy through the bloodline's heritage back through time. We can have a conversation with someone who really needs healing or release. Maybe we can even help guide them to the light. It could be that the spiritual energy present on the other side of physical reality is so vast and active that if they do not have an understanding of it, they could become lost or confused in their emotions, mental projections and astral bodies.

This is why there are so many angels and spirit guides to help the souls transition as they are accompanied by the astral, mental and emotional bodies for a short while. Time is relevant or irrelevant depending on how you look at it, so what is a short time period? A day, week, month, 10 years, 250 years? It's not a specific protocol, however, a soul can be in the in-between for an immeasurable amount of 'time'. So we can work with these spirits, especially friends and family members through the Akashic Records.

A Friend's Journey into the Light

I had a friend who was passing because of cancer. The day before I contacted him I had a dream of him standing in front of a golden portal of clouds leading into the light. What a beautiful vision to behold! He knew he was going to go and continued to get things done in life while being very focused as a Karate instructor at his **dojo** of many years where he taught people from all walks of life.

As his condition became acute and he was no longer able to work, I sent him a message in an Akashic meditation that I would be available to work with him and I would be there as a bright green light on the other side and Babaji would also be with me as a bright white-golden light. As I connected with him in waking meditation, we saw the reasons for his cancer. In his understanding of yin & yang energy, through his filters, his personal energy that he was exerting in life was very yang, in fact too yang, or masculine energy driven. The yang energy was literally consuming itself by way of the cancer. There were parts of his whole being that didn't understand the yin, softness or feminine energies and so it was not available to him in a balanced manner. The area that the dojo was in, our original hometown area, was an old mining town and the depleted earth energy was not helping matters.

Upon entry into the soul body state we had a conversation

and I talked with him about the properties of yin energy and that he would soon be in a sea of yin or feminine energy. I knew the tendency of his soul as strong male yang energy would be to incarnate back into the local area as a male with yang energy working on the same mundane energetic principles. As we discussed these principles of yin and yang I took him with me into the Hall of Records Temple where we walked and talked as I heard him say "Ah, so this is what you do". I assured him that this lucid conversation and the visit to the Hall of Records was actually happening. As we continued over the course of a day Babaji now came with me in a meditation and brought my friend's Asian karate guru from the early 1900's. As Babaji and I explained the dynamic that was happening with the imbalance of Yin and Yang energy to the guru with my friend Scotty present.

His Guru then said "I have a place for him". Much of the communications were energetic and subtle, though as Babaji went with them both, I knew that they were going back to a place in time of the past and that my friend would incarnate as a female student under the guru's direction of martial arts. This would greatly balance or solve his whole-being imbalance of yin/yang energies. And so it was done, and as the story came to a close, I felt Scotty's soul leave me and a deep feeling of Oneness with the Universe and the Great Beyond welling up inside of me. He really had moved on. This inspirational story is an indicator of the powerful work that you can accomplish when working with those in transition from the other side of the veil and within the energy of the Akashic Records.

Let's talk about the dynamics of enjoined souls with human forms. We actually have two souls. We have a body soul and a celestial soul. Both are energetic and both carry integral parts of our histories of incarnations. We have a physical energetic or etheric body soul comprised of an etherio-plasmic energy substance. This light energy as the body soul has the genetic memory of our ancestors and our bloodline including our DNA and cellular memories of each lifetime. As we incarnate from one life to the next, the body soul exits a body with it's light and moves into the ethers until it is called into form again. The body soul generally will try to incarnate back into the family bloodline though not limited to that bloodline alone unless by karma. It travels from one body of existence to another. Meanwhile the celestial soul is a fingertip or fingerprint of God's light energy from Source usually from star systems in the cosmos or created in the First Moment. It is coming to the planet to have an observational experience in the earthly 3rd dimensional gallery of physical reality. The celestial soul will incarnate with a person's body soul and seat itself into a lifetime to see and feel if there's a match. If there is a harmonic match between them then there is a blending of the celestial soul with the body soul that takes place and they will continue to incarnate together from now on lifetime to lifetime.

Can an integrated celestial/body soul split apart? Yes, such as in actions of great trauma. If there isn't a resonance then the celestial soul will move on to find another body soul or body spirit to blend with. Can a person live with just the body soul? Yes. These individuals will sometimes have a simpler, more direct or a more elemental process of their approach to living. They may be less intellectual and live more from gut instinct while more connected to the earth and the family bloodline. There are many good aspects of this dynamic. The Native American tribes were very naturally powerful because they prayed continually and primarily to the earth, the sky and to the ancestors.

The same can be said for any of the other cultures on the planet as they evolve. We may notice great teachers or humanitarians who tend to draw attention to their ways and their higher vibrations of the fully integrated celestial souls. These people show us the tendency for the celestial souls to come and to blend with humankind in an expression of what is possible. As this interaction of the two souls continues they will start to reincarnate together as one more highly integrated soul, while the aspects of the two souls remain.

Now as the celestial souls are trying to find home with the right body soul, they are part of a group of 12 Souls with an Over Soul which in turn is part of a larger matrix of 12 Soul groups and an Over Over Soul with a larger group matrix back to what is called the **monad.** These Souls in their groups are having scattered incarnations in the world until they meet with each other to accomplish the Soul's Purpose or to work out and heal karma. Some in physical form, some out of form, in a seemingly chaotic yet synchronous dance of the universe.

Souls and humans are also evolving into an ascended state where as the soul and the physical body become one heightened expression. If that weren't enough, celestial souls can also be in more than one body simultaneously and even up to 12 bodies. A more common example would be: The same soul that is with an older person closer to the end of their life and simultaneously with a newly born infant or small child at the same time. One soul in two bodies.

So you can see there is a synchronistic yet divinely chaotic dance to the souls' journeys as they weave in and out of existence through incarnations, in groups, in blood lines, in more than one body, in the same or different parts of the world, and even on into great expressions of living a life where enlightenment, self realization and ascension can be achieved. This can bring the earthly incarnation process for that soul to a halt as they evolve and move on to other higher worlds or planes of existence. They are no longer tethered to the earth plane unless they want to come back. Soul energy with it's radiant qualities is much different than what we commonly have thought it to be.

Life Review
Self Guided Journey Meditation

As you begin to become more comfortable and relax, take some long slow and deep breaths. Whether lying down or sitting up just allow yourself to be as you continue to relax deeper. As you breathe in more pranic energy and oxygen causing you to go deeper, see now a bright golden spotlight shining down on you from above like a beam or shaft of light. As the beam grows brighter everything else in the room becomes dark or fades into the background.

As the golden beams shines down, a large book now appears on a table in front of you. This is your Book of Life, it is open to the current time and moment at the center of the book. The Eternal Now Moment. There is a large golden mirror which appears on the other side of the table hovering in the air. As you look into the book connecting with the energy of the Akashic Records, look up now into the mirror.

As you go back to the beginning of this current life, start at the beginning and go through the details of your life. Start with being born and your earliest years. Look at all the things you've participated in, or accomplished and achieved. Look at all life's happenings without judgement, just simply go from year to year. Scan through each year of your life, each school year, or each portion of your life that marked a change.

As you view into your life take your time over the coarse

of an hour. It may be shorter as 30-45 minutes or longer as 1-1.5 hours. Really sit and look remotely at everything you've lived in your life and just be with it. Try to be detail oriented. If you remember something out of sequence just allow it to come in and then go right back to your normal sequence of events. Be as detail oriented as you can. Follow this movie all the way up to your present time and moment. As you come back to the now, open your eyes, take a breath, get up and stretch, and a drink of water. You may want to go for a walk to reflect as you may have remembered details long forgotten. This process brings you self acceptance of viewing your life simply to watch, and accept who we have been and who we have become. Welcome home. You may now feel the presence of fullness within you. Notice how you feel as you move through the next moments, hours and days.

Blessings to You in your Life Review Process.

The 'variance of associative energies' implies a study of perception of the many varied frequencies of light and beings and how they interact with the Universe and our Soul energy.

Chapter 17

Variance of Associative Energies

*I*n the worlds of metaphysics and spirituality there are many comparisons, likenesses and cross references. These comparisons and cross references often keep the minds of those of us who are inquisitive natural born thinkers continually busy. The challenge with comparisons of scientific analysis and spiritual truths, understandings and / or philosophies are this:

Just the dynamic of the continuing comparisons alone is enough to keep many, many people caught between the worlds of understanding truths and denials. A natural example of this is that someone is drawn to the spiritual path for a certain reason, maybe they are just trying something new or maybe they are drawn to it by the connection from other lives and are unaware of anything surrounding that possibility.

Meanwhile, in this scenario, somewhere in the world modern science has announced that they figured out that the whole universe is connected as one expression and is vibrating in certain frequencies of harmony. At another place in the world, the spiritual guru of a person has instructed them to use the sacred **Om** chant. Sharing the meaning of the Om with the student and the story of how ancient Siddhas journeyed within. While in these deep states of meditation on the inner plane they heard a sound, a vibration. When they came back from these deep **trance** states, the way they described this sound was by naming this continual humming sound vibration Om. So which is the new student to believe the guru with ancient traditions or the new ways of science? The true answer is to always follow your heart and go with your gut feeling on which feels better to you. You may agree with both sides as a conclusion that, yes all things are connected and the modern world is now waking up to that basic realization and also that it has been known for a very long time, ages in fact, even though the associated press has finally come clean with the information for the masses. Modern evolution and classics of antiquity can both bring us indications of the natural laws of the Universe.

For my own journey, it has been the ancient traditions that hold the keys and that I gravitate towards in the classical studies of spirituality and mysticism. The new ways of science are often based on understanding these principles in light of current technological advancement. Sure this can and does help the world, as we are always changing, evolving and searching for the better ways to do things.

The ancient arts and sciences of philosophy, meditation and spiritual understanding are the true foundations and cornerstones of our history and development. To use the Truth to be good people. As often as we move forward with new scientific ways to collectively say "Look what we can do now" like children, much of it has actually already been done before in other ages. We often find ourselves going back to the roots of great spiritual paths, or to a time when we've tried everything else in life, except to finally look within for the hidden messages and answers within ourselves that bring us to self realization and enlightenment.

Remember the old saying: **'When all else fails, read the instructions!'**. Some great minds have embodied both the spiritual and the scientific alike such as Nicola Tesla and Albert Einstein. And there are many great thinkers and humanitarians among us who see both visions as unified parts of the whole creation, the world and humanity.

The 'variance of associative energies' implies a study of perception of the many varied frequencies of light and beings and how they interact with the Universe and our Soul energy.

Maybe at one point science thought or dreamed: If ancient forms of meditation bring these results then maybe if we study this scientifically we can create a pill or another physical variation that will give us the same benefits. We've tried it all and now after experimenting with manufacturing all the pills, supplements and contraptions, we are back to meditation. It's free, it's natural and it brings benefits that cannot be manufactured or a short cut taken in order to get to the Divine. The actual short cut is a direct pathway to the Divine and we can realize it naturally in a single moment and in every single moment. Again, yes, all things are good, God and of the Tao.

If you go to a guru and he gives you a technique you may ask "Teacher why should I do this?" And he will probably not answer or simply say, "Just go and do the technique." He knows that the magic is in finding the message for yourself. The insights found from within you by using the exercises will be transformative and the guru knows that. If something that you are using such as a supplement or an energy device helps you, by all means do it. Feel good and inspired! My point is to simply not be outwardly directed by it. You have the power within. *

In the world of metaphysics, there are many scientific

study groups out there that will eagerly challenge the ancient insights with the dynamics of modern science and new age technologies. There are also many new modalities for healing and connecting with spirit. Many are interesting and hold promise. Often much like the technological or scientific approach to energy we are looking for short cuts to accomplish things and possibly to only make money. You will have to be the judge as to what is truly for the greater good and what are just face value lip service evaluations. Attempts at short cuts to explanations of the greater Truths that need no play by play explanation. It's not a sports game. I remember a bumper sticker I once saw: "This is not Dress Rehearsal, This is Real Life!" There are many modalities and professors of them that spring up in an attempt to make movements happen for people with a brand new patented system supported by all the merchandising and accompanying products. Use discernment knowing that if you are being guided to something in particular then there is a resonance for you to explore it and possibly work with it.

Dealing with Entities

Often times we think that if we feel energy especially when we are starting out on our path and amassing information by experiencing different modalities that the energy sensations are of the Light. "Did you feel that? Oh, I really felt that! Wow! I can still feel that energy! Sooo Powerful! That person must be a master!" etc. Have we become energy junkies? If we find ourselves tethered to seeing a public figure over and over that projects energy of some sort and no one really knows what it is, or there is a looming mystery behind it, then do the math.

The Divine does not hide itself. Yes it is in all things and it surely will let you know if indeed it is the Divine at work. Often times there are dark forces that can appear as the light.

We may equate in life that things of an upper or elite class are higher in vibration, making them special. Not always the case. Sometimes there are 'deals made with the devil' so to speak. There are sometimes dark emulations around things that are bright and shiny. How many times have we heard reports of officials being corrupt in church, state or corporate business affairs? Bad decision making in the name of the holy dollar is not the way, truth or the light.

Sometimes there is darkness that hides in the light. These entities can move through the light affecting people as they may. Often times with all of these situations of dark dealings and crimes being committed on all levels of society as well as in church, state and with officials, there can be entities behind the people involved or that have come into the situation and are influencing the outcomes. Why? Because there's an energy grab. The true currency is energy. And the greater form of that currency is soul energy. Entities and dark forces are attracted to power and pure energy. They can feed on the light. They can sometimes even work through healers and those professing some new approach to the Truth.

This is why it's important to know. You don't have to dwell on it, although, it is of value to know of the existence and especially when working with others. You also won't want to dwell on it so much that it could attract those unwanted energies back to you. You may ask what does this have to do with the Akashic Records?

If you're going to truly use the Akashic Records for the greater good and as you're doing important and guided work with the Divine, then you should know more fully the inner workings of the playing field. You may actually use this book and the Akashic Records and never have a run-in with dark forces. Many do not. However if you have, and many of us have, this information can be informative, helpful and of great use in releasing and clearing these energies for yourself and for others.

As healers, teachers and light workers we use all of our experiences to gain knowledge, wisdom and insight into ways to protect ourselves and others to heal, clear, teach and for protection. In this way no experience is too terrible as it holds invaluable first hand information for the light worker. When you have to deal with these forces you can think of it as 'in the field' or 'on the job training.'

All things are made of energy and there are many different kinds of energy out there. That's why it is important that we keep our vibration high and clear. The brighter our light is, many opposing energies will shy away while others might be attracted to it. As your light is bright and clear it ensures that even if an entity comes in contact with your energy you will not feel much of a difference at all because the Infinite Light that is You gave to them what they needed and they moved on.

This is why I'm referring to the energies as associative. If you're working in the Records you are protected by your guides, angels and the Holy Spirit and may at times, depending on the situation, only see or feel certain filtered kinds of energies to continue and complete your work at hand. This is a great blessing of protective grace. Also you may see or feel all different variations of energies and entities as your working with people in the Records who are still in form or on the other side. And it seems the more energy work you do, the more sensitive you become to different kinds of energies and you find ways to work with them or around them or heal and clear them. This is God and the Divine working through us to accomplish what's needed.

Another example is that you may work with someone who has an entity that's been with them for a very long time. The dynamic is that it's a symbiotic relationship. Let's say the entity arrived early in a person's life during a childhood trauma. Let's also say that the person has grown up and lived all these years functionally, while still being triggered from the trauma intermittently through life though does pretty good overall. They could even be studying healing and energy work. The entity may be attracted to the pure energy of the spiritual work. The more powerful the entity the more energy they will want to assimilate in order to grow their own energy. For this person the entity may invisibly remain hidden to them because they cannot tell the difference between the actions of the entity or their own ego.

While studying healing work and energy work the entity is receiving large amounts of energy and the symbiotic presence of the entity could even make the person more psychic indirectly feeding their ego. And you might even feel extra energy coming from that person when you're around them. This could be the energy that 'they' have been amassing or the presence of the entity itself.

A challenge for many of us is this: When we feel energy, is the energy coming or going? Often while we feel a charge from the person's presence there is energy that can be secretly taken at the same time. From behind or around back of us while they are right in front of us! I say around back of us because I'm referring to a diversion. It could be taken directly from any chakra or energy center or any part of the body. Maybe after being with someone you notice you feel relaxed the first couple of times and eventually you notice that you just feel drained. You may feel so depleted, if you're spending long periods of time with them, that you become exhausted. They could be very psychic, and be able to manifest and may even exhibit mood swings and complete behavioral shifts. Be careful in dealing with these people.

The importance again of a situation like this is that it's time to use the Akashic Records to take a look and see what's going on. Could it be an alien presence? Multiple personality disorder? Past life karmas? Entities? Demons? Or all of the above? You be the judge. Rule number one: If you're in an energetically compromising situation take yourself out of it, because no good can come from it. Can someone with an entity sense the presence of entities in others? Yes. Learn to protect yourself and get clear.

Items for Clearing

Sea salt is good to use in the shower or bath to clear. Lavender water in a spray bottle is good. **Orange Calcite** is good as a mineral to use. I recommend two double terminated palm sized orange calcite crystals to be held during meditation to clear negative energy and rebuild core energy. **Sulfer Rock** and **Blessed Thistle** are two good items you can find at your local herb shop or new age store. They are used to clear unwanted energies and they work really well.

A **Native American smudge stick** made of **Sage** to clear your body and then the rooms of your house works really well to clear with the earth energies. Pets, animals, or conjuring animal spirits or familiars are very good in holding sacred space. **Sweetgrass** to burn with or after sage in gratitude.

Ganesha the remover of obstacles is a good deity to work with in dealing with unwanted energies. Ascended Master St. Germain, keeper of the Violet Flame (*protection*) can help clear and protect you and your space by focusing on a violet or deep purple flame. Call on Christ, Mother Mary, Babaji, and Merlin as well as many other qualified masters and guides for help on the other side. Call the one that feels appropriate for you and/or the situation at the time. They can all help you to hold sacred space. Arc Angel Michael is known to be very powerful for personal protection and safety.

I have found **Commander Ashtar** and **Ashtar Command** to be very helpful in clearing one's personal air space in the night, by calling them vocally. White candles hold sacred and holy space. As does your voice, use your voice to command clearing in your immediate surroundings and formulate a clearing statement such as the one below. The color blue holds a sacred clearing vibration for you.

You may use an ancient mantra for protection from unwanted energies such as **"HUNG VAJRA PHAT"** (pronounced Hoong Vash Ra Pay) This mantra will protect your body, energy fields and space. One of the best ways to sustain a clearing is to not continually think about it after you do it. Do not continually focus on the presence of entities! This energy of thought attracts them. Do not operate out of fear continually or anger. These vibrations keep a person's energy out of balance and can invite unwanted 'cling-ons'. Forgiveness and gratitude work wonders in shifting the energy.

Clearing Command: **"Any and All unwanted and negative energies which are not of the Light of God or here for my highest good, must leave this space immediately. Any energies, entities or beings that are here by deception must leave immediate by Divine right order of the Universal Law. I command you leave here now and be transmuted up into the Source Light of Creator God. So Be It, So Mote It Be, It Is Done, Amen.**

If you feel a need for help from an outside source, there are many qualified practitioners to contact (See Pg. 352). Often times just the dynamic of the healer as another person with their energy being is enough to clear away what we cannot from within ourselves. They can naturally hold space for you in healing and clear away and protect you by releasing those unwanted pesky energies that may be visiting or entities that may be with an individual can also be removed as well as in your home or living space can also be cleared. This section on clearing also pertains to the next chapter.

You are Sovereign. You have the natural abilities of ascension whether in the physical or in a transitory higher dimensional experience. You are Divine.

Chapter 18

Treatise on Extraterestrial Interactions & Energies

The information in this chapter is important to know for your advanced workings with others in healing and with the Akashic Records. Though not directly related to the Records, as you move through your spiritual or healing career you will find many individuals, sects, cults and groups who are attracted to seek out those who can read the Records or are attracted to the energy of the Records themselves. Often because it represents to them perceived power in the form of knowledge and if they could just tap into that knowledge then, yes, they could have more perceived power in the their own experience.

By Universal Law it doesn't really work that way, though they still try, and they should be aware of such surrounding dynamics as the natural built-in protector circuit of the Akashic for only the pure of heart to access the highest information.

As Hitler reached a point where he (and the entities, demons and E.T.'s working through him) decided he/they wanted to rule the world, he went to India and sought out the advice of a **Sikh** guru. As the story goes, he asked the guru how do I use ultimate power to control? The guru, knowing that extending both arms straight up with palms facing out was a powerful **mudra** to use, said to Adolph, "Just hold up one arm." We might consider that it at least lessened the outcome.

Often times many have wanted to control the destiny of the world and the course and direction of mankind. There are two very powerful properties that 'they' are not considering:

A. Creator God of Love

B. the Free Will bestowed to all Souls by Divine Right Order of Universal Law.

God naturally loves All of us equally (even the tyrants) and the cosmic energy of the Tao is being used by all to accomplish all things. These two principles make for an interesting if not colorful planet. The radiant Soul energy of God in human form has naturally transmuted and thwarted many hair-brained attempts to destroy or dramatically alter our culture by the dark forces. Our global society is already a dynamically colorful and elemental, and dare we say sometimes primitive environment, and it has been decided by those who are the Divine Watchers that Universal Law must be used to restore harmony when and where the opportunity is available. Often times Universal Free Will is used by deception of disempowering the masses with fear by directing their minds with advertising, television network media and propaganda. Have you had your programming today? In this way the minds, bodies and souls inadvertently become a battery to be used in mass to harness energy for the dark side. This is foul play by deception. We are not attempting to create conspiracy here, simply announcing hidden aspects of what is already in play so that you know how to work with energy in general when working with healing, clearing and the Akashic Records.

In the other worlds, galaxies, and universes exist other races of beings. Some are human or humanoid and others are very different in a multitude of ways. These other races of beings have different reference points of God, Self, and Society. Some are more unified and some are more rogue.

We have many qualities and life forms here on planet earth that make the environment of earth and it's elements, atmosphere and resources attractive. We as a race are attractive as well for many reasons. The differences between us and them have long since kept us guessing as most of this society has yet to know themselves as galactic citizens. The governments of the world have kept their dealings with extraterrestrial races top secret classified information since their beginnings. This secrecy has created an energetic separation here on the planet. The earth humans outside the governments who have been contacted by E.T.'s and beings from other races who are not dealing with our governments create a whole other paradigm. Many people from around the globe have received messages from aliens on everything from coming earth changes to spiritual enlightenment. Some of these people are known and many more who have remained silent. You may be well be aware of a few races that have been interacting with humans for a number of reasons.

The **Pleadians** are said to walk among us and to come and go imparting knowledge from their wisdom and even intercepting impending earth threats. They monitor the earth as do many other races coming and going silently. **Ashtar Command** of the United Federation of Planets patrols the galaxy to protect us and it from outside invaders and even galactic human and non-human threats as we are globally and galactically protected by treaties. Many of these races operate naturally from a perspective of what we would consider to be highly spiritually evolved, though, to them it is just naturally the way to be.

The **Arcturians** have interacted with the earth peoples as have the **Andromedans** and the **Sirians**. The Sirians have links back to Egyptian times and power sites of distant history's past. Some Sirians were rulers in Egypt. The **Annunaki** among other races battled for territories in the ancient parts of the world. In ancient times especially areas of Atlantis, Egypt, Babylon and Sumer to name a few, the preists and high priests were the go-betweens for rulers and the alien 'gods'.

Not only have we been visited continually throughout history, there is currently much concern about time travelling to the future and the past to influence events that could change our history and alter our future. There has been for decades talk about the coming new earth as an ascended and etheric model or new version of the earth and some will step into that model of the New Earth while others will remain here on the Old Earth ... or the old paradigm.

Recently there has been talk and speculation that these two Earths are now being integrated as one model. This may well be the reason for a lot of the energetic anxiety that we have been experiencing for the last few years and may continue with astrological and earth shifts. Could it be that all of this has been done by restructuring earth history through time travel? Think of the alien races travelling across the Universe to and from different star systems to arrive here. In a way they are time travelling light years every time they visit here. Are these visitations partially responsible for creating rifts or shifts in the space-time continuum?

Let's talk about Angels. The question has also been posed, are the angels really aliens? They are from what we would consider a different dimension, the 6th Dimension, where the Angelic Realm exists. And our understanding is that God has created the angels and put them in touch with us here by Universal Divine Law to protect humans and to be messengers of Divine information as well as help Souls transition from the earth plane to the after-life and even into the Akashic Records to find their next set of coordinates and mission. Are the Arc Angels the rulers of the legions of angels in that realm? Yes. Do they help humans? Yes. Do they bend the rules of Universal Law to sometimes inadvertently reside over humans? Yes, sometimes out of a direct need for a person or group's safety and well being. There are battles between light and dark being waged in other dimensions sometimes over these principles.

Yes it may sound dark, or like skewed information, though, how often do you watch humans in movies playing precarious roles and bending or breaking the laws in order to help someone, speak up for the greater good, or even save the planet? So the idea is not completely inconsiderable. They are under direct orders from Creator God to be loving, helpful and kind. These are beings which have been given great power and the orders to use it. In the angelic realms there was a great conflict that played out about how they would be perceived by humans as they were interacting with the humans and other issues concerning the usages of the light and the dark and the Divine Will of the Throne of God.

The angelic realms can be perceived as multi-layed spheres or worlds of dimensional energy much like the mental plane. **Michael** is loved by countless millions for his protection and strength of justice. **Metatron** is known as the King of the Angels and has the ultimate strength and power in that realm. Lucifer was God's most beautiful angel and has also been referred to as Satan. We all know the story of how he fell from the heavens into other worlds. There are stories that will tell you that Satan as this previous arc angelic being has been playing 'lord' to this world for quite some time through seduction and power. Keep in mind that these angels were all brothers and sisters working together at one time. Metatron plays a similar role by often intercepting and answering the prayers sent to God. It has been said by those who have interacted with Metatron that he is the only one who can withstand the vibration of True Creator God Source and is the go-between for the Light of Creator and the lower realms. Some who seek power often resort to Metatron as they may find through Hermetic study that Metatron has something to do with residing over the matrix of physical reality as a watcher and guardian.

There are many mandalas and sacred geometries that illustrate the flowing and creation of existence on the earth plane. Two of these diagrams are the **Flower of Life** coming to us from ancient Egypt/Atlantis and **Metatron's Cube** from the ancient study of alchemy and the angelic world. It is known that Metatron's Cube is the geometry that was used as a layout template in constructing the floor plans for many cathedrals built around the world.

One issue whether resolved or unresolved within the angelic realm and the inter-dimensional connections that govern this 3rd dimension is the dynamic of other beings playing God to the beings of this world. By the truest nature of Divine Universal Law, this should not be, though it often exists by ordering of light dimensions or out of a need for creations or our protection and even by what we might call a 'white lie'. Bending the Universal laws, truth and physics.

There have been many of us who have had incarnations in the angelic realm. And many feel the connections and the effects here now in human form. There are those of us who have come directly from the angelic realm and sometimes struggle with gravity, laws of nature and interacting with people in human form. We can find our own personal answers concerning all of this within the Akashic Records.

Let's talk about the **Zeta Riticuli** aka the 'greys' and the **Anunnaki** aka the lizards. Not my favorite topic but it needs to be addressed. Yes, we can view them compassionately as children of God. These are what could be called parasitic races. The greys have been rumoured to actually be a portion of human civilization from the future whose evolution as a race was devolving. As the evolution of the greys went downhill through their own genetic manipulation and tampering, they travelled back in time from the future to try and use learn from, borrow and manipulate human gene codes as a way to reconstruct their own physical make-up. This has included inter-breeding, abductions of humans, implants, and masking of dreams in order to work with or borrow individuals during their night sleep. They have laboured trying to find ways to cure their own race and have made secret deals with governments for the trade of their technology in order to continue their studies on earth life here.

Another newer agenda of theirs is now the 'soul blending' with humans so they can have a physical 3D experience and enter back into incarnations. The problem with this is that they have already been compromised. Their intentions are skewed and while it may work to some degree, it is another backward's engineering program that brings those involved with it dark power. It changes people and takes their soul. While their soul presence may somehow still be linked to them as to not circumvent Universal Law, their soul may no longer be prominently linked to their bodies. This can cause all sorts of unexpected differentiations rifts in healthy consciousness and physical ailments.

Once you suspect or know there is a 'presence' of this nature in your midsts, or you have already been through this, you only need to announce or command:

"By Divine Right Order of Universal Free Will any and all beings who are here by deception must cease and desist as this is my Body, my Space and my Soul, I Am Divine, now go and do not return!"

Often people's dreams have been masked with elements from their own memories. This makes it a challenge to get a handle on what's actually happening though if you know this is a possibility and you really study and look at the dream, you can catch it. Once it's been recognized by you as a deception, it will stop.

They can enter into a human's energy field simply if the human is out of harmony. Anger, tension, stress and fear are perfect opportunities for these intruders to sneak into a person's energy field. If your light is pure, bright and strong, meaning: no anger at self, others or God and in harmony with All of life, love and joy within you are clear and protected. At that vibration, you are of no use because:

A. They cannot connect with you or get in to your matrix to steal energy.

B. Because you are directly connected with the Divine Light of God, which directly honors Free Will and Ultimate Loving Truth.

These beings are aliens with advanced toys & sciences and quarky almost dark side outer space thought patterns. Sounds very Looney Tunes doesn't it? Yes, all are God's creatures though if they come in peace and for the greater good you would know it. Remember the movie 'Mars Attack?' So don't let curiosity kill the cat. Stick with what you do know, such as which races you're already aware of that you know for sure are on the right side of the Light and helping humanity. The greys also often work as henchmen for the reptilians or Annunaki.

Spiritual energy is often confused with the scientific and/

or the metaphysical approach to physics of outer space or anything that's beyond our planet and known 3D reality. We really are a curious race, we have beautifully evolved bodies with advanced energy fields and a beautiful planet as well! These are some of the reasons we are attractive to other races.

Many scientific exploring minds would rather read a scientific journal rather than anything that deals with spirituality. This is the denial tendency that eventually goes in the direction of creating the 'greys' race. They are interested in the advancements of technology through creating and using energy, though no real respect for the energy itself, spiritually or otherwise.

The reptilians or Annunaki are an equally challenging subject. They have also been referred to as the Nefilim or dark angels. Their approach is that they helped to engineer our DNA at one point in our history. So should we be in cahoots with them or working for them? They would like to think we exist because of them and that they should therefore control us. As with the greys, many of our government officials and world leaders have conferred with this race. Again we are a primitive race and can easily be swayed by scientific bling or anything greater than what technologies we have bben able to create on our own. Show someone advanced technology or energy dynamics that are not of this world and they immediately take it as a heroic gift that the Universe has bestowed upon them, even if they don't understand it, and even if it's ultimately of dark origin. Such is the case with the **Arc of the Covenant** and such are the **crystal skulls**.

If somebody that you never saw before gave you a rock and said that you could talk to God through it and when the voice comes through the rock it would float, you would challenge it until you saw the rock float and the voice coming through and then you would think you were the most special person in the world that God had actually sought you out to keep secret the only floating rock with his voice coming through it. Just one question...Are you sure the voice is God's? Hmmm.

The reptilians have been referred to in great detail through conspiracy material. Everything from shape shifting to sub-human identities, living underground in the inner earth, and being from a hidden planet **Niburu** that's on a wide elliptical revolution around our sun. Some have even said that the moon is hollow as a synthetic satellite from which they rule the earth. Conspiracy material is very detailed on exposing the dark side. One problem with it, is that it has such a charge of energy around it that even if you wanted to do something about all the looming alien darkness in the world, there isn't much that can be done, because in being exposed to the material you are presented with the possibility of being directly disempowered through the fear of it. So please use kid gloves when taking this information in. Sometimes there's not much you can do with the information except be paranoid. Don't go there.

So what I'm saying is: DO NOT LOOK AT THE PINK ELEPHANT. DO NOT THINK ABOUT THE PINK ELEPHANT. THE PINK ELEPHANT IS EVIL. Do you get it? There are no negatives: Focus is Focus. There may always be dark. Be the Light! Radiate your own Goodness connected to God Source no matter what.

The real challenge with these folks (reptilians) is this: they are from the 6th dimension and can step down to physical reality but not for very long without technology. There have been some that have lived on the earth through history. In South America there are hidden underground tunnels that ran down from a Catholic church. When investigated, strange murals were found that depicted a lizard man in a hood standing in a field of extinct healing herbs. Strange ancient symbols surrounded the painting. The story handed down was that the lizard man was a loner and came to the villages very seldom, though, was kind and helpful to humans offering healing and knowledge. We know that there are some good lizards though most are untrustworthy by our standards. Yet another example of a race with advanced toys and technologies that are really not operating from what we would consider to be the goodness or god-ness of Creator God's love. We are a trusting and patient people though we can also be a bit gullible at times too. The lizards are also reported to be involved with snatching of humans and children.

These groups and individual reptilians work as entities to people of this world. They connect their energy with those who have a lust for power and as they vibrate through them many of the world's atrocities are committed. Their main operatives here secretly seek power and control through the military industrial complex along with the Zionist and the cabalists. They are reported to have been behind the inception of the Catholic church and go back all the way to the warring 'gods' of the Old Testament. In these biblical texts there is a conflict or misinterpretation of the writings in the chapters and books that are actually talking about multiple gods warring with the earth people and their own kind as opposed to only referring to Creator God. The possibility exists that all the references to 'gods' and God were distorted or changed to simply translate as 'God' in the rewriting of these ancient texts.

These aliens are largely responsible (among other things) for keeping current earth human life in an evolutionary stasis. That is, they have covertly and by deception of manipulating Universal Law when possible (much like a crafty lawyer) ruled, controlled, and stunted the spiritual and social growth of the planet. Could we end up another stunted race with advanced toys? Anything's possible, that's why the spiritual avatars and masters have been visiting the planet, to tip the balance.

So where is the relevance of all this? Here is the real kicker. The greys and the reptilians are interested in working through people here on the planet as leaders, public figures and even energy workers.

Some refer to this as 'blending'. With the agreed consent of a human or by deception based on the promise of some power(s). The human is tricked into giving up their Soul energy to the alien being or group of beings, thus becoming an instrument for them. The human's perception of what's really happening is masked. Their soul energy is being compromised and they are being used as a spokesperson for the alien entities. The aliens may be deceased or out of body, seeking a blending opportunity, still in body though in a different dimension, or here in a human form already blended with a human and looking for more humans to convert into a compromised blended state. The promises of power for the individuals being approached is attractive. More energy, psychic abilities, energetic abilities, persuasion over others including the opposite sex. This does not come without a price. As the soul of the afflicted individual becomes blended with the alien energy, their mind becomes compromised as more of that person is now moved off into another dimension of reality where they still exist, though, just a shadow version of who the person once was and would have been: the full clear organic human expressing in the here and now.

The is risky business, and if you're around someone who has underwent this blending process they will try every trick in the book to convince you that it's the way, the truth & the light. They may be using terms such as Christ and God, though the energies are more Satanic if anything. This is vampirism at it's finest. Remember the statement earlier in the book. The true currency is Souls, and that's why the Akashic Records exist. For your own Soul to advance through 'Knowing the Self' in the best way possible as an organic natural individual expression of the Divine human race. We are a young race, though we have God potential that has been kept from most of us and everyone or everything else that knows of this, wants to find some way to tap into it and make it work for them.

Your soul, your multi-layered energy body, your chakra system, your organs, your brain, your physical body. These are yours and yours alone. That is the Divine Will and Truth of Creator God.

So now you can see why this is of importance to know when using the Akashic Records. There are all kinds of energies and beings out there doing all kinds of things to gain power and use the earth plane as a playground for their needs or uses. Please take the opportunity to read and to know this information, though, don't let it be your stumbling block of fear. Your strength, knowing and clarity is why this knowledge is being given. All of the talk about the variances of associative energies and alien energies is so you can simply know the difference. You may know it now intellectually without having to experience it first hand energetically or in the physical, though if you do, you will now know what to look for and when it is present when dealing with others in your healing, clearing and intuitive work.

Sometimes as with many other things in the intuitive world, you will know or see things that you can't really say or do anything about, this is often a challenge for those of us who want to help others. It's hard to call the kettle black. Be watchful and vigilant and you will find the best ways to help with vigilance. Just make sure to be aware of what you're dealing with in order to keep your own body and energy fields clear of interference. Having the life force or soul energy sucked out of you by an entity or alien presence is not an option. Use the knowledge and wisdom of these pages to strengthen your practices of protection, personal clearing and continue on your own spiritual journey knowing that there is definitely a difference in organic earthbound evolution of the spirituality of humanity and the short cuts and metaphysics of alien presences and workings. The good alien races know this and they completely abide and respect our growth as another galactic race, helping where they can, through guiding from a distance and communicating positive messages to some of us from time to time that we share with others here. Messages of promise, guidance, hope, strength, peace and well being.

Some aliens are really good at mind control. They love to plant thoughts into the mind field of others and even directly into the brains of others. This is a direct neglect for that person's free will of choice and serves the perpetrator's own needs and desires. This can give them the upper hand in a situation, such as getting you to do something with them or for them.

Often times people report that they've had dreams where everything was out of place just enough to know something was going on. Some hypnotist and psychics even enjoy these tactics of dream masking (also a Satanic control tactic). Be aware of your thoughts. Especially if you're receiving compromised messages not to do the things you love, such as paint or have fun, etc. They could be synthetic messages generated from an outside source that harmonically keep people stuck by re-circulating thoughts of failure, anger, fear and pain.

Let's talk about the **crystal skulls**. In the metaphysical and new age communities the crystal skulls have had a 'wow factor' of epic proportions. We have heard about these skulls more recently with the resurgence of interest in metaphysics and introduced in a book called the *Chariots of the Gods* in the 1970's. I have spoken about these from time to time with individuals who really do not understand what they are dealing with. When you feel huge surges of energy is it always good? Are you sure? How do you know?

I believe the crystal skulls are an open conduit. Both a transmitter and a receiver. Why would someone or something create an exact representation of a human skull out of crystal? Crystals are known to be energy conduits. With Creator as the watcher of the Universes, I believe that the alien races that were responsible in manipulating our DNA over history for evolutionary purposes have used these crystal skulls to amplify the genetics and cause powerful evolutionary transformation to occur over short periods of time. They may also have been used to shape shift down into the lower dimensions of 3rd dimensional reality by aliens, entities or other worldly beings that could not sustain a presence here without the help of such a transmitter/receiver.

The other concerns with these skulls is that they are being used to receive a long range broadcast from deep space which is vibrationally influencing humanity, human consciousness and our group mind by using cosmic star energy as the carrier and producing a signal from a destination. We talked about energy earlier in the book as a dynamic that those within the metaphysical, new age, healing and spiritual communities want to have a tangible experience of.

It's not necessarily always the most pure and clear energy emanations or vibrations that some seekers are energetically coming in contact with. As we discussed in the previous chapter, and important in relation to the skulls, we sometimes don't know whether energy is coming or going. So as we become more clear we might now notice that when energy is being taken from us. In a scenario where energy is being taken or given we may be used as a biodynamic hydro-electric battery. We may feel an energy surge that feels like a spiritual presence or experience. Closer sentient examination and exposure to this dynamic will reveal to you results and characteristics of when this dynamic is present or happening. You will become more aware of it. Much in the same way that after certain exposures to true higher vibrational spiritual energy we are now able to sustain it in the mind, body and energy fields for longer periods of time consistently, continually and/or permanently.

This is important. Most people just want to have an experience based on word-of-mouth referrals to feel the energy of the crystal skulls even for prolonged periods of time. Can dark energy heal? Yes. Can dark energy give you psychic experiences? Yes. So do your homework. All things are God and yes it is important to not live in fear, thought it is important to use discernment. Especially if you are tending along the higher clearer paths of understanding your soul, yourself and mystical places like the Akashic Records. You create radiant fields of clear spiritual energy when you step into your own power. All others in other dimensions as well as those here on this plane recognize this.

Mind control whether en mass or localized and focused could create specific outcomes therefore influencing the path of humanity. Ask yourself as you listen for the silent answer. Do the ascended masters use crystal skulls? Does Christ use crystal skulls? Does the Dali Lama work with crystal skulls? As you isolate the vibratory answers you'll gain personal insight.

The skulls are of alien origin and very ancient, and it's dare I say, of questionable use. Most people that I've met who are working with or have worked with the crystal skulls are looking for a powerful energy experience some without the aspirations of anything spiritual. Some have become ill from being exposed to amplified non-earthly energies. For some, the circus of energy is more appealing. And this is a direct reflection of why so many different things are happening simultaneously here on the earth. Everyone wants a piece of the action here. Whether something is transmitting either locally from the planet here or from off-world over long range through space to and from here, manipulative results could be achieved through individuals and groups of the human race including the manipulation of evolution or devolution.

Here's an example of energy. If you are empathic to feeling different types of energy vibrations. Notice how you feel around some law enforcement or government officials and their offices as well as lawyers and courtrooms. These are people and places who are deciding the fates of others sometimes for the greater good and sometimes corruptly. Because of this there are charges of energy that circulate around these individuals and places which contain a full spectrum of vibrations including entities and angelics which can be both light and dark. Some of these folks are of the light and some are corrupt. Another reason why the angelic realm is so directly involved with these places and players. I'm not speaking out against government or law enforcement. There are many honorable people upholding the great good for us all and they should be applauded and respected for their commitment and service work.

You be the judge. The darker energy of places and around certain groups or individuals has a charge of energy that the common person might feel as uplifting depending on what level they are at. If someone is in an emergency, help is there or on the way. Sometimes with more subtle introspection in the midst of people who are in direct contact with a lot of people, both of the light and dark side, you can feel an undertow of the current of energy.

It could be an amazing experiment to clear a group of

police officers with a smudge stick of sage after being in the field on their shift just to see what the differences are in the surrounding energies. My point is that there is a tangible energy experience on the earth plane, and all number of different energies can come through, angelic, demonic, alien and more. In another associated example if you go to a hospital you can feel the overall feelings, frequencies and vibrations of the people there open for healing as well as the spirit of healing.

Could Satanic forces be harnessing humanities minds through rituals with the crystal skulls? Possibly. The fact is that the crystal skulls are here now and that groups and individuals are harnessing their energy as an external power source for many uses, both known and unknown, and there are others in other dimensions connected to these people. Use kid gloves when dealing with these skulls. Many who are using them are seeking more energy and you may not benefit in the long run by being pulled into the undercurrent energy tow surrounding these transmitter/receivers. Get out to nature and lead a clear happy, joyously and earthly grounded life. The ancient Tai Chi masters had a great balance with this as a natural conduit between the earth and sky.

Where are we going with all this? The Akashic Records are based in the mystical and spiritually higher vibrations. Be mindful of the energies you're working with. You are primarily human and you have the knowledge and wisdom within you, even if you are not yet aware of it, to bring the greatness of creation through you, both energetically and as a unique expression of Creator God here in human form.

You are Sovereign. You have the natural abilities of ascension whether in the physical or in a transitory higher dimensional experience. You are Divine. You don't need to wade through the trenches of being leached on by unseen forces who need energy in order to connect with the earth plane. Be clear and free.

Higher frequencies sometimes do not have that energy buzz we often search for. You do not have to judge it, just take it all in and consider these possibilities as new ideas that can bring expanded knowing to your understanding of it all. Is all this interesting as a unique creation of the Universe? Of course it is...Do you want to be an energy slave to it or a self realized master? Be your own master. Listen from within and be guided by your own inner knowing.

The main challenge for most of the UFO crowd is this: They tend to confuse beings from outer space or elsewhere with spiritual masters or advanced levels of spiritual energy. Just because a being has advanced technology doesn't make them anymore aware of God or Love than you or I and sometimes less. The beings who are aware of God will tell you the same thing. Just because a being uses energy in ways that we do not yet know of does not make them a spiritual master.

This is another confusing manipulation: Some 'alien blended' people will use all the terms that a light worker might, such as Christ, God, Higher Self, Spirit, etc. This could be done by deception to open up a person for soul energy vampirism. Because the person who has already given up their soul for the 'blending' is compromised and may be sincerely or severely confused about core levels of giving, receiving or taking energy form others. Beware of people trying to bring alien presences to you in spirit form. They seek your soul energy or to come through you to have an earthly experience as they are out of body or in another dimension. These creatures are from different races and have different agendas. They may be very persuasive through their human earthly channel.

Use extreme caution. The races who truly respect you

will not try to come towards you, into you, or come at you. Just be present and aware. The preservation of the human race and your own soul may depend on it. Space is vast and this planet is an oasis, make sure that gypsy space travellers aren't feeding on your soul energy and intending to 'stick' around. As stated before spiritual beings will always respect every part of your space, soul, journey, body and home without question. If someone or something is in question, get a second opinion or give them a copy of this book

I'm writing about these dynamics here in this book because these are things that need to be known about in relation to being clear and having a clear or untethered experience of using your intuition as you open up into the Akashic Records. We love to scare ourselves, and often those who start down the metaphysical path become side tracked with conspiracy theories. We may at times buy into fear in a never ending quest for hidden or dark knowledge that we can't really do anything with. We may at times be held stalemate and must release this or come to grips with it from a much larger perspective or wisdom that compassionately all things are of God. This will help us supersede seemingly alarming scenarios and all the 'what ifs' in order to move forward.

Many teachers will tell you to just not focus on all of this. And while that is important, everyone out there is not a highly evolved spiritual master yet and most of us have energies that would better serve us to be cleared. Assimilate the info, file it and use it if and when needed.

This information is meant to open your eyes through the knowing of the dynamics. Some of you may have even experienced this yourself or know someone who has. Don't become lost in it. Simply know it for what it is and then continue to stay focused and rooted in the Healing, Love, Joy and Powerful Radiance that is You!

Tut

18" x 24" acrylic on etched brass

The key to healing all of
the atrocities in the world is
spiritual awareness.

Chapter 19

Histories, Evolutions & Futures of the Human Races

$\mathcal{D}$imensions and realities, ever constant though ever changing. Supreme Truth and the reflections of our own personal truths in relation to it. How much is our own truth in alignment with the greater truth? This is a question that we can continually ask ourselves. Just focusing on this question alone can inspire greater levels of self realization, enlightenment and knowing.

In the higher dimensions above the 3rd dimension there's a constant play between light and dark. As the grand play and exchange between light and dark continues, we experience the changes here in the 3rd Dimension. For many of us here on the spiritual path and those of us who are healers and intuitives (and we all are), we all have from within us this recognition of the light and the dark and we try to explain it to ourselves in a silent story. When asked, we paint a picture or weave a tapestry that may bring understanding or healing to the listener in the moment.

Creator God and the Divine always has a plan and uses the darkness, unbeknownst to it, as a catalyst. This happens here in the world as we look at world affairs. Those who bring pain and suffering or war and death know the power of the light. They cannot approach the radiance of the masters who are holding space for all of the rest of humanity. The many millions of monks and saints that have visited the earth plane and held sacred space for all to occur. In this way they are loving and guiding so that humanity might awaken to it's own greatness through creative and reflective moments of knowing.

We experience moments of this when ever there is a calamity caused by earth changes, weather patterns or man's pollution or war. We collectively see the suffering and sometimes we even spring into action with compassion. There should never be a question of answering any call in a moment of need no matter what the issue is. Every time we answer this Divine compassionate call, it brings us together as a community. We shouldn't have to have calamity to come together though. Much the same way family may not talk and even have ill feelings towards each other. Until a death in the family occurs and it's too late to right the wrongs. Regret is one of the hardest things to recover from. Many never do, though not impossible with inner child healing and guided self help. Often this can bring a natural opening to compassion and healing for all involved.

Every time we answer a compassionate call we are changing our reality both as individuals and as a world community. Especially as a world society where the response is magnified when many people are involved. We change the collective karma of the human race, an issue that is rarely discussed. Most of us are concerned with our personal karma and personal gains in life, though often the collective karma has made it a struggle for us and we focus on survival.

Our history has been changed many times and continues through time travels in an elusive quest for control, power and a search for circumventing looming events that have either been speculated through scientific calculations, looked at as a possibility along the event horizon, or predicted psychically. These time travels and the worm holes repeat themselves sometimes creating loops in realities. Have there been multiple realities concerning our history? Yes. These move in and out of prominent positions of change as our history books are diluted and written in ways which allows for change by the agreed upon group consciousness of humanity or certain things are blatantly left out or omitted. If people are not aware of an event within the constructs of the group mind, it is easier to be re-written. Both humans and aliens have continued to intercept, change and influence history as we continue to change as a civilization. For alien races this is an interesting concept as they arrive from very far away by means of natural travel, by bending the space time continuum, or by means of star gates.

Christ changed the outcome of humanity's path by taking on the karma of the world of His times single handedly, though, everyone involved with that movie was playing roles in the grand play that shaped the future of humanity.

Gandhi took on the karma of India by doing his historical fasts and speaking to the nation whose fate was changing from turmoil to one of peace. Many great ones among us have affected the course of history by way of the thoughts, words and deeds. Many tyrants have done the same and so the dance of light and dark continues though we have and are still making great strides of progress.

The group consciousness of humanity really wants to have it's cake and eat it too. We want a safe planet without too much world change or pollution although, we aspire to continue creatively developing a world full of life's luxuries. Most of us want to be wealthy or well off. We all want love and most of us have distorted reflections of true love. We all want the perfect piece of real estate while preserving the earth and conserving resources. The only real answer to what the masters have referred to as suffering or being constantly controlled by the ego is enlightenment. Enlightenment supersedes all forms of mental, physical and emotional suffering.

I've often wondered what our world would be like if our elected officials, federal, state and local as well as all police, military, doctors, nurses and lawyers were required to maintain a healthy holistic lifestyle. These are supposed to be the service people we look up to, correct? Can you imagine the effect it would have on the decision making processes of our world? This simple and powerful idea could restore harmony on so many levels. If you've ever changed your diet to a healthier program such as raw juicing, cleansing and taking supplements, you know what I'm talking about. The self clears up and better decisions and interactions with others start occurring very quickly and naturally. This can inspire great waves of having a more natural and loving and clear response to the world and all life. Better decision making is also a natural response of better living. Just imagine congress without fabulous babes, cash and prizes.

The Creative Human Race

It seems that our usual human mode of operandum as individuals and as a race is to see how much we can learn, how far can we go, how many things can we collect and how much wealth can we amass. As we look at the rise and fall of other races, empires and ages, we are now certainly as a planet at a fragile point. We as creative beings seem to be trying to out-build ourselves. If there is a vacant country side why not fill it up with paved roads and new houses even if they are only built well enough to bring an inflated profit, and then on to the next country side? We as a race seem to want to build, build, build, while we're not very practiced in conservation or balance.

The paradox is this: It's an expression of the Universal creative energy flowing through us. I'm not pointing to this as an activist, merely shining the light on a huge movement of creativity that comes through the human race's raw talents. What might lay in waiting for such an unbalanced culture? We have operated for a whole age in an unbalanced manner. When we as a race look back in centuries to come, we will see parts of the history of a world that is Hollywood's worst self destructive science fiction horror movie.

The future will find us living in a world of balance, green energy, advanced technology, and much less population and this will all evolve out of necessity. What can we do now to teach ourselves and others to snap into a higher state of consciousness? Often many have cried wolf and we've seen another day as a race and planet and so we continue to operate with our heads down and our blinders on.

The key to healing all of the atrocities in the world is spiritual awareness. If someone who runs a corporation or building company has a true spiritual understanding of a well balanced life and is doing their spiritual homework they will be more inclined to be of service to community rather than paying off the local city council (who may have pledged to keep a historic community intact) to bring in housing developments and big industry. Or to pay bribes to agencies or regulatory branches in order to dump toxic chemicals in remote and not so remote parts of the world.

To build around that one historic tree or historic landmark and to not interrupt so drastically the flow of nature is a step in the right direction. Our system has been unjust, corrupt, and ran by greed. Not to mention the homeless and diseased of the world. There is much good at work in the world which continues to balance the atrocities. When will we tip the scales as a race for good?

We need a true spiritual program in our lives. Spiritual not religious. We are still a primitive race for many reasons. We do have potential as some alien races say. It's no wonder we need so many incarnations to clean up our messes.

Creation of the Human Race

We as a race of humans were created by Creator God through stages of natural growth evolution and genetic re-wiring from off-world races at different intervals. The Universal Conscious of Creator God's hands at work by way of the Elohim, an advanced legion from the angelic realm who originally created humans and much more including the earth, and the animal, plant and mineral kingdoms. This was done by quickening processes of evolution and multiple manifestation techniques. They imported many beings from other star systems to get the planet up and running. Humans though in a seemingly evolutionary process have already been through stages of having had harmonious and advanced cultures on this planet and others.

The human race was created for multiple reason's. If you read any books on E.T.s, many will say that among the ancient visitors were the Annunaki who re-engineered our DNA by advancing it and limiting it though allowing us to evolve. If we were advanced builders, thinkers and workers, we could then create a world civilization capable of supporting an off-world space program which would really serve the curious interests of world rulers, god-like aliens and the elite, while the rest of the world is indirectly used as a work camp to support this. Some authors have even pointed to the concealing of the export of gold and other precious minerals mined from our planet for off-world trade and interests.

Much of the system of control of worldly affairs is about funnelling everything into our space program to get off the planet. While whole races here at home are starving, lost, sick, homeless and dying in all of the earth's countries, the corporate military industrial complex continues to look away to bigger and better things without informing everyone of what they're building, working on or have found answers to.

The answer is in the preservation of our peoples right here at home. True service and brotherhood. The great yogi **Paramahansa Yogananda** stated "Everyone thinks that they are doing the right thing" which gives us a compassionate perspective.

If you read other divinely channelled books such as the *Urantia Book* or *Keys of Enoch*, these books will indicate that we were created to be an advanced race of beings, like the Ascended Masters. With certain master-like capabilities demonstrated by the great Avatars (embodiments of God) who have visited our planet, such as Sai Baba, Babaji and Christ. In ancient India these abilities were referred to as the **7 siddhis** (gifts or abilities) including, invisibility, flying, instant manifestation, and bi-location, clairvoyance, becoming minute or becoming giant.

These are always considered to be rare and miraculous gifts endowed to the spiritual masters for what reason? It was never about the gifts. They were only given the gifts from Spirit because they had Wisdom in using the gifts. Only for the right reasons and usually to be of service to others. We have the capability of being advanced spiritual individuals and an advanced spiritual race. We are a primitive race and yet we are transforming again into an advanced race. The key to our balanced advancement is Spirituality, Awareness, and Conservation.

There is wisdom involved with using the Akashic Records,

and with all of the topics mentioned there is a good reason for it. You may now see the reason why the Hall of Records was set into place by the Elohim. With all of the evolving, changing, and linear/quantum activity of our space-time reality it is pure Universal genius to have a library of checks and balances for all the Souls who have ever visited or will ever visit the planet earth and an etheric stored template of literally everything here. The Akasha is the etheric stored template of our Living Library Planet Earth as well as every thought, word and deed of everyone and everything here. All things animate and inanimate.

We don't use the Akashic Records to spy on our neighbors, other governments, or find out about cheating spouses. These matters are better handled by a psychic. We use the Records to know who we are in relation to ourselves, others and the rest of the world (creation). We have been kept primitive for so long that 'knowing' doesn't seem very exciting does it? We all reach a point in life whether a pauper or a millionaire when nothing truly makes us happy in the material world except finding our true nature and our true self. It can be the ultimate quest and question. Every other thought, word or action is a distraction. The intention of finding your way can lead you down a road to successes you never thought possible.

For an alcoholic it could be getting sober and going to AA meetings and working the 12 step program. For this person, this is a miracle in their life. Or perhaps someone recovering from a life threatening illness or near-death experience and realizing that they had been a real tyrant to others. In their newly found lease on life to set things right they commence to acting completely different. Again for this person this is a miraculous occurrence in their life. Maybe someone has been angry for most of their lives and in their retired years they start to realize that they have an appointment with eternity.

In pondering this they may start to become more naturally hospitable to others.

These are real world examples of knowing the Self at a deeper level, finding the Path, or waking up to a new way of being. A Spiritual Experience based on wisdom gained or gathered through life changing experiences. We don't have to wait until we are in the narrows to start doing some self introspection. There are many ways in which you can use information and knowledge to gain wisdom for change. Thankfully we have many great sources for information including knowledge, healing and understanding from the Akashic Records. Start Now. Be the change in the world you wish to see as Mahatma Gandi said.

The Grand Cycle

As we look into the Akasha there are a few major factors for the future I would like to mention here. There are different considerations of what is to come.

First we have the traditional earth changes that come every 13-26,000 years in the great rotational cycle of our galaxy around the Great Central Sun. This brings us through the photon band or a pole of light which streams throughout the Universe. There are galactic clouds around the Center of Creation and in one place around this cloud band of gases, there is a part, split or separation in the galactic clouds surrounding the center where this band of photonic energy shines out from the Source Light of Creation across space.

The dynamic is this: Every 13,000 years we either are going into magnetic separation or a unified quantum oneness. And for all points in between there are many variations of expression while simultaneously under the influence of astrological occurrences. This creates anomalies in space - time and consciousness. When we're moving into separation we have definitive world changes such as severe weather patterns, war, suffering, cleansing by fire, etc. When we are headed into unity on the other side of the galactic rotation, we are experiencing oness, healing, falling away of the old ways that were built up during the separation.

The world is not going away anytime soon. The cycles from separation to unity will continue to occur. The great avatar Babaji has stated that he will remain on the planet until it turns into a star in the year 6,032. Human population will definitely ebb and flow during these cosmic cycles.

Each of us as souls who have been around for more than a few lifetimes have quite possibly lived incarnations during times of separation as well as incarnations during times of unity, giving much color and expression to our whole being persona and a resonance for being here now in form on the planet to witness the Great Shift once again.

In other words, some souls have seen it all. The last cycle of separation destroyed what we know as Atlantis. This book is being written in the winter/spring of 2013-14 as we enter the cycle of Unity not long after the winter Solstice of *December 21st, 2012*. No one was really sure what to expect, and many people had a different experience. Some of us didn't feel anything while others felt energy openings that were off the charts (your author included) and many varying experiences in between. So as we've moved past this time we now perceive that it's just the opening or beginning of a great cycle within the Grand Cycle that moves us into Unity. There are many changes on the wind for earth, society, and all of our race both as humans and as Divine Souls.

The earth changes are already starting to occur that will alter our existence here on the Mother Earth. Great land masses will be under water and others exposed as more and more earthquakes and tectonic plate shifts occur on the earth. Some land shifts will occur more gradually as the earth allows for relocation of it's inhabitants while water levels and weather patterns continue to change.

As the magnetic poles are being shifted the weather patterns are dramatically being altered with colder and longer winters and hotter summers and shorter springs and autumns. Many researchers and observers suggest that it wasn't global warming but global cooling in the long run that is the dynamic which could consume the earth. Global warming may well be just the dramatic climatic beginnings of a much larger scale global cooling trend.

A Trend in Technology

The next dynamic to be discussed is technology. Has anyone even noticed that technology has a tendency to want to interact with us and dare I say interface with us? It has a consciousness and an energy life just like everything else, synthetic by nature, though it is aware or alive. As a somewhat childlike race of beings who've had incandescent lighting and gasoline combustible engines in our earthbound automobiles, any form of technology excites us to a certain degree. We almost think of it as a luxury. This has been happening since the inventions of modern appliances for the home in the early 1900's. Many traditional things simply cannot or do not need to be improved upon although we still continue to redesign and manufacture lighter and even cheaper or more flimsy versions of the once sturdy tools and appliances we had.

Advancement is good, though we've had industrious global communities with a wealth of workers and questionable quality control in manufacturing of goods to be distributed globally resulting in a lot of household items that break down or can only be used a few times. Was quality ever the real focus in this scenario? So production and quality of tools and appliances is at a turning point, meanwhile the technological age has really taken off. It was only 4 decades ago we were watching the original Star Trek and they were using communicators. Now most people have mobile cellular phones which operate in the same way.

Digital everything is the modern way. Computers and computerized or automated belongings of every nature are a seemingly new way of life. The paradox is this: As you watch people in society using their text messaging via their 'smart' phone, you may notice that they are connected with the device. If you've ever been around someone who you are trying to work with or carry on a conversation with and they are texting at the same time, you know what I'm talking about. Their consciousness and attention is being connected to their hand held (smart?) device via their brain and senses. It's a 4th dimensional connection. This 4D connection they may experience while driving a car, motorbike or bicycle (though not very safe) working with others, eating, and any other functions.

Has anyone considered the implications of continuous connections with technologies? We've all seen the futuristic movies about robocop, robots taking over, and heard stories as far back as grade school about the stories of 'the beast' in the book of Revelations in the Bible, which some say already exists as a massive super computer. 'F***book' and other computer program platforms that are continuously live streaming and can take up large blocks of your focus time with your senses are another form of this 'blending'. If you are online as they call it or on the internet much of the time you may be seeing information about the implantation of microchips in humans.

If this does run it's course it will be only the beginning of android like technologies which seek to blend with humans symbiotically as a new form of life. This will take on many new controls of the human functions. The end result in this scenario is that human energy, brain functions and animate living tissue will be used as a battery much like the movie 'the Matrix'. We have known from scientific studies and inspirational movies such as 'the Secret' that the human mind and brain have enough energy to light up a city. It makes you wonder if other forms of life which seek expression here have considered this or may already know it.

As a simple minded child-like race of people in general we all tend to think of these modern sci-fi alterations as cool, unique and futuristic. And to a certain extent they will probably come to pass. The downside is this: As technology and computers advance along with new forms of governmental synthetic control, you may find everything is becoming conveniently done for you. With the implantation of a chip so much is known about you that it (the chip) and you can literally be talked to on a cellular, emotional, mental and physical level. You will have to do less and less with more being done for you. You would become a battery for a new form of humanoid blending with software and eventually hardware. The benefits might be argued with these software and hardware upgrades to your wetware (brains) though the human organic expression will be compromised which is of concern.

I see in the future a split of the human race into these human/androids along side the organic earthlings. We will also start to notice as this comes about, in our lifetime or beyond, that as we perceive technology blended with humans we now would recognize a free standing computer as a life form. Could this be what Star Trek the Next Generation was illustrating with the Borg? Travelling through space and assimilating everything in it's way. We need to be mindful as a race as to what's allowed to blend with us regarding technology. We have a Soul, brain and biodynamic energy generating fields that are of notice and importance to those beings and things who don't have them.

There will be an increase in multiple alien presences here on the earth as they are already here and have been here for quite some time, whether cloaked or invisible to the human eye, shape-shifters or very human in appearance and virtually indistinguishable to earth humans. These aliens will befriend humans bringing technologies forward that will advance society. There will eventually be alien races living among us openly. So this brings three major groups to the table: 1. Original organic humans

2. Androids and android-human hybrids
3. Aliens and alien/human hybrids.

In coming times there will be also be more cosmic bodies such as comets and meteorites impacting the earth and coming close to the earth therefore affecting the atmosphere of the planet and the gravitational pull and field. This could upset the balance of everything from communications to equilibrium, flooding, tidal waves, earthquakes and the list goes on.

The strange thing that I see in the Akashic Records is a cosmic radiation or virus coming down which may affect the earth population greatly. It seems that in the vision were it lands it cannot be treated quickly enough and kills instantly like an advanced stage of cancer. This 'cosmic cancer' could be from the radiation of a comet's tail that pass by the earth close enough to rain down debris or fall out. It may be that the elements from the fallout just don't set well with earth life. This is a consideration, so we will have to 'look into it' in subsequent visions and correlate with what others are 'seeing' in order to formulate how this will play out. If I've learned one thing about the Akashic Records it's that some meanings, visions or interpretations are literal and some are symbolic, and either way they come to represent a true picture of what will happen. So continue to look into the Records and practice your viewing, you may even want to share your findings with others who are working in the same modality or in similar ways of seeing.

Indigo Earth Mother & Daughter
24" x 36" acrylic on etched brass

Journey to the Akasha CD & Download

Feel the energy of the earth and the soil under your feet and how the earth supports your life, your physical body, your whole being and existence. The Great Mother nurturing your every thought, word and deed. We belong to the earth. Breathe deeply.

Journey 3

Shamanic-
Akashic
Journey

Divine Earth Spirit, Spirit of the Four Directions, Great Spirit, Ancestors, Elemental Kingdoms, Earth, Sky, Water, Fire, Air, Plant and Mineral Kingdoms, Animal Kingdoms, Divine Spirit Guides. Empower and surround us, work with us and through us. Accompany us on this Shamanic Journey into the Akasha.

Close your eyes. Breathing deeply, listen to your heart beat. Listen to the heartbeat of the earth. Relaxing...relaxing, going deep, relaxing deeper. Your eyes are growing very heavy and the light of day becomes darker and darker and darker.

The sun had rose in the east but now it's setting in the west as all of the many stars appear in the sky. The moon is rising overhead. See the beautiful stars filling the sky as you relax and continue to breathe deeply. See the stars and the constellations very clearly on this bright moonlit night. As you stand outside on the earth barefoot. Raise your arms now in your mind pointing your palms up to the cosmic stars. Drawing down the energy of stars. See the cosmic energy flowing into your hands, into your eyes, into your face. In through the top of your head. Down through your body activating and energizing your whole body and all of your energy fields and systems. Feel this energy coming out the bottom of your feet and connecting with the earth. You are between the heavens and the earth. With the energy of great Father Sky running through you. Feel your feet on the earth. Feel the energy of the earth and the soil under your feet and how the earth supports your life, your physical body, your whole being and existence. The Great Mother nurturing your every thought word and deed. We belong to the earth. Breath deeply.

As you look to your left on this moonlit night, you notice a soft clear running stream that disappears up into the distance. It's very gentle, it's reflecting the moon light. Trickling, flowing, a beautiful stream for all the little beings and creatures that exist from it's life giving energy.

Start to walk along this stream, looking at the beautiful stream, the wide open skies, the stars. See the soft gentle clouds whispering past the full moon as you continue to walk along the stream. The air is so clear and it's the perfect temperature. As you continue to walk you're coming up to a clearing and you see giant sacred symbol of the Four Directions etched into the soil. As you walk closer, you see that native colors have been used. You feel the energy as you step into the circle. You feel the lay lines and the energy of the north, the south , the east and the west meeting and intersecting in the center of this circle. You can feel it in your heart. This is the energy of all creation merging with your heart, your mind your soul, your body. As you put your hands up over your head and look up into the stars you notice that your feet are becoming lighter and lighter. Your body is becoming lighter and lighter. Your mind is becoming clearer and lighter. As you continue to breathe deep your feet leave the ground. As you're levitating up over this giant sacred mandala. Continuing to rise, continuing to rise. Up into the Great Spirit of the Sky. Sailing, soaring with the eagles, hawks, ravens, doves. Soaring straight up higher and higher now, climbing higher, the moon appears as if it is coming closer, and we now start to reach cloud level. We now start spiraling like a great bird, spiraling upwards, your body becomes lighter and lighter all the time as you fly faster and higher. Coming close to the moonlit clouds, you soar straight into the clouds trusting, though you can't see, know that answers await on the other side. Flying, sailing, soaring through the mists higher and higher. Soaring higher and higher now. As we look down we see the whole planet earth. Through the clouds we can see the distant horizon, the atmosphere, as we are up in the etheric field of the planet.

It seems that time and space has shifted. That we are in an alternate reality. The earth is still very real, the time is very different and space is very different also. Flying now and sailing out over the oceans the clear blue womb of the Mother, we see the continent of South America and all it's many sacred sites. Come closer to South America as we fly sailing and soaring looking at the coastlines. We are now flying closer and closer to the countryside which is Peru with many ancient mystic places. Mysteries of unforetold adventures awaiting us there.

As we start our downward spiral coming closer and closer, sailing and soaring flying in spirals over Peru, we see down in the distance, the sacred ancient site of Machu Pichu. See the green mountain sides and the steep rocks as you sail closer like a giant condor. See the clouds and the mist rolling through the mountains changing. This is a different time and place and a different time and space. This is the world of the Shaman. Continue your spiral down sailing and soaring as you come closer, coming closer. It almost seems like you're flying too fast as you continue to drop deeper and deeper through the atmosphere and the air fields coming closer to the mountains as you continue to soar. But you're in a different time and space, normal realities no longer apply here as you fly faster and faster straight down towards the earth you see giant sacred markings etched out into the earth. What do these markings look like?

Descending faster and faster coming very close to the earth, coming very close to Machu Pichu. Continuing your descent faster and faster. Once you come so close to the earth it looks like you will crash into it, but as you merge with the earth, you go right into the earth, you go right through the earth. You are now in the lower worlds, in the underworlds, going deeper, sinking deeper and faster. Looking around what do you see? Rocks, tunnels, elemental beings, keepers of the earth. What are the colors of the earth?

This is where you can meet your animal guides, your ancestor guides, your spirit guides. The Spirit of the Mother Earth. They are all here in the tunnels and passage ways. Continue flying through the earth. You may be moving through what appears to be solid matter though you know it's not in this dreamlike yet very real shamanic state of consciousness.

Looking at the animal spirits, the earth guides, the earth keepers, you may see faces and beings coming out of the stone. Standing guard ready to assist, humbly watching you pass. Flying now through this great tunnel system, you see an opening up ahead, a light as you start to fly. Gradually upwards, gradually upwards. Ever so gracefully peacefully gliding to a large opening. You start to ascend again up through the earth to the surface. Straight up your body is being pulled. Straight up through the soil. And as you come out up to the surface you find yourself at the ancient sacred site, the Temple of the Moon. You're in this grand ancient stone temple.

Created by the ancients. There's a huge circular hole cut right in the middle of the ceiling where the full moon is shining a shaft or a beam of soft yellow moon light, very powerfully down through the opening straight down onto an altar in the middle of the room.

As you walk across the Temple of the Moon to the altar, you notice that in the moon light lies a very ancient book. It looks almost as if the cover is made of some sort of skin. It's very ancient looking. This is your Book of Life. As you're here your spirit guides gather around you, your animal guides. You have a feeling or a knowing as you look into the book that you will get some answers here. Across the room on the other side of the altar, is a large black unpolished stone which reflects no light. As you look into this ancient Book of Life you see archetypal symbols, tribal symbols, cosmic symbols, native symbols. What do they look like? Look at their shapes forms and colors. These are the patterns of life woven through all time and space.

Look up from the book into this large black unpolished stone. Out from the void you see your guides starting to appear coming out of the stone, your animal guides, your spirit guides, your native guides. Coming out of the stone into the room to surround you. They are very thankful to be here with you on your journey to accompany you for healing and healing the earth.

Look back down at the book as the pages start to turn. They turn to a future time. What do the symbols appear as. What is the cosmic message? What is the healing message? These archetypal symbols are so strong that you can almost feel them in your body. Feel them in your body now. These light codes are healing your body.

Look up into the mirror again the black void mirror from the unpolished stone. How do you appear? What do you see? Where does the shamanic tunnel of vision connect to?

See the vision, dream the dream. Open your eyes and look deeply into the stone, into the earth, into yourself. As the images start to appear they grow clearer and clearer, sharper, brighter. You can hear them through the earth. You can feel it through the earth. These visions are healing you as you are healing yourself you are healing the earth.

Your spirit guides here as your intermediaries to the underworld, the lower worlds, the realms of the shaman and the earth's keepers. Look back down into the book once more. As the pages start to turn they magically they magically stop on a recent past moment. When energies shift, in the mind, body, heart or soul had occurred and healing was needed in that moment but was unnoticed.

Looking into the book we see archetypal symbols. Mystical ancient symbols. Tribal symbols of healing. These light energy symbols are beaming light into our bodies. Healing us, healing that moment. The energy of the symbols is so strong in this book that we can feel it connecting through us. We can feel it in the earth, we can feel it in our body. Look up into the unpolished black stone one more time. When was this moment? What happened in this moment?

This healing is occurring, your spirit guides , your animal guides, the shamans of the underworld are healing you here, through the tribal symbols of your Book of Life. They are all present now surrounding you. They have a message for you, a vibrational sound message. What is the sound? What is the message, what are the words, what is the song?

As the moonlight shining through the center of the temple we feel ourselves start to levitate again as your feet leave the ground. You feel yourself levitating as your feet leave the sand. Being drawn up through the center of the temple into the moon light and out into the open sky. Flying in this dream like state of consciousness. Sailing, soaring out over these ancient beautiful parts of thc carth. The energy is so high and clear flying through the sky out over the mountains. Out over the canyons, the valleys, the lost cities, the lakes, ancient statuaries, carvings in mountain sides.

We're going to a very powerful place. As we start our descent down into a mountain valley. Sailing along we land on a mountain at the ancient Doorway of Aramamuru. The stone temple star gate used by the ancients. Carved into the side of the mountain under the starlight of the night. We step into a doorway. There is a vibrational tone that your spirit guides are singing. Hear the tone as you place your hands and your forehead on the surface your body merges through the stone doorway. And you go deeper and expand and you find yourself flying through the cosmos out through the star systems. Pure positive energy of creation.

Complete silence, the void of deep space, the beauty of all the star clusters being created, the solar systems and universes. With your guides flying right beside you. Your guides with the help of the star energy starts to bring back lost parts of your Soul. Missing Soul pieces or Soul fragments are brought home back to integrate with you as you're flying out here to gather them all. As you're flying through space you see the planet earth and the moon and the sun and the other surrounding planets in orbit. You start flying towards the Earth, the Earth is now calling you home.

And you notice that time has shifted the closer that you get. The moment is starting to seem more real again. As you're coming closer and closer to the atmosphere and you see the earth slowing turning in the light of the sun you start your descent into the physical world of planet earth. Entering into the atmosphere in the warmth of the sun. Spiralling downwards, sailing, lofting you see the country in which you reside and you glide closer and closer to the surface through the clouds taking in the fresh air of the higher atmosphere. The wind is breezing past you. Coming closer to the surface you see the lakes and the hills, the streets, the cities, continuing downwards you see your home town region and your home. Coming closer sailing down see it all.

Be thankful for all of the information and the healing that you've learned on your journey. Thanking your spirit guides, thanking God, all of the elementals, Great Spirit, as you continue down to your hometown and you see your home. Coming closer to your dwelling as you move down into your dwelling and into your space and back into your physical body. Take a deep breath. Start to gently move your arms and legs and feel the energy of the earth supporting you. Feel the healing energy running through your body the energy of the sky. Give Thanks.

Thank You Great Spirit, Om, Peace, Amen

© 2012 Bill Foss

St. Germain

Chapter 20

Using the Stargate for Soul Retrieval

$\mathcal{I}$n the previous journey we experienced what I call *Shamanic-Akashic* energy as a blend of Akashic and Shamanic energies. As we go into the Akashic Records and continue to work with the energy of the Records and the energy of the Soul continuing to open the intuition and continuing to heal karma from other lifetimes and this lifetime, the feel of working in this capacity actually can start to have the likeness of Shamanic work.

As you are working with shamanic energy, know that it is deep work. How clear is the person working with you on this deep level? We know that when we work with a spiritual healer that the Divine has an ultimate goal to reach us through the healing. Shamanism is based on the work of the inner planes or what they call the **Shamanic State of Consciousness**. Traditional shamans travel through these altered states of consciousness with the help of mind altering herbs or without the herbs or roots and also with the help of animal spirits also called **familiars**. These 'familiars' are very powerful because as spiritual beings in a multidimensional universe having a human experience, the animals are always rooted in the Eternal Now without judgement. Their clear energy holds space for the healing of bringing back soul fragments as well as clearing away negative energies and/ or entities which are no longer needed or are not beneficial for a person. So when you work with shamanic energy it can be very deep and very powerful. Akashic Records work also deals with the business of the Soul. In the Records we work from the soul energy as our point of reference, so we can go into the Akashic Records through the Soul energy reference point and work remotely, though very vividly on a sensory and visionary level. One of the main gifts, advantages and dynamics of working through the Records is that it is remote work. So you are experiencing and yet not directly experiencing simultaneously. When working with the shamanic energies you are involved with remote work though the different planes of existence that you visit and by accessing the Soul from that different reference point of the altered state realities including deep connections with the earth energies. Sometimes the shamanic work can leave a person feeling a little raw or open, bringing uncomfortable energetic experiences to the table as everything shifts and realigns in life.

What I call *Shamanic-Akashic Healing* refers to a new modality and blend of the shamanic and akashic energy to achieve even greater results that brings soul retrieval remotely through the Records as opposed to only journeying in S.S.C. (shamanic state of consciousness)

There are a number of ways that we can work with the Akashic Records to achieve Shamanic like results without the use of mind altering substances. When mind altering or mind opening substances are used in conjunction with spiritual journeying, it forces the mind's eye or third eye to open to other dimensions not normally available through everyday waking state normal life sensory perception.

From ancient times there are two different view points and guidelines associated with the spiritual journey work:

A. That the use of herbs, alcohol or other mind altering substances is okay, allowed or common during ritual for the individual and the culture.

B. That the best and clearest way to get in touch with Spirit is by being completely drug and substance free.

I tend to agree with scenario B. In scenario A. we may find powerful shamans, medicine doctors and others who work with a litany of different spiritual energies to acheive a multitude of outcomes. In some ways there could be spiritual ego which is generating spiritual power as a currency. You be the judge, though I think you will often find that the spiritually clear, clean and sober way is the best way to achieve results in other dimensions.

When a person uses drugs or alcohol it tends to open a person energetically to all number of strange beings, entities and psychic connections with others that are not truly beneficial for a person's life or path. It is known to short-circuit the etheric field and/or open a person temporarily that allows other uninvited energies to connect with them or contact them. It also can either dull the senses or make them more acute.

If you do use alcohol or drugs, how does it really make you feel? After the initial buzz wears off, where are you then? How do you feel about yourself and others the next morning or day? There is the consideration that some shamans are using sacred herbs and should be honored as a sacred practice and a traditional part of their culture. When this has been brought into the modern or western world, it has had a multitude of varying effects.

A common reoccurring theme for humans is that once we have felt energy or the effects of a sacred substance we want more of it. Not always, but there is the possibility of certain people to adapt addictive qualities from working with altered states of reality. They may find that as they visit an altered state that they are searching for something they can't seem to get from everyday life. This is an excellent opportunity for that individual to move away from this type of continual journeying and try the natural approach of guided meditation. Even the elders will tell you that it's a sacred sacrament and should be respectfully honored as such. If you are going to do something of this nature you may want to travel to a sacred place like Peru and work with a traditional tribal shaman and then hold space for the experience by honoring it as a one time experience instead of continually indulging. Again I am not suggesting to anyone that you go try mind altering substances. You are your own person and have to go within and meditate on what's best for you.

As we look into our other lives and even earlier moments of this lifetime we may find times and moments when or where we suffered trauma. Maybe there is a moment from childhood when we were neglected or even felt abused. If there are times from your childhood that your conscious mind has blocked out, I would tend to think there is a traumatic experience being blocked from your conscious mind. This is the way the mind experiences self survival so we can continue with a relatively normal life. Though often our life experiences can be reflections that are colored by these traumatic and hidden experiences hidden in our subconscious minds and creating any number of mind numbing or challenging situations for us in everyday life.

The masters sometimes refer to this as suffering of the

ego. If pieces of memory are missing, work needs to be done. You may want to find a qualified practitioner to work with and move forward knowing that you will make progress in healing.

Another aspect of the nature of working with the Akashic is it's tendency to be remote even if we are connecting with it from inside the body or heart. We often in the guided journeys tend ourselves up and out of the conscious mind, body and energy fields, and out creating a passageway up into the Records and then after our Akashic reconnaissance mission or query for information coming back down the passageway and back into the body. This has different advantages. First we are consciously telling our intellect and subconscious mind that we are creating a pathway up and out to gather information and to have an experience and then we come back and close the path way so we have created a practiced, naturally conscious way to open up, journey out, come home and close the portal. This is much different from running around being psychically open in every moment looking into everything and everybody that gets in your way.

Most women and even some men who are in touch with their feminine energy side, really feel energy with their etheric field. We call this **empathic** or may refer to them as an 'empath'. Some of us have learned to feel with our energy fields as a result of being opened through traumatic life experiences. Sometimes people just open in this way. The ego, whose original job description is survival of the human form, is in charge of this dynamic. The ego may deem this as a special quality and for some people the ego will not want to lower this hyper alert awareness of the empathic field for fear of it being lost if it is closed or turned down. So the problem with this is that they start getting energetic sensations through **physio-etheric** biodynamic traits of being afraid not to get information continually. It's another form of being hyper alert. Do you see the paradox? How can the Akashic Records help this person? Visiting the Akasha can directly bring relief to this person by showing them to journey up and out with their senses, their mind and their soul to get the information remotely as an alternative to what they were previously receiving directly through the over excited or continually open etheric fields. This will be a special gift and dynamic for that person to know, experience and practice.

In Journey 3 we experienced a Shamanic-Akashic Journey and the energy dynamics associated with both the shamanic and akashic realms together in one guided journey experience. What is the benefit of doing this? The benefit is that we access the shamanic realms, energies and benefits by way of our own personal journey instead of the traditional shaman doing things for us.

When someone else journeys for us we may go back into the world and experience anything from dramatic to subtle changes or even conflicts. As certain things are changed, cleared away from us or added to us without our own doing or knowing from the process we get an increase in core soul energy that can spike our thoughts words and deeds with more power than we've been used to carrying for a while if ever. Like a 60 watt light going to a 150 watt light instantly. The benefit of the guided Shamanic-Akashic process is that you are personally in control and involved with the process consciously, subconsciously and super-consciously. You are having your own guided journey experience to bring back your own soul energy and are involved in your own clearing with the help of the facilitator.

The Familiars

Native American shaman with animal guides

© 2012 Bill Foss

Sky Dragon

Journey 4

Shamanic-Akashic Guided Stargate Soul Retrieval Journey

*Y*ou may want to have some sage in the form of a smudge stick and a glass of water. and a Native American flute or drum recording as a background for your meditation though not necessary. You can also use the *Shaman-Akashic Journey* on the *Journey to the Akasha CD*.

You may want to cover your body with a light blanket to make it feel safe as you journey out.

Relax and start taking some long slow deep breaths. As you continue to relax, relaxing down even deeper, you now feel a soothing peaceful comfort coming over your whole body. As you continue to relax, become aware of every part of your body relaxing, slowly from the tips of your toes all the way up your feet and legs, all the way up your spine, your front and back sides, your arms and up over your head as this relaxing power of spirit relaxes you even deeper. As your guides now stand around holding space for you, see them clearly, recognizing who is there. Your personal guides, your guardian angel, arc angels, ascended masters, family members, Native American guides and healers from the other side. As you relax now down, down, down deeper they are holding healing space for you.

See now many animal spirits gathering around you. What do they look like? Are there any current or past pets that show up for you?

As you are there in the room picture now a bright spotlight from above, a beam of light coming down around you as everything else in the room goes dark and moves back as you are now in this field, stream or beam of white light. You feel that your body is now becoming lighter and lighter. As you continue to see the beam you now start to float as you are being drawn up into this beam of Divine energy. Up, up & away as you float through the ceiling and up out into the night sky. See now the heavens and the stars, the towns below becoming smaller as you now see the glowing horizon of the earth's atmosphere. As you continue to move up you notice now that there are tiny orbs of glowing light that dance as a stream. Millions of orbs are making up this stream of bright white light. These are all the souls that have ever visited the earth plane. As these orbs stream around you, extend your finger and touch one as it expands a vision to you. Notice what the vision is, where you are, who you are with, is there a special message? As you continue to rise you reach out your other hand and touch another orb as it expands opening up a streaming movie of visions. Who is there, what do you see?

As you come up into the clouds floating up you now feel a gentle pressure in your body as you come through the floor of a great hall. The Hall of the Akashic Records. And as you stand there in awe of the tall arched ceilings and beautiful stain glass windows you now see. The cosmic energy of the stars beams down through the stained glass and dances in colors across the floors moving with energy.

As you look out you can see through the walls and the ceiling as they are semi-transparent revealing eternity. Your view pans out across eternity as you are now here looking out across all space and time. The vastness of the ever after. The stream that has brought you here is beaming up, cascading in the middle of the temple as it continues up all the way back to Source Light of Creation as you see it overhead in the distance. In the middle of the hall are a set of crystalline spheres that concentrically grow smaller one inside the other all the way down into the center disappearing into beyond. These spheres are singing with special tones, special vibrations that you cannot hear in normal space time reality. These vibrations and musical tones are clearing your body, clearing your energy fields and your physical body in every way. Clearing you out, leaving you feeling lighter. Lifting your vibration with their bright colorful tones. The Music of the Spheres.

As you now look to the north end of the grand hall you see a very large ancient stone ring. A star gate with ancient Akashic symbols and markings you have never seen before around it. You now have the sense that you are to journey through this ancient portal out through the Universe. As you start walking over towards the north end and the star gate across the vast floor, the symbols on the star gate start to light up and glow with golden energy. There are 7 steps leading up into the stone ring. As the stargate now engages and a rainbow field of energy is shining in the stargate, your guides now appear around you, here in the Akashic Records Temple, All of your animal spirits of familiars. Appearing as they let you know they are going with you. As you walk over to the giant ring of stone with glowing symbols and the rainbow field, ascend now the stairs with your guides.

1...2...3...4...5...6...7

You start to float and hover before the rainbow field as you are now being pulled into it's field like a giant vortex. And as you start to fly, so free you are expanding out into space! And you see all of the stars, heavenly bodies and colorful cosmic formations. As you're flying with your guides you see your power animal spirits with you, flying on both sides of you, and as you expand flying very fast and free, you feel the energy of the stars. The cosmic power of the stars streaming into you here in the void of space. There is only the void of space and the power of the energy of the stars. And as the stars shine to you they reflect and refract back to you parts of yourself that had been lost in space. Parts of your soul that had fallen away as you'd flown here before during sleep or the dream state. As you've now come to reclaim your beautiful unique Soul, that is yours! And it comes streaming right back into you as you fly around the heavens of the universe in a grand swooping circle. And you now see a bright white glowing energy around your body as a great force field as you know this is your Soul coming back. With even more velocity as you give thanks to the stars, heavens and universe and your guides and animal spirits, you now fly back through to the milky way galaxy and our solar system as you pass all the planets. Pluto.... Uranus....Neptune...Jupiter...Saturn...Mars....Earth... Venus... Mercury... and the Great Sun as you come back to the Earth. Coming down to our beautiful planet you now see the glow of the horizon and atmosphere as you come back down to your country, to your city, town or countryside. Back to your house, as you come back down into the ceiling and back down into your physical body. Take a deep breath, wiggle your toes and fingers and Give thanks for your guides and the animal familiars holding sacred space for your personal *Guided Shamanic-Akashic Soul Retrieval Journey*.

Be gentle and kind to yourself and no alcohol or anything else for 24 hours after your journey so that the soul energy really has a chance to seat back into you without becoming fragmented again.

Blessings to You on your Path, Namaste!

Earth Prayer
24″ x 36″ Acrylic on etched copper with crystal frame

As we are able to remember our childhood events, thoughts, words, actions, feelings, we embrace them and visualize our inner child with us now in guided meditations which are constructed to bring us closer as we merge with parts of ourselves which we may have been disconnected from.

Chapter 21

Healing the
Inner Child

As we traverse the many levels, perspectives, and modalities involved with self discovery and personal care and self healing, we will sooner or later inevitably be lead to reconnect with a part of our self called the 'Inner Child'. This part of our psyche represents very intricate and detailed parts of our personality that contain everything we've experienced, observed, learned and created during childhood. The benefits of working with our own 'inner child' can be nothing short of amazing. We can experience personal healing results by working on this level that may not be available from other modalities. Maybe in other modalities we are working with the same issues from different angles, though there are certain pieces or parts of our being that really listen to change, healing and release work through contacting or connecting with the inner child.

Your inner child is a wonderful little person and when we go back through guided meditation, we may have all kinds of emotions come up. The more we move forward in life the more dear these memories can become as we look back. These childhood moments can seem to have happened long ago and just yesterday at the same time. We will look at the childhood experiences and the inner child healing here in this chapter from the perspective of the Akashic Records among others.

As we look at our family, brothers, sisters, mother and father, and then back through our grand parents, aunts & uncles, cousins and others. We start to see more clearly who they are and who they have been in reference to our changing perspectives over the course of our lifetime. How did we see them as children? How do we see them now? What were the changes in our perspectives with family members as we grew up? As you gather more information about your extended family including your bloodline, ancestors and distant relatives. You may find out about different tribes, or parts of the world that your family was from. Were there any people who were noted in history that you are related to? Over the course of family discussions and even developing a family tree you start to see why and how the family moved around geographically over the course of their lives and generations. What were their challenges and their accomplishments?

Inevitably as we work through discovering, knowing, or getting reacquainted with ourselves at a deeper level, we will start to reach into deeper perspectives about ourselves. For instance, times when we are going through periods of healing where habits are dealt with and more self love and a healthy sense of self esteem are needed or sought after. We may be brought to work with practitioners whether psychological counsellors or alternative healing or spiritual counsellors which will talk to us about the inner child. This perspective, brings us very powerful passageways to our deepest levels of healing. As we are able to remember our childhood events through thoughts, words, actions and feelings, we embrace them and visualize our inner child with us now in guided meditations which are constructed to bring us closer to them. We merge with parts of ourselves which we may have been disconnected from. As we come together with these childhood missing parts of ourselves we have very profound moments of healing that occur.

We all need to validate this part of ourselves naturally and from a healthy perspective. Sometimes when we've had childhood situations, abuse or losing a parent, then this work may hold some amazing keys to unlock ideas, emotions and tendencies that often hold us back from having a full and happy life. Maybe there were situations as a child which blocked your creativity and ability to express freely or just be happy as a child.

For any and all associated events 'Inner Child' healing work can be very helpful. If you've had deep traumas occur then seek out the help of qualified professional practitioners who can support you by helping you reconnect the dots. As you bring it up to the surface and you look at childhood experiences with your inner child present you can heal it just by viewing the trauma and sending it healing, blessings, acceptance and release at the same time. You support your child self as your adult self is present.

In a similar way that we discussed in earlier chapters about looking into the Akashic Records from the Soul perspective. Just by the act of looking alone, the energetic pathway holds healing and releasing powers while we gaze upon it without emotional investment to it in this moment.

When we do inner child work, emotions are okay to express because children usually express emotions more freely than adults. So we pay attention to the emotions as they come up and even inspire new emotions for your inner children as we are now the ones taking care of them, we are the parents. We are our own parents now in our adult stages of life. And we can inspire, nurture, love, guide, console and heal our own selves through this wonderful connection to our own childhood and the 'little you' that wants to come out and play.

How often have you thought about moments from your childhood? Reflections of good moments or reflections of challenges. Are there any times that you have memories that just seem to be emotionally numbing? Another interesting perspective for you to consider: How many of your current moments are silent connected reflections of things you experienced in the first years of your life? Do you unconsciously play out those tendencies from time to time? This silent stream of elemental information coming to you via your childhood can be beneficial, or could hold you back.

If there are things that you've wanted to accomplish in life and it just seems like no matter what you try there is something holding you back that you can't quite figure out, may I suggest here that some childhood or 'inner child' healing is in order. The Akashic Records is a great way to accomplish this. We can also heal our family too as we are all connected through our DNA to the rest of our bloodline, generations of relatives, ancestors and immediate family members.

You may talk to your child self and heal many things. You can envision your current self as the person responsible for their well being. You can talk to them and let their presence shine reflections of who you truly are back to you giving you personal levels of introspection previously not known.

How would you take care of your personal inner child? Would you make sure that they had nutritious things to eat? What about having fun, would you make sure there are some interesting and fun things to do? There are many things to consider when thinking of taking care of a child, and we can reflect those back to ourselves, in personal hygiene, career, having fun, feeling safe, and so on. Have fun taking care of your inner child and develop a new and personal relationship with them. They can give to you in ways you never thought possible.

Theatre of Dreams
A Shamanic Dream and it's Reflections in Life

A Dream that I recently had was very earth shaking. So vivid that I want to share it with you here and show you how the dream coincides with other healing work in life for me and possibly you the reader and others.

As the dream starts I was on a beach between 2 beach houses where I was staying. As I walked through the sand facing the ocean directly between the 2 houses I stopped as there were 2 cats, one black and one black and white. Being a cat lover I went to pet them. I noticed as they were at my feet that they had mangled my left foot. I became alarmed in the dream as I continued limping around the house to the right into the beach house where I was staying with friends. There in the house I began telling a lady friend I had known for years, who was a massage and energy practitioner herself, in real life, to look at my foot! It was bleeding, mangled and I could see the bone coming out of the skin. It was very vivid. I couldn't feel anything from it in the dream and felt lucidly that it was probably either because we were in the dream state or that I was numb with pain.

So just then, while sitting reclined on the floor with my feet propped up, laying back the room became dark and after a few moments there was a crash of lightning and I heard a drum. There was a silhouette of a figure standing at my feet wrapped in a Native American blanket. The figure had long dark hair and 5 feathers sticking up around his head. I sensed the figure was male. As the room was dark again the lightning crashed once again in sync with sound of a thunderous drum. Again seeing the drums at my feet and the figure I now knew who was visiting me. I sat up and touched my feet to the drums as I sat forward. Reaching out I touched the male figure standing at my feet, as the lightning crashed again and the thunderous drum sounded.

It was Babaji! I was having a dream visitation from the Immortal Himalayan Saint. Babaji stretched out his hand and announced " There's some dark energy in here" and as he pointed towards me he directed his finger away from me and I saw some dark or dissonant energy move away from me and then dispersed. It is always a very humbling experience to have a visitation from Babaji, because whenever he makes a dream appearance, I know that it is really happening.

At that point I moved into the next room where my friend Natasha sat looking at what appeared to be a TV screen or monitor. There was an image of my previous girl friend on the screen and as she pointed to the figure she said "Look we can make her do different things" The static figure became animated. Babaji's voice then said "The soul of the 5 sisters is a very powerful shaman from another lifetime" I knew he was speaking of the 5 sisters of which my friend Natasha was part of.

I had been in a relationship with one of the 5 sisters and had been friends of their family for years before that. Years ago in a dream I saw that their body souls were separate, though a singular celestial soul was operating through the 5 bodies. As discussed in previous chapters, a celestial soul can operate in more than one body at the same time while linked to separate body souls. In this story it was in order to gather sensory input of 5 different simultaneous lives being lived in the same immediate family. A unique dynamic illustrating that the characteristics of soul energy is not what we think it is. Souls can operate simultaneously and continually along the space-time continuum in many different directions, while still providing a silent, singular and localized expression of it's presence.

As I awoke, I was a bit startled, I had known that I had a visitation from Babaji as the energy was very high in the room and it was hard to go back to sleep.

As I now type, I'm revisiting a shamanic center in Austin, Texas where I had several nights ago attended a shamanic drumming and journeying circle. As we all introduced ourselves and then layed down, the facilitator, Karen, began to drum. As she continued to drum I waited patiently for any lucid visions, pictures or dreams to surface. As I lay there much to my surprise out of nowhere I saw an image of my mother (in this lifetime) grabbing me by the shoulders and shaking me very hard while yelling. She was so mad her teeth were clenched together. It was a startling image. It had come up to be healed.

The next thing that I saw was an image of myself as a teenager walking quickly away or 'running away' as I had known that this symbolized my yearning to leave the small town I grew up in because of my early childhood experiences and because of feeling so out of place for so many years. As we came up out of the drumming meditation we shared our experiences.

When it was my turn I shared the story of the previous dream that I had about Babaji. As I told the story I realized that there were some things that were strangely synchronistic. At the center here in Austin there were 2 cats, one black and one black and white. Also the facilitator Karen bore a striking resemblance to my friend Natasha in the dream. Shorter red hair and glasses. Could it have been the shaman facilitator? Maybe. Could the person in the dream have been representing both people? Yes. My left foot became mangled symbolizing both trouble in moving forward and walking wounded with my feminine or left side. This dream, story and sequence of events was all about healing my own issues with my mother, women, and even more so my own feminine side.

Another interesting detail is that the facilitator, Karen, announced that she was working with Black Panther as a protecting animal guide (familiar or power animal). I have also worked with Black Panther for years. Often times when I've facilitated group or individual journeys for people they have commented from time to time on a huge black panther walking up the steps of the Akashic Records with them or in front of them. Black Panther energy as a familiar is known to symbolize hidden power from the feminine and getting in touch with our own dark side. Darkness is the place for seeking and finding answers, for accepting healings, and for accessing the hidden light of truth.

So as the opening within myself played out over the next week, I felt a little off my game and I knew that I was opened by spirit to accomplish some deeper healing. I felt an energetic opening around my heart and spine in the back up into my neck.

The image of my mother shaking me in anger at a very young age had come up from deep within my subconscious mind and my cellular body memory to be healed. As I spoke with my friend Diane, another shamanic practitioner who has been a dear friend for years and who actually facilitated my very first soul retrieval, she shared with me intuitive information she was hearing. She said to ask all of my guides and spiritual masters and teachers on the other side who would like to step forward and facilitate the completion of the healing.

As I went into silence later that night and asked, Mother Meera stepped forward. I understood in the moment why and it was a complete synchronicity of spirit for her to be the one to complete the process. Two weeks prior to the shamanic circle and after the dream with Babaji I went to see Mother Meera, a true Indian saint, an avatar or living master, in Austin Texas. She was traveling to a few US cities to see people for public **darshan**. This is the amazing process that I experienced while being in her presence. A room full of people at the Universalist Unitarian church one at a time filed silently to the front where she sat on a chair. The energy coming from her was very noticeable and powerful even at a distance. As I knelt before her she held my head with her hands for about a minute and then raised my head to look directly into my eyes for another minute. As I returned to my seat I could feel her spiritual energy or rather the spiritual energy of Creator God working very powerfully through her. I received many messages that day as well as healing energy. The interesting correlation I want to make here is that the early childhood exchange between my mother and I and the recent exchange with Divine Mother Meera were completely different. Opposite you might say, though we know all things are love and I'm not disowning my mom anytime soon because of it, though I am experiencing deep healing because of the dream, the shaman's circle and the meeting with Mother Meera. What an amazing journey. I wanted to be sure and include it for you here to witness as you may have had similar experiences.

The power of dreams to help us heal is a great vehicle for our spirit guides on the other side to work with us in healing as well as the reflections of all our past experiences. Mirroring back to us what is buried deep down inside that needs healing. Your inner child and your spiritual helpers are always with you as you investigate and start your journey along the path of self healing.

All the Very Best Wishes
in Your Healing Process. Be Well.

As you reach for the door it magically opens to you. As you move inside The Hall of the Akashic Records. And as you stand there in awe of the tall arched ceilings and beautiful stain glass windows you now see. The cosmic energy of the stars beams down through the stained glass and dances in colors across the floors moving with energy.

Journey 5

Akashic Inner Child Healing Journey

*R*elax and start taking some long slow deep breaths. As you continue to relax, relaxing down even deeper, you now feel a soothing peaceful comfort coming over your whole body. As you continue to relax, become aware of every part of your body relaxing, slowly from the tips of your toes all the way up your feet and legs, all the way up your spine, your front and back sides, your arms and up over your head as this relaxing power of spirit relaxes you even deeper. As you relax now down, down, down deeper your spirit guides are holding healing space for you.

Find yourself now in a beautiful outdoor setting. Very bright blue skies and white puffy clouds. Very lush green grass and trees that extend into the distance. The temperature is perfect as you feel the gentle breeze on your skin. See the sun dancing through the trees as the wind gently moves the branches and the shade dances under the trees across the grass. See the beautiful flowers of all different kinds. There is a small stream in the near vicinity, hear it trickling gently in the background as you also see and hear the birds. The are different varieties of rocks, pebbles, bushes and plants.

Feel the soft plush grass under your feet as you see the beautiful bright blue sky and white puffy clouds. Up ahead in the clearing you see a beautiful crystalline staircase. You see the shimmering pastel pearlescent colors of blue, pink, green, gold, and white as this staircase is glowing and vibrating with energy. As you walk over to the stair case and touch the banister it vibrates to your touch welcoming you, singing with energy.

You decide to do it, you take the first step and then, another...and then another, as you climb higher & higher... up, up & away. Continuing to climb up, it almost seems as if your feet are gliding up this stairway to heaven as you continue to rise. You feel yourself moving away from the earth as it disappears below and you see the celestial bodies of the heavens as you are gliding up.

As you move up you enter the bright white clouds. Everything is white and you cannot see where you're going, but that's okay, your heart knows the way as you continue up. As you come out and look out across the sea of clouds, you find yourself in from of a grand temple, the Hall of the Akashic Records. There are 7 steps in front of you leading up to the front door, let's climb the steps
    ... 1..2...3...4...5...6...7.

There is a lion and a lioness respectively on the right and left side of the door. They are very real and as you look down into their eyes, they look up with a gentle loving gaze, as you stroke their manes. They will stand watch for you while you are in the Hall of Records.

As you reach for the door it magically opens to you. You move inside The Hall of the Akashic Records. And as you stand there in awe of the tall arched ceilings and beautiful stain glass windows you now see. The cosmic energy of the stars beams down through the stained glass and dances in colors across the floors moving with energy.

As you look out you can see through the walls and the ceiling as they are semi-transparent, you look out across eternity. You are now here looking out across all space and time. The vastness of the ever after. The stream that has brought you here is beaming up, cascading in the middle of the temple as it continues up all the way back to the Source Light of Creation as you see it overhead extending in the distance back to the Great Light.

You see at the other end of the hall, as you walk across the floor, a door close to the front of the hall as you're facing north. As the door opens there is a small child standing now in the doorway and looking around. The child looks across the hall to you and seems to have a longing in his/her eyes to connect with you. As they come out of the doorway into the hall looking at you and you are walking towards the child.

As the child comes closer you notice that this child bears a striking resemblance to you when you were a child. This is You. This is You as a young child. As we are meeting them here in the Akashic Records where all things are possible. And as you come together with the child, kneeling down to greet them, you give your inner child, your little self a hug. It has been a long time. As you remember back looking deeply into the child's eyes. Smiling now at each other, you are both excited about being reunited. There is a sense of home and nurturing that comes with this connection.

So as you hold the child's little hand you stand now in the middle of the great Hall of Records as your mother and father appear. They look young now as they did from the time period when you were a little child. Behind them there is a great window that disappears into eternity. As you see your mother and father standing there in front of the window, now behind them their mother's and fathers, and behind them their mother's and fathers, and behind them their mother's and fathers. On & on & on. The generations of all your distant relatives lining up all the way back into the light of eternity. As you're standing there with your child self you both look at each other as you're holding hands and you raise your other hands as a beautiful golden light starts to come from your hands and from your hearts as it beams out across the room. This golden healing power of love reaches your mother and father and moves into their hearts as they now receive this golden healing power of love light and it moves right through them to, and their mothers and fathers, and their mothers and fathers, all the way back through the ancestors of the family all the way back into the source light of creation.

As this happens a beautiful glowing explosion from Source Light of God's Creation sends the golden loving energy back through the hearts of all the generations, all the way back from source down through the lineage as it reaches your mother and father and comes back to you. And the golden healing love energy now comes from the hearts of your mother and father beaming back into your own hands and hearts of you and your little self, your inner child.

With your inner child you lovingly look at your parents as they are smiling at you, and you smiling to them. The whole family has been healed all the way back across eternity. And the Source Light of Creation has shined that light again all the way from the beginning through them healing the ancestors, the bloodline, your whole family on your mother's side and your father's side of the family. Your whole family receives the benefits of the healing that has been experienced here today.

And as you look at your little one there is so much love you now feel between them and you that you reach down and pick them up and hold them in your arms, laughing, smiling and rocking them. You say to them "I Love You, and I will always be here for you" and the child now feeling at home and peaceful with you, puts their head on your chest as if to go to sleep. And in an instant the child starts to merge back into you, right into your chest. As your inner child has now found their way home, back to you to remain inside where they will always be with you and you with them. And you can talk to them any time you wish, through communication, through visualization, through your heart. You can always come here to the Akashic Records and connect with them hear as well. They will always meet you here.

And so now feeling full and complete once again, giving thanks for the healing and connections that have occurred today, you move back across the hall to the front door stepping out and saying goodbye to the lions as they purr. See the light glistening in there eyes. As you walk back down the steps:

7...6...5...4...3...2...1...

Looking out across the sea of clouds you step back onto the crystalline stair case and glide back down, down, down to earth and the earth comes closer, and back to your continent...and your country...and your countryside...and your neighborhood...and your house... and your house and back down into your body. Wiggle your fingers and toes, take a deep breathe and blink your eyes. Welcome yourself back to physical reality. Go to a mirror and look into your own eyes, your reflection. See if you can see the extra energy of what you've just accomplished in the healing. Has extra light been brought back to you? Does anything feel changed or different. Give your self credit and thanks for doing the work.

Thank You Divine Spirit for this Healing with my little loving Inner Child. Om, Peace, Amen.

You now have the tools of Knowledge, Wisdom and Power to continue your journey into the future and to let unfold the greatness within you as you use this new found information for expanded consciousness within you. You are the greatest expression. You are the Dream in the Dreamer's eyes of ecstasy.

Chapter 22

Welcome Home to New Ways of Knowing

$\mathcal{A}$s you read this book and consider the information, energy techniques and guided forms of meditation used here, you are being put in touch with new ways of perceiving and new connections from beyond that you may or may not have previously known about. As you now know new ways of considering or observing through the Akashic Records you have been given a whole new set of parameters to operate from which includes your opened and expanded senses, your Soul, your past lives, your energy fields, mind and physical body, your physical reality and more.

You have been reading about some of the ever so subtle dynamics of the Soul, it's intuitive powers and the pathways into higher mind dimensions which contain the record of truly all that you are (the I Am, your I Am Presence). You may want to re-read the information here in the book or digest it and come back to it and see how you interpret it over time. New information can sometimes come with a bit of natural conflict as we've been so used to processing our usual life's information from the senses, our emotions and our responses in the usual ways. So when we get new info it can sometimes jostle things loose or maybe it catapults you straightaway into new higher ways of being for your life. This can truly put you in touch with your soul's purpose, your heart's desire and your life path. Consider that you have just been given the keys to a mansion that holds all the knowledge of everything that ever was, is, and is to be. You now have a great new set of tools in your tool chest for working with your own life, soul, mind and path as well as working with others on their healing path of self discovery and greater self knowing.

These are things that we always have available to us in every moment of every lifetime. We can access healing of self knowing through various modalities or spiritual path's from around the world and many of their interesting techniques. We can also access the Akashic Records which is in no way more important than any other form of healing, though it supersedes all other modalities as it streams with the very considerations and existence of all things. So consider going to the source for top shelf information and healing.

You now will have the opportunity to participate in levels of reality you might not have found any other way, though everything is perfect and guided in our inquiries and our path. If you have been guided to the Akashic Records for study, healing, and reading there is good reason for it.

We have talked about many dynamics and issues in certain chapters discussing other energy anomalies and events besides the Records or that are akin to it and some that are not related though you need to be aware of.

One of he Earth's primary purposes is a home for the Divine Celestial Souls to enjoin with human minds and bodies and to have an earthbound experience utilizing the senses, mind, emotions and physical body for observations of self, interaction with others and the world. If you look deep into the Records you will perceive such dynamics. I'm sharing this here because I feel it's important as a platform of knowing from which to work. This is one major dynamic of physical reality. The Souls as radiant beings of Creator God's Love and Light are here by directive of the First Moment Light Source of Creator God to experience this world. So there are many, many other dynamics and actions that happen here that are perceived as negative or deciding factors of the earth plane. This is consciousness playing out all it's many scenarios creatively.

We sometimes think that we are helpless in the midst of current events or affairs. This is not the case. You only have to realize the true direct perceptions born of no emotional conflict and you step onto a different playing field or new quantum program. The energy and dynamics of life here in this paradigm can be like playing *'Spock chess'*. Remember Spock from Srar Trek with his multi-level chess board? You can apply this principle of 'Spock chess' to the adjoining dimensions as well. Ultimately Creator God will not allow anything of great evil to interfere with our journey. We always have the tools and opportunities here in the physical to rise above impending dangers and doom and realize our own divinity and greatness as well as everyone's. It only takes one moment to become self realized or enlightened and we come back time after time after time for the dramatic experience of being in human form. It's like finishing school for the Soul.

This is the realm where the Souls who have enjoined with humanity have come to experience animate life and conscious mind, body and heart with the soul. For that reason among others this is a special place or realm. Often times in our recent past many catastrophes and calamities have been thwarted by the sheer presence of the radiance of

Souls en mass incarnate as humanity. This is a power that has never truly been addressed. Whether it be epidemics, corporate blunders or earth changes. The souls have a powerful radiance that has answered many events with the silent yet powerful light of spirit. A dynamic that has really not been figured out, paid attention to, or a way found to control it. This is the unspoken power of humanity, the love and the joy of souls being enjoined with a human body. This recognition shows up in our history time and again as we experience the spirit of the human race, and how it's come together in times of need.

The darkness has sought to harness the Light in general and the radiance of the Souls. There is True Light that exists as power coming from these Souls. The Light uses the dark to accomplish change. You are the Light, the Power and the Radiance of God's Love, Light and Joy. Who wouldn't want that? We have also talked about in previous chapters some of the characteristics surrounding the needs for awareness, protection and clearing. You now have the tools to move forward and to know yourself at greater ways in the perfect moment.

So it is my hope that you will use these tools of wisdom to seek your greatest reflection and sense of Self. To use this knowledge in unison with anything and everything else that you've learned and applying it where applicable to create a greater spiritual experience, or dynamic for your life.

Practice accessing the Records. If you already do access them, there are always new levels of knowledge and perception that you can gain. You can access daily, frequently, periodically or maybe you wait for the right moment in life as it becomes apparent to you that a dream, death or situation with family, friends or others around you become relevant to the knowledge. You then know why this book of knowledge was brought to you, so you could understand, practice or share the information in order to know how to help others. You now have the tools of Knowledge, Wisdom and Power to continue your journey into the future and to let unfold the greatness within you as you use this new found information for access to expanded consciousness within you. You are the greatest expression. You are the Dream in the Dreamer's Eyes of Ecstasy.

Gradually over time with each one of your journeys you fill in yet another empty chair of the orchestra that is you, the director. As you find more and more of the players or actors of your incarnations, you learn the real truths about 'You'. These are available to you through spiritual readings and you may even have confirmation of cross references through dreams or readings with different readers.

The great thing about finding your own incarnations within the Records and your Book of Life is that it is a special and personal confirmation for you. It is a gift that you can give yourself this knowing. And it comes to you naturally as you are ready. Their are certain seats that will not be filled until you are ready to know more and the enigma may be that you are always ready to know yourself at the deepest levels. So move towards this knowing through deep access to your Soul's records of incarnations here in the Akashic Records. The closer you come it will compliment every thing else you are studying in life spiritually and all other aspects.

To Know Thyself. Through observation, this is the greatest instruction from Creator God to all Souls. And then your moments of Enlightenment and Self Realization will be upon you. Bringing you great awareness of it all. As you look into the Akashic Records, your Soul and it's journey, your other lifetimes in this world and beyond, the cosmos and all the other dimensions. You will have a knowing that simply Is. Enjoy! and Many Blessings to You in your Great Moments of Knowing Yourself. Namaste, Bill Foss, 2/13/2014

You have entered the Realms of The Akashic Records and Middle Earth. The ordinary perceptions of time, space and physical realities no longer apply here.
You have come to ask the Oracle of your Soul the Nature of Your True Essence.
I will help guide you, your feet already know the way.
Looking Now into the impermanence of the moment. Is the chalice half empty or half full? Deep within this inquiry yet in plain sight, The space between the two is both the impermanence and the eternal. That which you seek or deeply desire to know is right in front of you at all times, hidden in plain sight. It is this dynamic that holds you in reason until the right moment for you to truly know who you are and why you have come. That Moment is Now.

the
Magic
of
Merlin

BILL FOSS

Magic of Merlin CD & Download

"Light is only Light and make sure that your Light is pointed in the right direction."

300

Journey 6

The Magic of Merlin

Relax. Take Three deep breaths. Relax...relax even deeper. This is a safe place and this is a sacred space. I would like you to visualize a rainbow colored ball of energy at your heart. And as you continue to breath in and breath out slowly, relaxing, I would like you to visualize this rainbow colored ball of energy growing bright as the sun lighting up every thing in your presence, everything in this room. There are no shadows. This room is shining very brightly in your presence.

As you continue to grow brighter in this light, this light now shines out, pervading all the walls of this room. Shining out brighter, shining forth through the walls. Out into the neighborhood, out to cover all the surroundings and all the property in which you are now present. As this rainbow colored ball of light grows brighter and brighter out from your heart. It now goes out to engulf the whole countryside. growing brighter, the whole countryside is shining very brightly in your light.

As it continues out now surrounding the whole country, the whole continent in which you live, the whole continent is shining very brightly in your light. As this light continues to grow out, shining forth now out across the seas. Across the waters of the ocean, spreading, spreading. We now see this rainbow colored ball of light engulfing the whole earth, the whole planet as it spreads slowly, shining, shining, encompassing, engulfing. See now the whole world shining very brightly in your light.

You may have noticed that as the whole world is shining very brightly in your light, that you have ascended up over the planet. As you look down the planet is turning very slowly, and you are floating here above the planet watching the earth slowly rotate.

As you look down you may see tiny pin points of light on all the many different continents. These are all your many lifetimes on this planet. Planet Earth, where your Soul came into human form and played out lifetimes. Just notice where they are, notice the groupings, different regions of the world as the world turns slowly by. And continue to relax.

Turn now your gaze away from the earth and look up directly into the sun, see the brightness of the sun. The energy of the sun is so warm. Feel the cosmic rays of the sun coming in through the top of your head, your crown chakra and in through the eyes, in through the face. The sun is so bright it's almost blinding you. That's okay, let it take your sight away trusting.

Feel the cosmic rays of the sun nourishing you coming in through your head and your face, your senses, your eyes. Down into all the energy centers along the spine. Down through all the meridian points of the body. And as the solar rays of the sun are coming through, from above, so the earth energies are coming up from the planet above which you are floating, and coming through the bottoms of your feet. Waves of energy coming up and entering the bottoms of the feet with the grounding, soothing earth energy and. And connecting these two energies, solar and earth, connecting all of your chakra points and all of the meridians of the body.

Healing, Balancing and Energizing...
Healing, Balancing and Energizing...
Healing, Balancing and Energizing...

Turn now your gaze away from the sun and look back down towards the planet earth. As we are floating here in space between the sun and the earth. See the clouds, see the earth turning and the blueness of the planet and the ocean, see the whiteness of the cloud patterns here from space.

As we see the earth turning slowly. We will start very, very gently spiralling like a giant hawk, like a giant eagle in large spirals down towards the planet. Descending down, down as you relax even deeper. The earth is turning slowly as you relax even deeper going down, down, down. Spiralling down, spiralling down continuing to spiral down. Sailing, swooping, flying, falling. Circles and circles. Relaxing even deeper going down, down, down...down, down, down.

Coming closer to the clouds now, coming closer to the atmosphere. As we continue to spiral now we're starting to sail into the clouds of the atmosphere. See the white puffy clouds, the very soft clouds of all different shapes and sizes. Moving, churning. As we enter into the clouds everything becomes white and bright. We see the mists of the clouds. Passing us, passing us, as we continue to spiral and we're descending down, down, down, down. The bright white mist of the clouds all around us. Occupying all space around us. It's all continuous, seamless, timeless oneness. Everywhere we look is white.

As we continue to spiral down, spiral down keep sailing, flying, sailing, spiralling down, through the clouds. As we're in the clouds we're in a perfect state of oneness with all that is, all that ever was and all that is to be. As we start to come out of the clouds on the other side continuing our spiral down towards the planet, see the brightness of the oceans and the continents and all the greenery and all the trees. Time has somehow shifted. We are not in the ordinary manner of time as we once new it. We are now in the timeless ever presence of the Akashic Records. We are now descending down, down, down, spiralling, sailing, coming close, noticing the continents as we fly. We see the ocean we see North America, South America, we see Africa, and Europe, Asia, Australia.

As we continue to spiral we start to come closer into the northern hemisphere off the coast of Europe we see the British Isles, and we see the United Kingdom.

In this ancient timeless place we are now entering a space known as Middle Earth. The magical mystical realms that have governed these areas long before the existence of our present times and days and ages. The days of ancient. Time has shifted now. As we continue to spiral down over the countryside and we see the continent coming closer down over the countryside, we see the rolling hills, the grass and the green as we continue to spiral down. We notice several ancient sacred sites, which now in the presence of Middle Earth are available to us in their true original state.

Directly below us as we continue to spiral down several hundred feet below us we see Stonehenge. This ancient power site for many magical, mystical and spiritual gatherings. As we continue to spiral down, down, down. Coming closer we see the ring of stones from the top. The perfect ring of stones. We start to fall faster and faster towards the earth. Faster and faster as we just start to fall, free falling. Towards the earth down, down, down. Falling faster and faster. Falling straight down. Very quickly now, very swiftly falling down, it looks as if we will fall flatly upon the earth.

As we come closer to Middle Earth and moving through the stone rings, we plunge deep down into the earth of Gaiatri, Mother Earth. The deep richness of Middle Earth.

Down into the earth. See the deep dark soil, smell the richness of the water and the soil as you look around. In this altered state, look around, go ahead look around. What do you see? You may see many, many timeless and ancient earth keepers. Earth devas, angelics placed here long ago in this timeless suspended state and place. As they seek to be of service to all of the elements, you may see the rock creatures the beings of stone standing guard, living breathing rock forms placed here long ago by those who knew to do so for the earth. Also notice if you see any animals in the area. Any animal forms moving through the soil moving through the earth. Smell the deep richness of the earth as we continue down, down, down.

We land now in what appears to be a large passageway. Very hollow passageway which goes off into the distance as we look around. We notice that there is a very vast tunnel system that goes off in many different directions. Here in Middle Earth we may see groups of ancient Druidic tribes moving through the tunnel systems with staffs calling up light from source to light their way as they walk through this very vast tunnel system which connects from this continent to Europe and to Africa. And as we have met the earth spirits, the earth keepers notice in this different altered time reality their presence and the rich vibration coming to you, coming to your body from the earth as you move effortlessly through the elements. And as we are walking along the ancient rock corridors these stone passageways, this huge passageway, we have the feeling that we are headed north and so we just let our instincts follow as we are walking through this tunnel system, the light of our soul shining, lighting the way for us. As we walk along here the water trickling down the walls. Smell the richness of the cool earth breeze. Hear it whistling through the tunnel systems.

We are going to see an old friend. A very special old friend and teacher has been waiting here to meet with us for a very long time. As we continue walking north, it's very hard for us to know exactly how long we've been walking. We've lost our since of time and space. As we continue down this dark passageway headed north. And as we come to what looks to be the end of the tunnel, it is not necessarily the end but it opens up into a larger room where there are rock formations and a waterfall and there are wonderful light sources. And this looks to be a dwelling and an ancient study. You may see many carvings or ancient symbols in the rocks. You may see sculptures, symbols, power sources here. Just up ahead you see a form sitting quietly against the rock, against the chiselled and sculpted rock quietly studying.

We have come to see Merlin, the ancient magician. Grand wizard of the ages and Merlin is motioning to us, 'Come closer'..."Come closer" he says. "So you have come to see Merlin". Yes we have come to see you Merlin. We have come to see what we can learn from you. What will you show us today? What will you teach us? What will you have us know?

Merlin has been here for a very, very long time living in Middle Earth with the earth keepers guarding the ancient and sacred knowledge. And so Merlin, as he calls up light from Source to light the way. Standing up with a gentle smile as we look notice what Merlin looks like. A very gentle, gentle soul, a very old soul. Wise and full of Wisdom. As he points across the room we notice that there is a very large unpolished black mirror on the wall.

Merlin what would you have us know? And Merlin says "Look, Look deeply into the mirror as you are looking deeply into yourself. Scry...scry, through the waters of the void and the mist. Look into the unpolished surface and see the images coming to you now. Coming forth, there is a story, an ancient story of which you are part and it is time for you to know your place in all of this. You have earned the respect and the attention to look into the magical mystical realms and see, see now may the veils be lifted. And there is a message here for you as your spirit guides are with you. So what is your question? What is your purpose? What is your desire?"

Turn now from the ancient mirror and look into the center of the room. There is now a gigantic stone ring. And in this stone ring appearing before you from Merlin's wand a bright blast of light and there is a window to another time, to another place. And what is this time? What is this portal? Merlin, what is this portal?

"Dear Ones, this is a portal back to Atlantis. This is the master crystal of Atlantis, as it turns slowly emitting light. Clockwise, the platform rotating counter clockwise, the outer ring rotating clockwise. You will notice that the crystals are aligned on the outer rings, very intricate system like a finely tuned watch, that are turning and spinning in different directions. Emitting light, this is the source, a very wonderful Source that was used for their race as they called from Source. To Source from Source. "

"And as the crystals align and line up with the master crystal and the energy pulsates and glows with it's own resonance, you now have a knowing of the source or the earth, the earth keepers the earth spirits. And you may now have access to this energy beaming through different time space reality from this axiontal alignment you may heal the planet to perfection and bring peace, joy, harmony, good fortune, stamina and stabilization of all the peoples of the world. Inspiration and creativity. Joy and responsibility, harmony with all."

"This is the right use of true power. Light is only light. And make sure that light is pointed in the right directions, always as you call from Source. And as you use your voice, as the soul commands out into creation from the voice make sure that to use your words wisely. Every utterance, every syllable, every word is a command to the elements, earth, air, fire, water. Heaven and earth, all the plant, animal, and mineral kingdoms, the devas, the angelics."

"Learn to use your words wisely and as you call...call forth for the enjoyment. Call forth for the peace, harmony for humanity. Call forth perfection. Call forth for the planet earth and healing of all the many upheavals their have been. Call forth peace for the emotional state of humanity. Call for peace for the weather patterns. Know your true power. True power is not force. True power is resonance. True power is observation, communication, with a voice to the elements. Conjuring correctly, calling from Source. From known elements of this world and from the ethers. Call forth to your purposeful need from your heart's desire. That which is needed in the moments to be utilized for your comfort and your joy. To be of service to society, humanity and others. Go now, my children and be free. Be inspired. Live life harmoniously and creatively. To inspire the human spirit. Live in harmony with nature. Respect it's powers. Use the elements wisely and be of service to all."

And as Merlin waves his wand once more, the portal fades, as this ancient elder has spoken his wisdom. He now beckons us to come with him. And he starts to float up. As we following him we are floating up. With Merlin we are floating now. Floating, floating becoming lighter here in the tunnel and we start to float up in this huge stone rock room hewn from the earth, this room as we come close to the ceiling. We gently glide right through the stone, the rock as we are in Middle Earth. And we continue to rise, rise, rise. floating, floating, rising through the rocks. Seeing the rocks, stones, pebbles, earth keepers, all of the devas, all of the minerals, the underground creatures, the moisture, the smell, the pungent smell of the earth. As we continue to rise. Nearing the surface of the planet now.

And as we come to stand upon the earth we find ourselves inside the ring of Stonehenge once more. And the clouds gather as the Druidic circle of ancient elders stand just inside the stone ring. Calling up light, calling up blessings, calling forth prayers from Source for the crops. Calling forth prayers from Source for all of the animals. Calling forth prayers from Source for all of the trees. And the clouds overhead are starting to turn in a clockwise direction. As we're standing here with Merlin in the center of this giant healing energy vortex from Source. Here in ancient Middle Earth. Merlin calls forth one last blessing of well wishes.

As he calls forth the Spirit of the East, the Spirit of the South, the Spirit of the West, the Spirit of the North. The Spirit of the Earth. The Spirit of the animals, the Spirit of water, fire, earth and air.

That we may be of humble service to humanity and to the earth, to all of these. That we are able to balance, heal, and send wellness to walk as a light upon the earth and give resonance and show the way. To observe and see the world as it truly is, without conflict. Showing forth those who would tend towards the light. Showing those who want to come into the light. Into the presence of their own true selves.

Showing them the way. As they step into the trueness and the simplicity of the moment and the trueness and the simplicity of the next moment, and the next moment, and the next moment. The streaming impermanence of every streaming simplistic moment. Timelessly and effortlessly creating the oneness.

As Merlin now raises his wand and calls up light from the sky, as lightning comes down and strikes his wand. His staff he holds high and drives down into the earth sealing the well wishes, the calling, the Source, the command. And in the same instant we notice that our feet are feeling lighter. As Merlin's eyes connect with ours, he gently looks towards the earth again as he starts to fade and sink into the earth and the Druids become the timeless void.

Like the wind we start to float above Stonehenge as we're sailing now, sailing now up into the vortex of the clouds. Up, up & away. Sailing into the clouds, ascending, ascending, ascending into the clouds. Ascending up into the clouds, everything is white, it's churning bright white again. We feel the resonance of being super charged with inspiration and feel the lightness of Spirit. And feel the lightness of our true nature. Light as a feather able to do anything. Able to accomplish every single dream, wish, hope, every goal that we set out we are in alignment with.

And as we're flying through the clouds we start to have a resonance that we're coming into the current time and space. the current time and space here in the present, here in the now. As we start to come out of the clouds we see the earth in this time in this moment spiralling down spiralling down, coming closer to the place that you live. Continuing to slowly fall towards the earth. Sailing and flying light as a feather. As you come closer to the earth you see the countryside that you know. And as you're coming dropping closer to the earth, you see the building that you know where you are now. And as you come in closer and closer you come back, back, back down into the building, into the room, into your body, back into the present moment. Taking a few deep breaths...

Thank You Mother Earth, Earth Keepers, Merlin and the Ancients for Blessing us with your tomeless wisdom and magic. Namaste, Amen

Planetary Logos, Earth Spirit, Holy Spirit, Elemental Kingdoms, Devas and Earth Keepers, Realms of Pan, Angels and Arch Angels of the Light of God. Kuthumi, El Morya, Quan Yin, Djwahl Khul, Sanat Kumara, Dererkara, St. Germain, Serapis Bey, Buddha, Sananda, Mary of Magdala, Mary of Sephoris, Babaji, Merlin, Spirit of the Four Directions, Great Spirit, Holy Toa, Empower and Surround Us this Day. Manifest your Wholeness, your Wellness and your Oneness, in our Thoughts, Words and Deeds. Guide Us as we Call from Source in Co-creation with the Creator Manifesting from our Heart's Desire to our Purposeful Needs. Bring Joy and Inspiration, Light, Service...Inspiration to Humanity. Om, Peace, Amen.

Sai Baba

24" x 36" acrylic on etched and torched copper

Glossary of Terms

Akashic Records - A sanskrit term meaning sky, space or ether. A living energetic library of every past, present, future moments of every person, place or thing, animate and inanimate. Used by God and our Souls to determine the advancement, healing and karma of the lifetimes lived.

Alchemy - The defining goals of alchemy are often given as the transmutation of common metals into gold (known as chrysopoeia), the creation of a panacea, and the discovery of a universal solvent. Alchemy is the art of liberating parts of the Cosmos from temporal existence and achieving perfection which, for metals is gold, and for man, longevity, then immortality and, finally, redemption. Material perfection was sought through the action of a preparation (Philosopher's Stone for metals; Elixir of Life for humans), while spiritual ennoblement resulted from some form of inner revelation or other enlightenment (Gnosis, for example, in Hellenistic and western practices)

Alta Major - Influenced by the 3rd Ray, Alta Major is a minor center but functions as a major center. The throat center connects with it at the moment that the Antahkarana (all mental processes as the Atman is forming) is starting to be built. Alta Major is connected with the Carotid body, which monitors oxygen content in the blood and controls respiration. Strong influence of the throat center. When Alta Major is fully developed, it forms a communication center between vital energy of the spinal column (kundalini) and the energy of the two head centers (Crown and Ajna or 3rd Eye). Alta Major is the physical correspondence to the Antahkarana. Alta Major has powerful link with cerebellum (voluntary muscle movements), medulla oblongata (breathing, heart rate and blood pressure, also connections with Throat, Heart center and spine. Alta Major development leads to an acquired

313

and conscious control of one's dharma or Soul work on earth. It has the power to bring down intuitive vision into consciousness. It is the healer's conscious link with the Higher Mind. Through the Alta Major center the Spiritual Will of the Crown center is balanced. Alta Major center is particularly related to sleep and to the working out of past experiences in sleep. It is helpful to go to sleep with the consciousness gently focussed in the Ajna center.

Annunaki - According to Zecharia Sitchin, Nibiru (called "the twelfth planet" because, Sitchin claimed, the Sumerians' gods-given conception of the Solar System counted all eight planets, plus Pluto, the Sun and the Moon) was the home of a technologically advanced human-like extraterrestrial race called the Anunnaki in Sumerian myth, who Sitchin states are called the Nephilim in Genesis. He wrote that they evolved after Nibiru entered the solar system and first arrived on Earth probably 450,000 years ago, looking for minerals, especially gold, which they found and mined in Africa. Sitchin states that these "gods" were the rank-and-file workers of the colonial expedition to Earth from planet Nibiru. Sitchin wrote that Enki suggested that to relieve the Anunnaki, who had mutinied over their dissatisfaction with their working conditions, that primitive workers (Homo sapiens) be created by genetic engineering as slaves to replace them in the gold mines by crossing extraterrestrial genes with those of Homo erectus. Ancient inscriptions report that the human civilization in Sumer, Mesopotamia, was set up under the guidance of these "gods", and human kingship was inaugurated to provide intermediaries between mankind and the Anunnaki (creating the "divine right of kings" doctrine). Sitchin believes that fallout from nuclear weapons, used during a war between factions of the extraterrestrials, is the "evil wind" described in the Lament for Ur that destroyed Ur around 2000 BC. Sitchin states the exact year is 2024 BC. Sitchin says that his research coincides with many biblical texts, and that biblical texts come originally from Sumerian writings.

Andromeda / Andromedans - A community of oneness. No cities, just 'villages'. Transport is teleportation or small above-ground craft. Dwellings and buildings tend to be circular or ovoid in shape. Construction materials are organic-based, natural fibre or crystalline in nature. Small to large families and community activities are important. Trade and a barter system rather than currency. No political structure, instead a council of wise elders which guides the planets within the Andromedan system who work together by consensus. Children are conceived the same way as on earth. Children are raised with the understanding that all community is family and can expect support, advice or guidance from anyone. Education begins from birth and extends to equivalent of the earth age of 30. Life spans average to 800 earth years. Andromedans are gifted craftsmen, musicians and sculptors. Sculpture consists mainly of 'light sculptures' using technology to 'bend' light waves which is then enhanced with colors. They are programmed with music and sound. Some are large enough to walk through and interact with. Andromeda's sky is a purplish hue. The greens are more vibrant than on earth. They have a common trees there that are scarlet. They have atmospheric phenomena similar to the aura borealis where there is a display of rainbow colours in the sky. Andromeda has smaller oceans, than earth. There is no measuring of time, except by the seasons which are similar to earth but without the extremes. Andromedans are explorers and have long been travelling to earth, in space craft, by teleportation and communication through channelling and telepathy. They did at one time have bases on earth during the age of Atlantis. Diet is vegetarian, and almost all food is grown on the different worlds within the system or traded for. Communication is telepathic and empathic, but music and sculpture could be described as a communication for Andromedans. As a people they are very fun-loving. They like to balance work with lots of relaxation and play. Entertainment is a big factor for them.

Arcturia / Arcturians - This group of beings settled in the constellation of Arcturius. These races of humanity are very private, and for very specific reasons do they get involved with Earth. They think of themselves as healers. They carry a strong pride of technology in the arts of physical healing, and emotional and spiritual bodies. They have been known to intervene in the ancient past to help resolve very serious conflicts in our area of the Universe by sharing their unique ability to show others how to integrate their belief systems and feelings to resolve conflict. They can be very silent, and can and will keep very much to themselves. They as a group, have done much to help raise the overall levels of consciousness in our Universe.

Ascension - The rise of the 'Christ-consciousness' in mankind to the point that the individual is beyond the powers of reincarnation and karma. The word 'resurrection' as found in the New Testament is best translated as 'ascension'. After millennia of reincarnation, the soul finally gets off the wheel of karma in 'ascension'. The transformation of a person's current ego with the light body into an ascended state of existence being able to move between dimensions including the earth plane.

Asanas - A body position, typically associated with the practice of Yoga, originally identified as a mastery of sitting still. In the context of Yoga practice, asana refers to two things: the place where a practitioner (or yogin, in general usage), yogi (male), or yogini (female) sits and the manner (posture) in which he/she sits. In the Yoga sutras, Patanjali suggests that asana is "to be seated in a position that is firm, but relaxed" for extended, or timeless periods. As a repertoire of postures were promoted to exercise the body-mind over the centuries to the present day, when yoga is sought as a primarily physical exercise form, modern usage has come to include variations from lying on the back and standing on the head, to a variety of other positions. However, in the Yoga sutras, Patanjali mentions the execution of sitting with a steadfast mind for extended periods as the third of the eight limbs of Classical or Raja yoga,but does not reference standing postures or kriyās. Yoga practitioners (even those who are adepts at various complex postures) who seek the "simple" practice of chair-less sitting generally find it impossible or surprisingly grueling to sit still for the traditional minimum of one hour (as still practiced in eastern Vipassana), some of them then dedicating their practice to sitting asana and the sensations and mind-states that arise and evaporate in extended sits.

Ascended Masters - Spiritually enlightened beings who in past incarnations were ordinary humans, but who have undergone a series of spiritual transformations originally called initiations in Theosophy. The Ascended Master Teachings refer to the Sixth Initiation as Ascension. According to the Ascended Master Teachings, a 'Master' (or 'Spiritual Master') is a human being who has taken the Fifth Initiation and is thereby capable of dwelling on the 5th dimension. An 'Ascended Master' is a human being who has taken the Sixth Initiation and is thereby capable of dwelling on the 6th dimension. An 'Ascended Master' is a human being who has regained full union with his 'I AM Presence.' When a human being has regained full union with his 'I AM Presence,'that state of full union is referred to as 'Ascension' Technically, a human being 'ascends' when he takes the Sixth Initiation.

Arc of the Covenant - Is a chest described in the Book of Exodus as containing the Tablets of Stone on which the Ten Commandments were inscribed. According to some traditional interpretations of the Book of Exodus, Book of Numbers, and the Letter to the Hebrews, the Ark also contained Aaron's rod, a jar of manna and the first Torah scroll as written by Moses; however, the first of the Books of Kings says that at the time of King Solomon, the Ark contained only the two Tablets of the Law. According to the Book of Exodus, the Ark was built at the command of God, in accordance with the instructions given to Moses on Mount Sinai. God was said to have communicated with Moses "from between the two cherubim" on the Ark's cover. Many researchers now believe that the arc was actually a long range communication device used between earth and the 'gods' who were guiding and/or controlling humanity at that time.

Astral Plane - The 5th Dimension. The 'other-wordly' plane of existence closest to the 3d physical reality. This dimension acts as a go-tween for all of the many souls, spirits and entities interacting with humans or going on to experience other worlds.

Also associated with psychic activity.

Atlantis - Over 11,000 years ago an island nation located in the middle of the Atlantic ocean populated by a noble and powerful race. The people possessed a great wealth of natural resources found throughout their island. A center for trade and commerce the rulers of the land held sway over the people and land of their own island and into Europe and Africa. Atlantis was the domain of Poseidon, god of the sea. When he fell in love with a mortal woman, Cleito, he created a dwelling at the top of a hill near the middle of the island and surrounded the dwelling with rings of water and land to protect her. At the top of the central hill, a temple was built to honor Poseidon which housed a giant gold statue of Poseidon riding a chariot pulled by winged horses. It was here that the rulers of Atlantis would come to discuss laws, pass judgments, and pay tribute to Poseidon.. To facilitate travel and trade, a water canal was cut through of the rings of land and water running south for 5.5 miles (9 km) to the sea. The city of Atlantis sat just outside the outer ring of water and spread across the plain covering a circle of 11 miles (1.7 km). This was a densely populated area where the majority of the population lived. Beyond the city lay a fertile plain 330 miles (530 km) long and 110 miles (190 km) wide surrounded by another canal used to collect water from the rivers and streams of the mountains. The climate was such that two harvests were possible each year. One in the winter fed by the rains and one in the summer fed by irrigation from the canal. Surrounding the plain to the north were mountains which soared to the skies. Villages, lakes, rivers, and meadows dotted the mountains. Besides the harvests, the island provided all kinds of herbs, fruits, and nuts. An abundance of animals, including elephants, roamed the island. For generations the Atlantians lived simple, virtuous lives. But slowly they began to change. Greed and power began to corrupt them. When Zeus saw the immorality of the Atlantians he gathered the other gods to determine a suitable punishment. Soon, in one violent surge it was gone. The island of Atlantis, its people, and its memory were swallowed by the sea.

Awareness - having knowledge or perception of a situation or fact. Concerned and well-informed about a particular situation or development.

Ayurvedic - the traditional Hindu system of medicine, which is based on the idea of balance in bodily systems and uses diet, herbal treatment, and yogic breathing. Based around the principles of the elements: Earth, Water, Fire, Wood, Air. From Sanskrit āyus 'life' + veda 'science.'

Bhodisattva - in Buddhism one who has attained prajna, or Enlightenment, but who postpones Nirvana in order to help others to attain Enlightenment.

Brain Waves:

Beta brainwaves (38 - 15 Hz) - Are the brainwaves of our "normal" waking consciousness, of our outward attention, of logical, conscious and analytical thinking. High frequency beta ("splayed beta") is seen with restlessness, stress, anxiety, panic or while our inner critic or commentator is active. Splayed beta can be differentiated from the low frequency beta of the awakened mind, when thinking feels clear, alert, creative and to the point.

Alpha brainwaves (14 - 8 Hz) are seen when we are in a relaxed state, daydreaming or visualizing ("sensualising" seems to be more appropriate as imagination in all senses - hearing, kinesthetic, smell, taste etc. - stimulates alpha waves. Your visual sense may not necessarily be the strongest for you. Some people rather feel an inner knowing). We need alpha waves as the bridge to the lower frequencies of the subconscious (theta), if we want to remember the content of our dreams or our meditation, or if we want to retrieve information from our subconscious. For this reason alpha is especially important in combination with other brainwaves.

Theta brainwaves (7 - 4 Hz) Represents the subconscious. We see theta during dream sleep (REM sleep), meditation, during peak experiences and creative states. In theta we find unconscious or suppressed parts of our psyche as well as our creativity and spirituality. Theta images are usually less distinct and colorful than alpha images, sometimes of a blueish color, but they often feel more profound and meaningful. As long as we only produce theta brainwaves, their content will stay inaccessible to our waking mind. We need alpha to bridge the gap between theta and beta brainwaves to consciously experience or remember theta content.

Delta brainwaves (3 - 0.5 Hz) Are the brainwaves of the lowest frequency and represent the unconscious. If we only produce delta we will find us in dreamless deep sleep, but we also see delta in various combinations with other brainwaves. They may then represent intuition, curiosity, a kind of radar, hunches or a "feeling" for situations and other people. Delta is often seen with people who work in therapeutic environments or professions and with people who have had traumatic experiences and have developed a "radar" for difficult situations.

Gamma brainwaves (100 - 38 Hz) were detected later than the other brainwaves, less is known about them so far. They have been seen in states of peak performance (both physical and mental), high focus and concentration and during mystic and transcendental experiences. A lot of research is currently being done on gamma brainwaves in the 40 Hz range during meditation. One of the characteristics of gamma waves is a synchronisation of activity over wide areas of the brain. Gamma brainwaves are not easy to detect because of their low amplitude and can only partly be displayed on the Mind Mirror screen. Sometimes they may be seen as a narrow frequency band at 38 Hz.

Bermuda Triangle - (also known as the Devil's Triangle) is an area bounded by points in Bermuda, Florida and Puerto Rico where ships and planes are said to mysteriously vanish into thin air or deep water. Over the years, many theories have been offered to explain the mystery. Some writers have expanded upon Berlitz's ideas about Atlantis, suggesting that the mythical city may lie at the bottom of the sea and be using its reputed "crystal energies" to sink ships and planes. Other suggestions include time portals and extraterrestrials including rumors of underwater alien bases.

Bön - The pre-Buddhist religious practices of Tibetans and

Tibetic peoples of Nepal that are "imperfectly reconstructed [yet] essentially different from Buddhism" and were focused on the personage of a divine king; A syncretic religion that arose in Tibet and Nepal during the 10th and 11th centuries, with strong shamanistic and animistic traditions. This shamanic indigenous religion is not Buddhism, but is sometimes regarded by scholars as a substrate form of Buddhism. A set of popular beliefs in which local shamans try to heal people using ideas sometimes ascribed to Bön. Shamans may divine deities' wishes, have supernatural fights with deities, or be possessed by deities. These shamanic practices are common in the Tibeto-Burman speaking ethnic groups, such as Magar, Tamang, Tibetan, etc.

Buddhism - A religion and philosophy indigenous to the Indian subcontinent and encompasses a variety of traditions, beliefs, and practices largely based on teachings attributed to Siddhartha Gautama, who is commonly known as the Buddha (meaning '*the awakened one*' in Sanskrit and Pāli). The Buddha lived and taught in the eastern part of Indian subcontinent some time between the 6th and 4th centuries BCE. He is recognized by Buddhists as an awakened or enlightened teacher who shared his insights to help sentient beings end suffering through eliminating ignorance, craving, and hatred, by way of understanding and seeing dependent origination and no-self, and thus attain the highest happiness, nirvana. The originating teacher of Vipassana.

Bloodline - Direct line of descent; pedigree. Your ancestors, relatives and heritage.

Chakra - (in Eastern thought) each of the centers of spiritual power in the human body, seven in number along the spine from tailbone to crown of the head. From Sanskrit chakra '*wheel* or *circle*'.

Chi (also ki,ka) The vital force believed in Taoism and other Chinese doctrines, spiritual and religious practices, thought to be inherent in all things. The unimpeded circulation of chi and a balance of its negative and positive forms in the body are held to be essential to good health in traditional Chinese medicine. Literal translation: energy. Also known as ki (*Japanese*) and ka

(*Egyptian*)

Christianity - Is a monotheistic religion based on the life and oral teachings of Jesus as presented in the New Testament. Christianity is the world's largest religion, with approximately 2.2 billion adherents, known as Christians. Most Christians believe that Jesus is the Son of God, fully divine and fully human, and the saviour of humanity whose coming was prophesied in the Old Testament. Consequently, Christians refer to Jesus as "Christ" or the Messiah.

Clairaudience - (*French - clair meaning 'clear' and audience meaning "hearing"*) A form of clairvoyant extra-sensory perception in which a person acquires information by paranormal auditory means. The ability to hear in a paranormal manner. May refer not to actual perception of sound, but may instead indicate impressions of the "inner mental ear" or "*the 3rd ear*". Perception of sounds, voices, tones, or noises which are not normally audible. A clairaudient (person) might hear the voices or thoughts of the spirits, messages from God, angels, masters, gurus, or persons who are discarnate, or on the other side.

Clairsentience - (*French - clair meaning 'clear' and 'sentience' is derived from the Latin sentire, 'to feel'*) A form of clairvoyant extra-sensory perception wherein a person acquires psychic knowledge by feeling. One of the six special human functions mentioned in Buddhism. Refers to a person who can feel the vibration of other people. There are many different degrees of clairsentience ranging from the perception of diseases or sickness of other people (*aka medical intuitive*) to the thoughts or emotions of other people. It differs from third eye activity in that instead of vivid pictures in the mind, a very vivid feeling can form. Psychometry is related to clairsentience.(*Psyche and metric, which means 'soul-measuring'*).

Clairvoyance - (*French - clair meaning 'clear' and voyance meaning 'vision'*) is used to refer to the ability to gain information about an object, person, location or physical event through means other than the known human senses, a form of extra-sensory perception (E.S.P.). A person said to have the ability of clairvoyance is referred to as a clairvoyant -'*one who sees clearly*'.

Consciousness - The quality or state of being aware especially within ones self. A sense of one's personal or collective identity, including the attitudes, beliefs, and sensitivities held by or considered characteristic of an individual or group. Totality of conscious states of an individual.

Cuneiform - Denoting or relating to the wedge-shaped characters used in the ancient writing systems of Mesopotamia, Persia, and Ugarit, surviving mainly impressed on clay tablets: a cuneiform inscription.

Crystal Skulls - The crystal skulls are human skull hardstone carvings made of clear or milky white quartz, known in art history as "rock crystal", claimed to be pre-Columbian Mesoamerican artifacts by their alleged finders;

The results of these studies demonstrated that those examined were manufactured in the mid-19th century or later, almost certainly in Europe during a time when interest in ancient culture was abundant. Despite some claims presented in an assortment of popularizing literature, legends of crystal skulls with mystical powers do not figure in genuine Mesoamerican or other Native American mythologies and spiritual accounts. The skulls are often claimed to exhibit paranormal phenomena by some members of the New Age movement.

Dharma - In Hinduism the principle of cosmic order. Virtue, righteousness, and duty, esp. social and caste duty in accord with the cosmic order. In the teaching of the Buddha, one of the fundamental elements of which the world is composed. Dharma means 'the Law' as well as life that is lived in accordance with the law (whether legal statutes or natural law). Dharma in this latter sense is 'the path of righteousness', the way of 'correct', 'appropriate', 'decent', or 'proper' behaviour. The different religious traditions of India are conceived as so many variations of what is considered a life of purity and goodness

De ja vu - *(French - literally 'already seen')* is the impression that one has already witnessed or experienced a current situation, whether through dreams, the waking state, visions or a momentary lapse of reason.

Dojo - A room or hall in which judo, karate, kung-fu, tai chi and other martial arts are practiced.

Ego - A person's sense of self-esteem or self-importance: a boost to my ego. Psychoanalysis the part of the mind that mediates between the conscious and the unconscious and is responsible for reality testing and a sense of personal identity. Compare with id and superego. Philosophy (in metaphysics) a conscious thinking subject.

Elohim - A group of special or higher order of angels who are in charge of utilizing the creation forces of the Light of Creator God. Known also to work with the Council of Twelve and as guardians of the Akashic Records.

Empathy or Empathic ability - The action of understanding, being aware of, being sensitive to, and vicariously experiencing the feelings, thoughts, and emotions of another in either the past or present time line without previously having those feelings, thoughts, and emotions fully communicated in an objectively explicit manner about the person, feelings, or situation. Someone known to use empathic abilities may be referred to as an 'empath'.

Enlightenment - Spiritual revelation or deep insight into the meaning and purpose of all things, communication with or understanding of the mind of God, profound spiritual understanding or a fundamentally changed consciousness whereby everything is perceived as a unity. Freedom from desire and other worldly passions. For Hindus, as for Buddhists and Jains, enlightenment ends the cycle of reincarnation. Souls are held to enter many different bodies through the course of their existence. In each of the lives they lead they develop spiritually. Enlightenment is a state of freedom from the ignorance that causes suffering.

E.S.P. (Extra Sensory Perception) - Psychic abilities including but not limited to: mind reading, future sight, second sight, de ja vu, remote viewing, etc. Involving the acquisition or effect of past, present or future information that cannot be deduced from presently available and normally acquired sense-based information or laws of physics and / or nature.

Etherioplasma - the term is a combination of ether (the invisible energy that carries the human spirit that survives each death to form a new physical body) and the plasma energy that transfers the subtle electromagnetic forces from the soul to the human form that the human spirit use to help animate the human form. Etherio – plasmic. The actual measureable yet invisible energy substance of the Soul.

Familiars - Familiar spirits *(sometimes referred to simply as 'familiars')* were supernatural entities believed to assist witches and cunning folk in their practice of magic. According to folklore, they would appear in numerous guises, often as an animal, but also at times as a human or humanoid figure, and were described as *"clearly defined, three-dimensional... forms, vivid with color and animated with movement and sound"* by those who have come into contact with them, unlike later descriptions of ghosts with their "smoky, undefined forms. Also referred to as Animal spirits who work with Shamans of different cultures as well as in Native American spirituality.

Flower of Life - The Flower of Life is a name for a geometrical figure composed of multiple evenly-spaced, overlapping circles. This figure, used as a decorative motif since ancient times, forms a flower-like pattern with the symmetrical structure of a hexagon. A "Flower of Life" figure consists of seven or more overlapping circles, in which the center of each circle is on the circumference of up to six surrounding circles of the same diameter.

Grace - It has been defined as the divine influence which operates in humans to regenerate and sanctify, to inspire virtuous impulses, and to impart strength to endure trial and resist temptation and as an individual virtue or excellence of divine origin. It can also be perceived as divine intervention, blessings that were not asked for or even undeserved blessings.

Gregorian Time - The system of dates used by most of the world. The Gregorian calendar was proposed by the Calabrian doctor Aloysius Lilius and was decreed by, and named after, Pope Gregory XIII on 1582-02-24. It corrected the Julian calendar whose years were slightly longer than the solar year. It also replaced the lunar calendar which was also out of time with the seasons. The correction was achieved by skipping several days as a one-off re-synchronization and then dropping three leap days every 400 hundred years. In the revised system, leap years are all years divisible by 4 but excluding those divisible by 100 but including those divisible by 400. This gives a mean calendar year of 365.2425 days = 52.1775 weeks = 8,765.82 hours = 525,949.2 minutes = 31,556,952 seconds. Leap seconds are occasionally added to this to correct for irregularities in the Earth's rotation.

Guardian Angels - An angel assigned to protect and guide a particular person or group. The appearance of guardian angels can be traced throughout all antiquity. The concept of tutelary angels and their hierarchy was extensively developed in Christianity in the 5th century by Pseudo - Dionysius the Areopagite.

Guru - a Sanskrit term for *'teacher'* or *'master'*, especially in Eastern or Indian religions. The Hindu guru - shishya tradition is the oral tradition or religious doctrine transmitted from teacher to student. A teacher and guide in spiritual and philosophical matters. A trusted counselor and adviser; a mentor. A personal spiritual teacher. the syllable 'gu' meaning 'darkness' and 'ru' meaning 'that which dispells'

Hatha Yoga - Traditional hatha yoga is a holistic yogic path, including disciplines, postures (asana), purification procedures (shatkriya), gestures (mudra), breathing (pranayama), and meditation. The hatha yoga predominantly practiced in the West consists of mostly asanas understood as physical exercises. It is also recognized as a stress-reducing practice.

Hinduism - The predominant religion of the Indian subcontinent, and one of its indigenous religions. Among other practices and philosophies, Hinduism includes a wide spectrum of laws and prescriptions of *'daily morality'* based on the notion of karma, dharma, and societal norms. Hinduism is a conglomeration of distinct intellectual or philosophical points of view, rather than a rigid common set of beliefs. Hinduism is formed of diverse traditions and has no single founder. Among its direct roots is the historical Vedic religion of Iron Age India and, as such, Hinduism is often called the *'oldest living major religion'* in the world.

Hopi - The Hopi are one of many Native American cultures in the Southwestern United States. When first encountered by the Spanish in the 16th century, these cultures were referred to as Pueblo people because they lived in villages (pueblos in the Spanish language). The Hopi are descended from the Ancient Pueblo Peoples (Hopi: Hisatsinom or Navajo: Anasazi) who constructed large apartment-house complexes in northeastern Arizona, northwestern New Mexico, and southwestern Colorado. They lived along the Mogollon Rim, especially from AD 1100s–1300s, when they abandoned their large villages. No researchers have been able to determine the reason, although it is likely that a drying of water sources would have forced the people away.

I Am That I Am or Holy I Am Presence - The Self begins with that which is the permanent atom of being and the cause out of which the effect proceeds. We call this cause the I AM THAT I AM, the Presence of the I AM, or the I AM Presence.

I find that God by any name can be reduced to this sense of the eternal Presence. It defines being, and I see it as a sphere of intense light that marks the point of my origin. It is the permanent part of me, of which I am very aware, and the point to which I will return at the conclusion of this life.

Illumination - In theology, light or divine light is a term used to refer to an aspect of divine presence, specifically an unknown and mysterious ability of God, ascended masters, angels, or human beings to express themselves communicatively through spiritual means, rather than through physical capacities. In this context, *'light'* can carry the full range of divine or else human - understandable concepts ranging from pure emotion up to concepts and conceptualizations. Hence human beings are said to be recipients of knowledge, "truth," or "illumination," originating from God (in a transcendent reality) to human beings in the *'known universe,'* through spiritual means.

Incarnation - literally means embodied in flesh or taking on flesh. It refers to the conception and birth of a sentient creature (generally a human) who is the material manifestation of a soul, entity, god or God, whose original nature is non-physical. In its religious context the word is used to mean the descent from Heaven of a god, or divine being in human/animal form on Earth.

Introspection - (or internal perception) Is the self-examination of one's conscious thoughts and feelings. The process of introspection relies exclusively on the purposeful and rational self-observation of one's mental, physical, emotional and spiritual state; however, introspection is sometimes referenced in a spiritual context as the examination of one's soul. Introspection is the act of human self-reflection, and opposite to external observation.

Intuition - The ability to understand something immediately, without the need for conscious reasoning. The ability to acquire knowledge without the use of reason. The act or faculty of knowing or sensing without the use of rational processes; immediate cognition The word 'intuition' comes from the Latin word '*intueri*', which is often roughly translated as meaning '*to look inside*" or '*to contemplate*'. Intuition may provide us with information that we cannot justify by ordinary means.

John Dee - Dee was an intensely pious Christian, but his Christianity was deeply influenced by the Hermetic and Platonic-Pythagorean doctrines that were pervasive in the Renaissance. He believed that numbers were the basis of all things and the key to knowledge, that God's creation was an act of numbering. From Hermeticism, he drew the belief that man had the potential for divine power, and he believed this divine power could be exercised through mathematics.

His cabalistic angel magic (which was heavily numerological) and his work on practical mathematics (navigation, for example) were simply the exalted and mundane ends of the same spectrum, not the antithetical activities many would see them as today. His ultimate goal was to help bring forth a unified world religion through the healing of the breach of the Catholic and Protestant churches and the recapture of the pure theology of the ancients. Simultaneously with these efforts, Dee immersed himself in the worlds of magic, astrology and Hermetic philosophy.

He devoted much time and effort in the last thirty years or so of his life to attempting to commune with angels in order to learn the universal language of creation and bring about the pre-apocalyptic unity of mankind. A student of the Renaissance Neo-Platonism of Marsilio Ficino, Dee did not draw distinctions between his mathematical research and his investigations into Hermetic magic, angel summoning and divination. Instead he considered all of his activities to constitute different facets of the same quest: the search for a transcendent understanding of the divine forms which underlie the visible world, which Dee called "pure verities".

Reincarnation - The soul or spirit, after biological death, begins a new life in a new body that may be human, animal or spiritual depending on the moral quality of the previous life's actions. This doctrine is a central tenet of the Indian religions, Hinduism, Buddhism, and is also held in belief by esoteric groups of Judaic and Christian mystism. A belief that was held by such historic figures as Pythagoras, Plato and Socrates. Also a common belief of Druidism, Spiritism, Theosophy, and Eckankar and is found in many tribal societies around the world.

Disincarnate - Having no material body or form. Souls who are between lifetimes of incarnation.

Kabbalah - It's definition varies according to the tradition and aims of those following it, from its religious origin as an integral part of Judaism, to its later Christian, New Age, and Occultist syncretic adaptations. Kabbalah is a set of esoteric teachings meant to explain the relationship between an unchanging, eternal, and mysterious Ein Sof (no end) and the mortal and finite universe (God's creation). While it is heavily used by some denominations, it is not a religious denomination in itself. It forms the foundations of mystical religious interpretation. Kabbalah seeks to define the nature of the universe and the human being, the nature and purpose of existence, and various other ontological questions. It also presents methods to aid understanding of these concepts and thereby attain spiritual realisation.

Karma - *Pali: kamma* means action, work or deed; it also refers to the principle of causality where intent and actions of an individual influence the future of that individual. Good intent and good deed contribute to good karma and future happiness, while bad intent and bad deed contribute to bad karma and future suffering. Karma is closely associated with the idea of rebirth in some schools of Asian religions. In these schools, karma in the present affects one's future in the current life, as well as the nature and quality of future lives - or, one's saṃsāra. In Hinduism & Buddhism, The total effect of a person's actions and conduct during the successive phases of the person's existence, regarded as determining the person's destiny. Once karmas are experienced and repaid, one may leave the cycle of reincarnation. Related to cause and effect and the law of attraction.

Knights Templar - Officially endorsed by the Catholic Church around 1129, the Order became a favoured charity throughout Christendom and grew rapidly in membership and power. Templar knights, in their distinctive white mantles with a red cross, were among the most skilled fighting units of the Crusades. Non-combatant members of the Order managed a large economic infrastructure throughout Christendom, innovating financial techniques that were an early form of banking, and building fortifications across Europe and the Holy Land.

The Templars' existence was tied closely to the Crusades; when the Holy Land was lost, support for the Order faded. Rumours about the Templars' secret initiation ceremony created mistrust and King Philip IV of France, deeply in debt to the Order, took advantage of the situation. In 1307, many of the Order's members in France were arrested, tortured into giving false confessions, and then burned at the stake. Under pressure from King Philip, Pope Clement V disbanded the Order in 1312. The abrupt disappearance of a major part of the European infrastructure gave rise to speculation and legends, which have kept the "Templar" name alive into the modern day.

Kriya Yoga - Described by its practitioners as the ancient Yoga system revived in modern times by Mahavatar Babaji through his disciple Lahiri Mahasaya, circa 1861, and brought into popular awareness through Paramahansa Yogananda's book *'Autobiography of a Yogi'*. The system consists of a number of levels of Pranayama based on techniques that are intended to rapidly accelerate spiritual development and engender a profound state of tranquility and God-communion The term Kriya Yoga was developed in North India from an ancient tradition. The root of the Sanskrit word literally means *'to do'* and a true 'Kriya' technique always involves work with the body and the mind simultaneously. Kriya is a form of meditation involving Tantric Shakti flow of subtle energy within the practitioner's mind & body.

Kriyaban - Student, practitioner or yogi studying and practicing the science of kriya yoga.

Kundalini - Described as a sleeping, dormant potential force in the human organism. It is one of the components of an esoteric description of the 'subtle body', which consists of nadis (energy channels), chakras (psychic centres), prana (subtle energy), and bindu (drops of essence). Kundalini is described as being coiled up at the base of the spine, usually within muladhara (base) chakra. The image given is that of a serpent coiled three and a half times around a smokey grey lingam. Each coil is said to represent one of the three gunas, with the half coil signifying transcendence. Through meditation, and various esoteric practices, such as Kundalini Yoga, Sahaja Yoga, and Kriya Yoga, the kundalini is awakened, and can rise up through the central nadi, called sushumna, that rises up inside or alongside the spine in the spinal fluid. The progress of kundalini through the different chakras leads to different levels of awakening and mystical experience, until the kundalini finally reaches the top of the head, Sahasrara chakra, producing an extremely profound mystical experience that is said to be indescribable.

Kyballion - The book was first published in 1908 by the Yogi

Publication Society and is now in the public domain, and can be found on the internet. The book purports to be based upon ancient Hermeticism, though many of its ideas are relatively modern concepts arising from the New Thought movement. The book early on makes the claim that it makes its appearance in one's life when the time is appropriate and includes variations of material found in the book of Proverbs. The Kyballion teaches 7 principles - Mentalism, Correspondence, Vibration, Polarity, Rythym, Cause & Effect and Gender.

Knowing Way of Truth and Light - The original Christ teachings which came from Atlantis. Also known as the Way Teachings, The Way, The Knowing Way.

Lakota - The Lakota are a tribe who live on the northern plains of North America. They are closely related by culture, language, and history to other tribes who together are often referred to as 'Sioux'. This includes the Dakota who live in Minnesota and eastern North and South Dakota. The Lakota are known as the Teton or Western Sioux. This both to their location (west of the Dakota on the plains) and to the dialect of Sioux they speak.

Love - An emotion of a strong affection and personal attachment. Love is also a virtue representing all of human kindness, compassion, and affection - The unselfish loyal and benevolent concern for the good of another. Love may describe actions towards others or oneself based on compassion or affection. Love refers to a variety of different feelings, states, and attitudes, ranging from pleasure (*"I loved that meal"*) to interpersonal attraction (*"I love my partner"*). 'Love' may refer specifically to the passionate desire and intimacy of romantic love, to the sexual love of eros, to the emotional closeness of family love, to the platonic love that defines friendship, or to the profound oneness or devotion of religious love, or to a concept of love that encompasses all of those feelings. This diversity of uses and meanings, combined with the complexity of the feelings involved, makes love unusually difficult to consistently define, compared to other emotional states. Love in its various forms acts as a major facilitator of interpersonal relationships and, owing to its central psychological importance, is one of the most common themes in the creative arts.

Lymph (glands) - Physiology a colorless fluid containing white blood cells, that bathes the tissues and drains through the lymphatic system into the bloodstream. Fluid exuding from a sore or inflamed tissue. Literary pure water.

Lemuria - A hypothetical "lost land" variously located in the Indian and Pacific Oceans. The concept's 19th-century origins lie in attempts to account for discontinuities in biogeography; however, the concept of Lemuria has been rendered obsolete by modern theories of plate tectonics. Although sunken continents do exist – like Zealandia in the Pacific as well as Mauritia and the Kerguelen Plateau in the Indian Ocean – there is no known geological formation under the Indian or Pacific Oceans that corresponds to the hypothetical Lemuria. It has been adopted by writers involved in the occult, as well as some Tamil writers of India. Accounts of Lemuria differ, but all share a common belief that a continent existed in ancient times and sank beneath the ocean as a result of a geological, often cataclysmic, change, such as pole shift.

Magic -The art of producing a desired effect or result through the use of incantation or various other techniques that presumably assure human control of supernatural agencies or the forces of nature. Magic has been practiced in many cultures, and utilizes ways of understanding, experiencing and influencing the world somewhat akin to those offered by religion, though it is sometimes regarded as more focused on achieving results than religious worship. Magic is often viewed with suspicion by the wider community, and is commonly practiced in isolation and secrecy. Modern Western magicians generally state magic's primary purpose to be personal spiritual growth. Modern perspectives on the theory of magic broadly follow two views, which also correspond closely to ancient views. The first sees magic as a result of a universal sympathy within the universe, where if something is done here a result happens somewhere else. The other view sees magic as a collaboration with spirits who cause the effect.

Mala - A string of beads worn around the neck or wrist, traditionally of 108 bead count, to be used for prayers, mantras and chants. From the ancient Eastern traditions, and can also refer to a catholic rosary.

Mandala - A Sanskrit word meaning *'circle.'* In the Buddhist and Hindu religious traditions sacred art often takes a mandala form. The basic form of most Hindu and Buddhist mandalas is a square with four gates containing a circle with a center point. Each gate is in the shape of a T. Mandalas often exhibit radial balance. These mandalas, concentric diagrams, have spiritual and ritual significance in both Buddhism and Hinduism.

The term is of Hindu origin and appears in the Rig Veda as the name of the sections of the work, but is also used in other Indian religions, particularly Buddhism. In the Tibetan branch of Vajrayana Buddhism, mandalas have been developed into sand painting. They are also a key part of anuttara yoga tantra meditation practices. In various spiritual traditions, mandalas may be employed for focusing attention of aspirants and adepts, as a spiritual teaching tool, for establishing a sacred space, and as an aid to meditation and trance induction. It's symbolic nature can help one "to access progressively deeper levels of the unconscious, ultimately assisting the meditator to experience a mystical sense of oneness with the ultimate unity from which the cosmos in all its manifold forms arises." The psychoanalyst Carl Jung saw the mandala as *"a representation of the unconscious self,"* and believed his paintings of mandalas enabled him to identify emotional disorders and work towards wholeness in personality.

Mantras - a sound, seed sound, syllable, word, or group of words that is considered capable of creating (spiritual) transformation when used as a written or chanted prayer. A sacred verbal formula repeated in prayer, meditation, or incantation, such as an invocation of God, a magic spell, or a syllable or portion of scripture containing mystical potentialities. Chanted individually and in groups both silently and aloud traditionally

108 times and with the use of a mala or prayer beads.

Mudras - In Sanskrit: *'seal'*, *'mark'*, or *'gesture'*; Tibetan, *chakgya* is a symbolic or ritual gesture in Hinduism and Buddhism. While some mudrās involve the entire body, most are performed with the hands and fingers. A mudrā is a spiritual gesture and an energetic seal of authenticity employed in the iconography and spiritual practice of Indian religions and traditions of Dharma and Taoism. One hundred and eight mudrasare used in regular Tantric rituals. In yoga, mudrās are used in conjunction with pranayama (yogic breathing exercises), generally while seated in Padmasana, Sukhasana or Vajrasana pose, to stimulate different parts of the body involved with breathing and to affect the flow of prana in the body.

Medula Oblagata - The lower half of the brain stem, which is continuous with the spinal cord, the upper half being the pons. It is often referred to simply as the medulla. The medulla contains the cardiac, respiratory, vomiting and vasomotor centers and deals with autonomic (involuntary) functions, such as breathing, heart rate and blood pressure. This is part of your brain stem that connects directly to the spinal cord and what I call your main core channel. It is located on the cervical aspect of the spinal cord and attaches to discs C-1, C-2 and C-3. These are in the throat chakra center that governs self-expression.

Scientifically, the medulla oblongata functions primarily as a relay station for the crossing of motor tracts between the spinal cord and the brain. It also contains the respiratory, vasomotor and cardiac centers, as well as many mechanisms for controlling reflex activities such as coughing, gagging, swallowing and vomiting. However, scientists are becoming more aware that the human body can and does absorb energy and that a form of solar energy or electricity operates it. The main input center is located at the medulla oblongata in the brain stem. This area of the body is called 'the Mouth of God' by the ancient Masters of Life. The life energy was called 'The Word' due to its vibratory rate, which is audible. The medulla oblongata is so sensitive; a pinprick would cause instant death. To tickle it would cause paralysis. Any other organ can be operated upon except the medulla oblongata.

Meditation - A practice in which an individual trains the mind or induces a mode of consciousness, either to realize some benefit or as an end in itself. The term meditation refers to a broad variety of practices (much like the term sports) that includes techniques designed to promote relaxation, build internal energy or life force (qi, ki, prana, etc.) and develop compassion, love, patience, generosity and forgiveness. A particularly ambitious form of meditation aims at effortlessly sustained single-pointed concentration single-pointed analysis, meant to enable its practitioner to enjoy an indestructible sense of well-being while engaging in any life activity.

Metatron's Cube - The name of Metatron's Cube makes reference to Metatron, an angel mentioned in apocryphal texts including the Second Book of Enoch and the Book of the Palaces. These texts rank Metatron second only to the Abrahamic God in the hierarchy of spiritual beings. The derivation of Metatron's cube from the tree of life, which the Talmud clearly states was excluded from human experience during the exile from Eden.

Metatron's cube contains every shape that exists in the universe God has created, and those shapes are the building blocks of all physical matter, which are known as Platonic solids (because the philosopher Plato linked them to the spirit world of heaven and the physical elements on Earth).

The pattern delineated by many of the lines can be created by orthographic projections of the first three Platonic solids. Specifically, the line pattern includes projections of a double tetrahedron (aka stellated octahedron), a cube within a cube (a three-dimensional projection of a tesseract), and an octahedron.

Monad - Was a term for Divinity or the first being, or the totality of all beings. Monad being the source or the One meaning without division.

Mysticism - from the Greek, mystikos, meaning 'an initiate') is the knowledge of, and especially the personal experience of, states of consciousness, or levels of being, or aspects of reality, beyond normal human perception, including experience of and even communion with a supreme being.

Neo Cortex - The neocortex consists of the grey matter, or neuronal cell bodies and unmyelinated fibers, surrounding the deeper white matter (myelinated axons) in the cerebrum. The neocortex is smooth in rodents and other small mammals, whereas in primates and other larger mammals it has deep grooves (sulci) and wrinkles (gyri). These folds allow the surface area of the neocortex to increase far beyond what could otherwise be fit in the same size skull. All human brains have the same overall pattern of main gyri and sulci, although they differ in detail from one person to another. The mechanism by which the gyri form during embryogenesis is not entirely clear. However, it may be due to differences in cellular proliferation rates in different areas of the cortex early in embryonic development.

Niburu - According to Zecharia Sitchin's interpretation of Mesopotamian iconography and symbology, outlined in his 1976 book The 12th Planet and its sequels, there is an undiscovered planet beyond Neptune that follows a long, elliptical orbit, reaching the inner solar system roughly every 3,600 years. This planet is called Nibiru (although Jupiter was the planet associated with the god Marduk in Babylonian cosmology). According to Sitchin, Nibiru (whose name was replaced with MARDUK in original legends by the Babylonian ruler of the same name in an attempt to co-opt the creation for himself, leading to some confusion among readers) collided catastrophically with Tiamat (a goddess in the Babylonian creation myth the Enûma Eliš), which he considers to be another planet once located between Mars and Jupiter. This collision supposedly formed the planet Earth, the asteroid belt, and the comets. Sitchin states that when struck by one of planet Nibiru's moons, Tiamat split in two, and then on a second pass Nibiru itself struck the broken fragments and one half of Tiamat became the asteroid belt. The second half, struck again by one of Nibiru's moons, was pushed into a new orbit and became today's planet Earth.

Om or Aum - is a mystical sound of Sanskrit origin, sacred and important in various Dharmic religions such as Hinduism,

Buddhism, and Jainism. It is placed at the beginning of most Hindu texts as a sacred incantation to be intoned at the beginning and end of a reading of the Vedas or prior to any prayer or mantra. It is used at the end of the invocation to the god being sacrificed to (anuvakya) as an invitation to and for that God to partake of the sacrifice. The Māndukya Upanishad is entirely devoted to the explanation of the syllable. The syllable consists of three phonemes, a (Vaishvanara), u (Hiranyagarbha), and m(Ishvara), which symbolize the beginning, duration, and dissolution of the universe and the associated gods Brahma, Vishnu, and Shiva, respectively. The name omkara is taken as a name of God in the Hindu revivalist Arya Samaj and can be translated as *"I Am Existence"*. Also refered to as the primordial vibrational tone behind all realities and dimensions. Monks and Siddhas have reported to hear this tone vibrating in the deepest levels of trance and meditation.

Om Mani Padme Hum - *"The jewel of consciousness is in the lotus of my heart"* and *"I bow to the light within"* are meditative translations to focus upon while using this mantra. Om coincides with the 3rd eye and forehead, Mani - back of the head, Padme - heart and Hum - throat. Visualizing a ring of God's Divine light through these centers while chanting this mantra clears away negativity, pain, fear and stress and brings compassion and healing to the heart, mind and body, while opening and blending what the higher teachings refer to as the Heart/Mind. Tibetan Buddhists believe that saying this mantra (prayer), Om Mani Padme Hum, out loud or silently to oneself, invokes the powerful benevolent attention and blessings of Chenrezig, the embodiment of compassion. Viewing the written form of the mantra is said to have the same effect. It is said that all the teachings of the Buddha are contained in this mantra.

According to the Dali Lama: "It is very good to recite the mantra **Om Mani Padme Hum**, but while you are doing it, you should be thinking on it's meaning, for the meaning of the six syllables is great and vast... The first, *'Om'* symbolizes the practitioner's impure body, speech, and mind; it also symbolizes the pure exalted body, speech, and mind of a Buddha. The path is indicated by the next four syllables. '*Mani*', meaning jewel, symbolizes the factors of method: (the) altruistic intention to become enlightened, compassion, and love. The two syllables, '*Padme*', meaning lotus, symbolize wisdom. Purity must be achieved by an indivisible unity of method and wisdom, symbolized by the final syllable '*Hum*', which indicates indivisibility. Thus the six syllables, '*Om Mani Padme Hum*', mean that in dependence on the practice of a path which is an indivisible union of method and wisdom, you can transform your impure body, speech, and mind into the pure exalted body, speech, and mind of a Buddha"

Omnipresence - The property of being present everywhere. This characteristic is most commonly used in a religious context, as most doctrines bestow the trait of omnipresence onto a superior, a deity or God. This also identifies the universe and divinity; in divine omnipresence, the divine and universe are separate, but the divine is present everywhere.

Hinduism, and other religions that derive from it, incorporate the theory of transcendent and immanent omnipresence which is the traditional meaning of the word, Brahman. This theory defines a universal and fundamental substance, which is the source of all physical existence. Divine omnipresence is thus one of the divine attributes.

Pleadese / Pleadians - Nordics are typically described as six to seven feet tall (about two metres) with long blond hair and blue eyes, and are commonly reported as being male. Their skin is said to range from fair colored to tanned they are reported to be in excellent physical shape, and they are sometimes described as wearing skintight clothing. During the 1950s, many contactees, especially those in Europe, reported beings fitting this description. Nordic aliens have been described as benevolent or even "magical" beings who want to observe and communicate with humans. Contactees have said that the Nordics are concerned about the Earth's environment or prospects for world peace, and may transmit messages telepathically.

Pineal Gland - (or the '*third eye*') is a small endocrine gland in the brain. It produces the serotonin derivative melatonin, a hormone that affects the modulation of wake/sleep patterns and seasonal functions. Its shape resembles a tiny pine cone (hence its name), and it is located near the centre of the brain, between the two hemispheres, tucked in a groove where the two rounded thalamic bodies join. The Pineal Gland has for long been associated with Esoteric Knowledge surrounding the spiritual, metaphysical aspects of consciousness and the Self. René Descartes, who dedicated much time to the study of the pineal gland, called it the 'Seat of the Soul'. He believed that it was the point of connection between the intellect and the body. Directly behind the root of the nose (3rd eye chakra) floating in a small lake of cerebrospinal fluid. It is our body's biological clock. The pineal gland has been supplied with the best blood, oxygen and nutrient mix available other than that received by our kidneys. It acts as a receiving mechanism capable of monitoring electro-magnetic fields and helping align bodies in space. With its central hormone, Melatonin, the pineal not only regulates sleep/ wake cycles and the aging process, but also appears to act as the Mistress Gland (sofia)* orchestrating the body's entire endocrine system and thus, energetically speaking, the chakra system. It is also responsible for shamanic states, visions, kundalini awakening e.t.c.

Pituitary Gland - An endocrine gland about the size of a pea and weighing 0.5 grams (0.018 oz) in humans. It is not a part of the brain. It is a protrusion off the bottom of the hypothalamus at the base of the brain, and rests in a small, bony cavity (sella turcica) covered by a dural fold (diaphragma sellae). The pituitary is functionally connected to the hypothalamus by the median eminence via a small tube called the infundibular stem (Pituitary stalk). The pituitary fossa, in which the pituitary gland sits, is situated in the sphenoid bone in the middle cranial fossa at the base of the brain. The pituitary gland secretes nine hormones that regulate homeostasis. The Pituitary Gland is known as the Master Gland of the Endocrine System. It's secretions regulate all the other Endocrine Glands. This gland represents one's ability to coordinate the different aspects of one's Life. Problems represent difficulty doing this. The Pituitary Gland is linked to the Hypothalamus, also located in the brain, whose function is to maintain Homeostasis in the body. That is the body's tendency to return automatically to its level of highest functioning. Metaphysically, this means aligning the frequencies of the physical and energetic bodies to homeostatically return to one's highest spiritual functioning. The pituitary gland is called the "*Seat of the Mind*" with the frontal lobe regulating emotional thoughts such as poetry and music, and the anterior lobe regulating concrete thought and intellectual concepts. The pineal gland is known as the '*Seat of Illumination, Intuition and Cosmic Consciousness*'. The pineal gland is to the pituitary gland what intuition is to reason. The glandular system also coincides with the chakra system.

Prana - The Sanskrit word for '*vital life*' (from the root prā 'to fill',). It is one of the five organs of vitality or sensation, prana "*breath*", vac '*speech*', chakshus '*sight*', shrotra '*hearing*', and manas '*thought*' (nose, mouth, eyes, ears and mind). In Vedantic philosophy, prana is the notion of a vital, life-sustaining force of living beings and vital energy, comparable to the Chinese notion of Qi. Prana is a central concept in Hinduism, particularly in Ayurveda and Yoga. It flows through a network of fine subtle channels called nadis. Its most subtle material form is the breath, but it is also to be found in the blood, and its most concentrated form is semen in men and vaginal fluid in women. Prana was first expounded in the Upanishads, where it is part of the worldly, physical realm, sustaining the body and the mother of thought and thus also of the mind. Prana suffuses all living forms but is not itself the Atman or individual soul. In the Ayurveda, the Sun and sunshine are held to be a source of prana.

Pranayama - A Sanskrit word meaning 'extension of the prana or breath' or more accurately, '*extension of the life force*'. The word is composed of two Sanskrit words, Prāna, life force, or vital energy, particularly, the breath, and 'ayāma', to extend or draw out.

Psyche - The totality of the human mind, conscious, and

unconscious. Psychology is the scientific or objective study of the psyche. The word has a long history of use in psychology and philosophy, dating back to ancient times, and has been one of the fundamental concepts for understanding human nature from a scientific point of view.

Psychic - Relating to or denoting faculties or phenomena that are apparently inexplicable by natural laws, especially involving telepathy or clairvoyance: psychic powers. A person appearing or considered to have powers of telepathy or clairvoyance. Of or relating to the soul or mind. From the Greek psychikos— *'of the mind, mental'*, is a person who possesses an ability to perceive information hidden from the normal senses through extrasensory perception (ESP), It can also denote an ability of the mind to influence the world physically using psychokinetic powers. Elaborate systems of divination and fortune-telling date back to ancient times. Perhaps the most widely-known system of early civilization fortune-telling was astrology, where practitioners believed the relative positions of celestial bodies could lend insight into people's lives and even predict their future circumstances. Some fortune-tellers were said to be able to make predictions without the use of ritualistic objects or special, spiritual, or energy tools for divining information. More so through direct apprehension or vision of the past, present or future. These people were known as seers or prophets, and in later times as clairvoyants and psychics.

Pueblo - The Pueblo people are Native American people in the Southwestern United States comprising several different language groups and two major cultural divisions, one organized by matrilineal kinship systems and the other having a patrilineal system. These determine the clan membership of children, and lines of inheritance and descent. Their traditional economy is based on agriculture and trade. At the time of Spanish encounter in the 16th century, they were living in villages that the Spanish called pueblos, meaning "towns".

Qi Gong - a practice of aligning breath, movement, and awareness for exercise, healing, and meditation. With roots in Chinese medicine, martial arts, and philosophy, qigong is traditionally viewed as a practice to cultivate and balance qi (chi) or what has been translated as *'intrinsic life energy'*. Typically a Qigong practice involves rhythmic breathing coordinated with slow stylized repetition of fluid movement, a calm mindful state, and visualization of guiding qi through the body. Qigong is now practiced throughout China and worldwide, and is considered by some to be exercise, and by others to be a type of alternative medicine or meditative practice. From a philosophical perspective Qigong is believed to help develop human potential, allow access to higher realms of awareness, and awaken one's 'true nature'.

Quantum Physics - The study of the behavior of matter and energy at the molecular, atomic, nuclear, and even smaller microscopic levels. In the early 20th century, it was discovered that the laws that govern macroscopic objects do not function the same in such small realms. In the realm of quantum physics, observing something actually influences the physical processes taking place. Light waves act like particles and particles act like waves (called wave particle duality). Matter can go from one spot to another without moving through the intervening space (called quantum tunnelling). Information moves instantly across vast distances. In fact, in quantum mechanics we discover that the entire universe is actually a series of probabilities.

R.E.M. (raphid eye movement) - REM sleep typically occupies 20–25% of total sleep, about 90–120 minutes of a night's sleep. REM sleep is considered the deepest stage of sleep, and normally occurs close to morning. During a night of sleep, one usually experiences about four or five periods of REM sleep; they are quite short at the beginning of the night and longer toward the end. Many animals and some people tend to wake, or experience a period of very light sleep, for a short time immediately after a bout of REM. The relative amount of REM sleep varies considerably with age. A newborn baby spends more than 80% of total sleep time in REM. During REM, the activity of the brain's neurons is quite similar to that during waking hours; for this reason, the REM-sleep stage may be called paradoxical sleep.

Rosicrucians - Studies or membership within a philosophical secret society said to have been founded in late medieval Germany by Christian Rosenkreuz. It holds a doctrine or theology "built on esoteric truths of the ancient past", which, "concealed from the average man, provide insight into nature, the physical universe and the spiritual realm." Rosicrucianism is symbolized by the Rosy Cross. In the early 17th century, the manifestos caused excitement throughout Europe by declaring the existence of a secret brotherhood of alchemists and sages who were preparing to transform the arts, sciences, religion, and political and intellectual landscape of Europe. Wars of politics and religion ravaged the continent. The works were re-issued several times and followed by numerous pamphlets, favorable and otherwise. Between 1614 and 1620, about 400 manuscripts and books were published which discussed the Rosicrucian documents.

Samadhi - Described as a non-dualistic state of consciousness in which the consciousness of the experiencing subject becomes one with the experienced object, and in which the mind becomes still, one-pointed or concentrated while the person remains conscious. In Buddhism, it can also refer to an abiding in which mind becomes very still but does not merge with the object of attention, and is thus able to observe and gain insight into the changing flow of experience. In Hinduism, samādhi can also refer to videha mukti or the complete absorption of the individual consciousness in the self at the time of death, usually referred to as mahasamādhi.

Sanskrit - Classical Sanskrit is the standard register as laid out in the grammar of Pāṇini, 4th century BCE and it has significantly influenced most modern languages of the Indian subcontinent, particularly in India, Pakistan, Sri Lanka and Nepal. The pre-Classical form of Sanskrit is known as Vedic Sanskrit, with the language of the Rigveda being the oldest and most archaic stage preserved, its oldest core dating back to as early as 1500 BCE. This qualifies Rigvedic Sanskrit as one of the oldest attestations of any Indo-Iranian language, and one of the earliest attested members of the Indo-European language family.

Shamballa - In Tibetan Buddhist and Indian Hindu/Buddhist traditions, Shambhala (also spelled Shambala or Shamballa; is a kingdom hidden somewhere in Inner Asia. It is mentioned in various ancient texts, including the Kalachakra Tantra and the ancient texts of the Zhang Zhung culture which predated Tibetan Buddhism in western Tibet. The Bön scriptures speak of a closely related land called Olmolungring.

Shaman/Shamanism - is a practice that involves a practitioner reaching altered states of consciousness in order to encounter and interact with the spirit world and channel these transcendental energies into this world. A shaman is a person regarded as having access to, and influence in, the world of benevolent and malevolent spirits, who typically enters into a trance state during a ritual, and practices divination and healing

S.S.C. (Shamanic State of Conciousness) - An altered state of consciousness involving traveling to other worldly parallel dimensions- the upper world, the middle world, the lower world and the land of the dead. A shaman will journey there to bring back pieces of a persons soul which have been fragmented or lost from them in order to achieve wellness and wholeness for the individual.

Siddha - A Siddham in Tamil(an Indian sub-continent dialect) means *'one who is accomplished'* and refers to perfected masters who, according to Hindu belief, have transcended the ahamkara (ego or I-maker), have subdued their minds to be subservient to their Awareness, and have transformed their bodies (composed mainly of dense Rajo-tama gunas) into a different kind of body dominated by sattva. This is usually accomplished only by persistent meditation. Siddhas are the liberated souls. They have completely ended the cycle of birth and death. They have reached the ultimate state of salvation. They do not have any karmas and they do not collect any new karmas. This state of true freedom is called Moksha. They are formless and have no passions and therefore are free from all temptations. A siddha has also been defined to refer to one who has attained a siddhi.

Siddhi - The siddhis as paranormal abilities are considered emergent abilities of an individual that is on the path to siddhahood, and do not define a siddha, who is established in the Pranav or Aum – the spiritual substrate of creation. The siddhi in its pure form means "the attainment of flawless identity with Reality (Brahman); perfection of Spirit." In the Hindu philosophy of Kashmir Shaivism (Hindu tantra), siddha also refers to a Siddha Guru who can by way of Shaktipat initiate disciples into Yoga.

Sikh - is a monotheistic religion founded during the 15th century in the Punjab region of the Indian subcontinent, by Guru Nanak and continued to progress through the ten successive Sikh gurus (the eleventh and last guru being the holy scripture Guru Granth Sahib. The Guru Granth Sahib is a collection of the Sikh Gurus' writings that was compiled by the 5th Sikh Guru). It is the fifth-largest organized religion in the world, with approximately 30 million adherents. Punjab, India is the only state in the world with a majority Sikh population. The central teaching in Sikhism is the belief in the concept of the oneness of God. Sikhism considers spiritual life and secular life to be intertwined. Sikhs also believe that all religious traditions are equally valid and capable of enlightening their followers. In addition to sharing with others Guru Nanak inspired people to earn an honest living without exploitation and also the need for remembrance of the divine name (God). Guru Nanak described living an "active, creative, and practical life" of "truthfulness, fidelity, self-control and purity" as being higher than a purely contemplative life.

Sirus / Sirians - Sirius is also known colloquially as the "Dog Star", reflecting its prominence in its constellation, Canis Major (Greater Dog). The heliacal rising of Sirius marked the flooding of the Nile in Ancient Egypt and the "dog days" of summer for the ancient Greeks, while to the Polynesians it marked winter and was an important star for navigation around the Pacific Ocean. Sirius, known in ancient Egypt as Sopdet is recorded in the earliest astronomical records. During the era of the Middle Kingdom, Egyptians based their calendar on the heliacal rising of Sirius, namely the day it becomes visible just before sunrise after moving far enough away from the glare of the Sun. This occurred just before the annual flooding of the Nile and the summer solstice after a 70-day absence from the skies. According to Al Bielek, "the Sirians were technical creatures and were not very political. The Sirians look very human in some respects. They are muscular but have vertical slit eyes, like a cat's eyes. They wear a covering over their hair, and it is suspected that they are bald. Sometimes they have strange things on their ears which could be communicating devices. They are approximately six feet in height and can pass for humans in the proper attire. At Montauk, they were generally affable and did their job."

Soul/Soul Group - The incorporeal and immortal essence of a person, living thing, or object. Souls which are immortal and capable of union with the divine belong only to human beings. 12 Souls are grouped together in a Soul Group which is governed by an Over Soul. 12 Soul Groups are governed by a Monad.

Solar Gazing - Hira Ratan Manek (HRM), among others, have proven eating any food. The method is used for curing all kinds of psychosomatic, mental and physical illnesses as well as increasing memory power and mental strength by using sunlight. One can get rid of any kind of psychological problems, and develop confidence to face any problem in life and can overcome any kind of fear including that of death within 3 months after starting to practice this method. As a result, one will be free from mental disturbances and fear, which will result in a perfect balance of mind. If one continues to apply the proper sun gazing practice for 6 months, they will be free from physical illnesses. Furthermore, after 9 months, one can eventually win a victory over hunger, which disappears by itself thereafter. This is a straight-forward yet effective method based on solar energy, which enables one to harmonize and recharge the body with life energy and also invoke the unlimited powers of the mind very easily. Additionally, it allows one to easily liberate from threefold sufferings of humanity such as mental illnesses, physical illnesses and spiritual ignorance.

Spirit Guides - A term used by the Western tradition of

Spiritualist Churches, mediums, and psychics to describe an entity that remains a disincarnate spirit in order to act as a guide or protector to a living incarnated human being. Traditionally, within the spiritualist churches, spirit guides were often stereotyped ethnically, with Native Americans, Chinese or Egyptians being popular for their perceived ancient wisdom. Other popular types of guides were saints or other enlightened individuals. The term can also refer to totems, angels, guardian angels or nature spirits.

Spirit guides are not always of human descent. Some spirit guides live as energy, in the cosmic realm, or as light beings, which are very high level spirit guides. Some spirit guides are persons who have lived many former lifetimes, paid their karmic debts, and advanced beyond a need to reincarnate. Many devotees believe that spirit guides are chosen on "the other side" by human beings who are about to incarnate and wish assistance.

Tai Chi - A type of internal Chinese martial art practiced for both its defense training and its health benefits. It is also typically practiced for a variety of other personal reasons: its hard and soft martial art technique, demonstration competitions, and longevity. As a result, a multitude of training forms exist, both traditional and modern, which correspond to those aims. Some of Tai Chi Chuan's training forms are especially known for being practiced at what most people categorize as slow movement.

Tantra or **tantric** - Defined primarily as a technique-rich style of spiritual practice, Tantra has no single coherent doctrine; rather, it developed different teachings in connection with the different religions that adopted the Tantric method. These teachings tended to support and validate the practices of Tantra, which in their classical form are more oriented to the married householder than the monastic or solitary renunciant, and thus exhibited what may be called a world-embracing rather than a world-denying character. Thus Tantra, especially in its nondual forms, rejected the renunciant values of Patañjalian yoga, offering instead a vision of the whole of reality as the self-expression of a single, free and blissful Divine Consciousness under whatever name, whether Śiva or Buddha-nature.

Since the world was viewed as real, not illusory, this doctrine was a significant innovation over and against previous Indian philosophies, which tended to picture the Divine as absolutely transcendent and/or the world as illusion. The practical consequence of this view was that not only could householders aspire to spiritual liberation in the Tantric system, they were the type of practitioner that most Tantric manuals had in mind. Furthermore, since Tantra dissolved the dichotomy of spiritual versus mundane, practitioners could entail every aspect of their daily lives into their spiritual growth process, seeking to realize the transcendent in the immanent.

Tantric spiritual practices and rituals thus aim to bring about an inner realization of the truth that "*Nothing exists that is not Divine*" (nāśivaṃ vidyate kvacit), bringing freedom from ignorance and from the cycle of suffering (saṃsāra) in the process. In fact, tantric visualizations are said to bring the meditator to the core of his humanity and oneness with transcendence. Tantric meditations do not serve the function of training or practicing extra beliefs or unnatural ways. On the contrary, the transcendence that is reached by such meditative work does not construct anything in the mind of the practitioner, but actually de-constructs all preconceived notions of the human condition. The barriers that constrict thinking to limitation, namely, cultural and linguistic frameworks are completely removed. This allows the person to experience total liberation and then unity with ultimate truth or reality.

Tao Te Ching - A Chinese classic text. According to tradition, it was written around the 6th century BC by the sage Laozi (or Lao Tzu, "*Old Master*"), a record-keeper at the Zhou Dynasty court, by whose name the text is known in China. The text's true authorship and date of composition or compilation are still debated, although the oldest excavated text dates back to the late 4th century BC. The text is fundamental to both philosophical and religious Taoism and strongly influenced other schools, such as Legalism, Confucianism and Chinese Buddhism, which when first introduced into China was largely interpreted through the use of Taoist words and concepts. Many Chinese artists, including poets, painters, calligraphers, and even gardeners have used the Tao te Ching as a source of inspiration. Its influence has also spread widely outside East Asia, and is amongst the most translated works in world literature

Thymus gland - The thymus is a specialized organ of the immune system. The thymus *"educates"* T-lymphocytes (T cells), which are critical cells of the adaptive immune system. Each T cell attacks a foreign substance which it identifies with its receptor. T cells have receptors which are generated by randomly shuffling gene segments. Each T cell attacks a different antigen. T cells that attack the body's own proteins are eliminated in the thymus. Thymic epithelial cells express major proteins from elsewhere in the body, and T cells that respond to those proteins are eliminated through programmed cell death (apoptosis). The thymus is composed of two identical lobes and is located in front of the heart and behind the sternum.

Tao - A Chinese word meaning *'way'*, *'path'*, *'route'*, or sometimes more loosely, *'doctrine'* or *'principle'*. Within the context of traditional Chinese philosophy and religion, Tao is a metaphysical concept originating with Laozi that gave rise to a religion (Wade–Giles, Tao Chiao; Pinyin, Daojiao) and philosophy (Wade–Giles, Tao chia; Pinyin, Daojia) referred to in English with the single term Taoism. The concept of Tao was later adopted in Confucianism, Chán and Zen Buddhism and more broadly throughout East Asian philosophy and religion in general. Within these contexts Tao signifies the primordial essence or fundamental nature of the universe. In the foundational text of Taoism, the Tao Te Ching, Laozi explains that Tao is not a *'name'* for a *'thing'* but the underlying natural order of the universe whose ultimate essence is difficult to circumscribe. Tao is thus *'eternally nameless'* (Dao De Jing-32. Laozi) and to be distinguished from the countless 'named' things which are considered to be its manifestations.

Tattvas - In Kaśmir Śaivism, the 36 tattvas describe the

Absolute, its internal aspects and the creation including living beings, down to the physical reality. The addition of 11 supplemental tattvas compared to the Sāṃkhya allows for a richer, fuller vision of the Absolute. Going from śiva to pṛthvī tattva we find the process of manifestation, the creation of the universe; going the opposite way we find the process of spiritual evolution culminating with the dissolution in Śiva. Tattvas divide into three groups: Ashuddha, or impure (material, sensorial, the organs of action, the mind and the ego), Shuddhashuddha, or pure-impure (the soul and its limitations) and Shudda, or pure (internal aspects of the Absolute). The impure tattvas are the domain of objectivity and duality, the pure-impure tattvas are the domain of knowledge and the pure tattvas are the domain of transcendental unity and non-differentiation.

Urantia Book - The authors introduce the word "Urantia" as the name of the planet Earth and state that their intent is to "present enlarged concepts and advanced truth." The book aims to unite religion, science and philosophy, and its enormous amount of material about science is unique among literature claimed to be presented by celestial beings. Among other topics, the book discusses the origin and meaning of life, mankind's place in the universe, the relationship between God and people, and the life of Jesus.

Violet Flame - The Violet Flame is a Divine gift and tool for everyone, given to us by Ascended Master Saint Germain. It is a sacred fire that exists on the Higher Dimensions. People with the gift of inter-dimensional sight have seen it. Cameras have captured it when it was not visible to the person taking the photo. The Violet Flame is Real and I invite you to use it to your great advantage. The Violet Flame is Spiritual Alchemy in action. Just as Alchemy is said to turn Lead into Gold, the ultimate purpose of the Violet Flame is to turn the Human into the Divine Human. Its action is to TRANSMUTE denser feelings, actions, deeds, karma, etc. into a higher vibrational frequency, which helps prepare us for our Ascension

Vipassana - In the Buddhist tradition means insight into the true nature of reality. A regular practitioner of Vipassana, is known as a Vipassi.Vipassana is one of the world's most ancient techniques of meditation, which was introduced by Gautama Buddha. It is a practice of self-transformation through self-observation and introspection to the extent that sitting with a steadfast mind becomes an active experience of change and impermanence. In the west, Vipassanā meditation is often referred to simply as *"insight meditation"*.

Wheel of Life - The bhavacakra (Sanskrit; Pali: bhavacakka; Tibetan: srid pa'i 'khor lo) is a symbolic representation of samsara (or cyclic existence) found on the outside walls of Tibetan Buddhist temples and monasteries in the Indo-Tibetan region. In the Mahayana Buddhist tradition, it is believed that the drawing was designed by the Buddha himself in order to help ordinary people understand the Buddhist teachings. The bhavacakra is popularly referred to as the wheel of life. This term is also translated as wheel of cyclic existence or wheel of becoming.

Yantra - Is the Sanskrit word for "instrument" or "machine". Much like the word "instrument" itself, it can stand for symbols, processes, automata, machinery or anything that has structure and organization, depending on context. One usage popular in the west is as symbols or geometric figures. Traditionally such symbols are used in Eastern mysticism to balance the mind or focus it on spiritual concepts. The act of wearing, depicting, enacting and/or concentrating on a yantra is held to have spiritual or astrological or magical benefits in the Tantric traditions of the Indian religions.

Zeta Riticuli - Referred to as the 'Greys' and are typically depicted as dark grey-skinned diminutive humanoid beings that possess reduced forms of, or completely lack, external human organs such as noses, ears or sex organs. Their bodies are usually depicted as being elongated, having a small chest, and lacking in muscular definition and visible skeletal structure. Their legs are shorter and jointed differently from what one would expect in a human. Their limbs are often depicted as proportionally different from a human's; their humerus and thighs are the same lengths as their forearms and shins, respectively. Greys are depicted as having unusually large heads in proportion to their bodies. They are depicted as having no hair anywhere on the body, including the face, and no noticeable outer ears or noses, but only small openings or orifices for ears and nostrils. They are depicted as having very small mouths, and very large opaque black eyes with no discernible iris or pupil. Sometimes Greys are depicted as having no noticeable nostrils or mouths. Also reports of alleged encounters state their height to be 2–4 ft tall.

Check out the monthly newsletter for:
- Meditation insights and tips
- Upcoming workshop locations
- Personal individual sessions
- CD's and Downloads
- New Art & More!

www.billfossworld.com

Masters
of Light

By BILL FOSS

Babaji

24" x 36" acrylic on etched copper

358

Glossary of
Spiritual Masters, Deities, Teachers, Avatars and Angels

Avatars

Babaji - A revered East Indian Saint the world over. Babaji's physical presence came into being on November 29th 203 A.D. As a young boy Babaji Nagaraj began his spiritual studies learning from sages and gurus, after being orphaned, sold into slavery, and then bought and freed by a wealthy and kindly trader. The term 'Babaji' means *revered father* in the East. The young sage after studying with a powerful guru attained immortality at the age of 16 when a golden body of light filled his presence, in the midst of his spiritual practices. He has been on the planet ever since, as he vowed to his sister, Mataji, to always stay in an immortal physical form on the planet. According to those who encounter this Yogi, he lives in the Himalayas with a small group of disciples, and appears to people the world over in dreams and in the physical to instruct in spiritual learning, give kindly advice, or help where help is needed. Like other Bodhisattvas, Babaji can appear at anytime in anyplace and in any form. He was Paramahansa Yogananda's guru and can be read about in the book '*Autobiography of a Yogi*' This amazing and powerful maha avatar, is one of many helping to guide and balance all life animate and inanimate on the planet.

Buddha - Sidhartha Guatama - A spiritual teacher from the Indian subcontinent, on whose teachings Buddhism was founded. The word Buddha is a title for the first awakened being in an era. In most Buddhist traditions, Siddhartha Gautama is regarded as the Supreme Buddha of our age, "Buddha" meaning '*awakened one*' or '*the enlightened one.*' Gautama Buddha may also be referred to as Śākyamuni (Sanskrit: 'Sage of the Śākyas'). The Buddha found a Middle Way that ameliorated the extreme asceticism found in the Sramana religions.

The time of Gautama's birth and death are uncertain: most

early 20th century historians dated his lifetime as c. 563 BCE to 483 BCE, He found a Bodhi tree and started to meditate. He told himself that he would not get up until he had found enlightenment. He meditated under the tree for 49 days. His mind is said to have become pure, and then, six years after he began his path. When the Buddha became enlightened, he knew the answer to suffering, and he knew how to defeat suffering: the Four Noble Truths. He asked himself if the world was ready for such a deep teaching. He decided to travel to a town called Sarnath to teach the people his new way. He taught about the Four Noble Truths and the Noble Eightfold Path. His original process is known today and through the ages as Vipassana.

Jeshua ben Joseph - Essene teacher from Galilee in Roman Judaea, who was baptized by John the Baptist, and was crucified in Jerusalem on the orders of the Roman Prefect, Pontius Pilate. Scholars have offered competing descriptions and portraits of Jesus, which at times share a number of overlapping attributes, such as a rabbi, a charismatic healer, the leader of an apocalyptic movement, a self-described Messiah, a sage and philosopher, or a social reformer who preached of the *'Kingdom of Heaven'* as a means for personal and egalitarian social transformation. Scholars have correlated the New Testament accounts with non-Christian historical records to arrive at an estimated chronology of Jesus' life. Christians traditionally believe that Jesus was born of a virgin, performed miracles, founded the Church, died sacrificially by crucifixion to achieve atonement, rose from the dead, and ascended into heaven, from which he will return. The majority of Christians worship Jesus as the incarnation of God the Son, and the Second Person of the Holy Trinity.

Mary Magdalene - or Mary of Magdala, was one of Jesus' most celebrated disciples, and the most important female disciple in the movement of Jesus. Jesus cleansed her of 'seven demons', (Lu 8:2, Mk 16:9) sometimes interpreted as referring to complex illnesses. She became Jesus' closest friend and then wife. Prominent during his last days, being present at the cross after the male disciples (excepting John the Beloved) had fled, and at his burial. She was the first person to see Jesus after his Resurrection.

Mother Mary - or Mary of Sephoris, variously called Saint Mary, Mother Mary, the Virgin Mary, the Theotokos, the Blessed Virgin Mary, Mary, Mother of God, and, in Islam, as Maryam, mother of 'Isa, was an Israelite woman of Nazareth in Galilee who lived in the late 1st century BC and early 1st century AD, and is considered by Christians to be the first proselyte to Christianity. She is identified in the New Testament (Mt 1:16,18-25, Lk 1:26-56, 2:1-7) and in the Qur'an as the Mother of Jesus through Divine Intervention. Jesus is viewed as the Messiah - the Christ - in both traditions, giving rise to the common name of Jesus Christ. The canonical gospels of Matthew and Luke describe Mary as a virgin. Traditionally, Christians believe that she conceived her son miraculously by the agency of the Holy Spirit. This took place when she was already betrothed to Joseph and was awaiting the concluding rite of marriage, the formal home-taking ceremony. She married Joseph and accompanied him to Bethlehem, where Jesus was born. In keeping with Jewish custom, the betrothal would have taken place when she was around 12, and the birth of Jesus about a year later. The New Testament begins its account of Mary's life with the Annunciation, when the angel Gabriel appeared to her and announced her divine selection to be the mother of Jesus. Church tradition and early non-biblical writings state that her parents were an elderly couple, Saint Joachim and Saint Anne. The Bible records Mary's role in key events of the life of Jesus from his conception to his Ascension. Apocryphal writings tell of her subsequent death and bodily assumption into heaven.

Patanjali - is the compiler of the Yoga Sūtras, an important collection of aphorisms on Yoga practice. According to tradition, Patañjali was also the author of the Mahābhāṣya, a commentary on Kātyāyana's vārttikas (short comments) on Pāṇini's Aṣṭādhyāyī as well as an unspecified work of medicine (āyurveda). Patañjali's place of birth is held to be 'Gonarda', in a 'country in the eastern division', and he described himself as a "Gonardiya" throughout his life. This corroborates Tirumular's Tirumandiram which describes him as hailing from Then Kailasam (Koneswaram temple, Trincomalee), and he famously visited the Thillai Nataraja Temple, Chidambaram, where he wrote the Charana Shrungarahita Stotram on Nataraja. In recent decades, the Yoga Sutra has become quite popular worldwide for the precepts regarding practice of Raja Yoga and its philosophical basis. 'Yoga' in traditional Hinduism involves inner contemplation, a system of meditation practice and ethics.

Sai Baba - (born as Sathyanarayana Raju (23 November 1926 – 24 April 2011) was an Indian guru, spiritual figure, mystic, philanthropist and educator. He claimed to be the reincarnation of Sai Baba of Shirdi, considered a spiritual saint and a reputed miracle worker, who died in 1918 and whose teachings were an eclectic blend of Hindu and Muslim beliefs. The materializations of vibhuti (holy ash) and other small objects such as rings, necklaces and watches by Sathya Sai Baba were a source of both fame and controversy; devotees considered them signs of divinity, while displayed in millions of homes and on the dashboards of cars, and lockets bearing his photo are worn by many as a symbol of good fortune.

He also started the Sri Sathya Sai Super Specialty Hospital in Puttaparthi, India as well as helping to found many schools and feed the hungry.

Deities

Pan - In Greek religion and mythology, is the god of the wild, shepherds and flocks, nature, of mountain wilds, hunting and rustic music, as well as the companion of the nymphs. His name originates within the Ancient Greek language, from the word *paein*, meaning *"to pasture."* He has the hindquarters, legs, and horns of a goat, in the same manner as a faun or satyr. With his homeland in rustic Arcadia, he is recognized as the god of fields, groves, and wooded glens; because of this, Pan is connected to fertility and the season of spring. The ancient Greeks also considered Pan to be the god of theatrical criticism. In Roman religion and myth, Pan's counterpart was Faunus, a nature god who was the father of Bona Dea, sometimes identified as Fauna. In the 18th and 19th centuries, Pan became a significant figure in the Romantic movement of western Europe, and also in the 20th-century Neopagan movement. Also considered in some circles to be ruler of the elemental and nature devas.

Gaia - Was the goddess or personification of Earth in ancient Greek religion, one of the Greek primordial deities. Gaia was the great mother of all: the heavenly gods, the Titans and the Giants were born from her union with Uranus (the sky), while the sea-gods were born from her union with Pontus (the sea).

Ganesha - also known as *Ganapati* is one of the deities best-known and most widely worshipped in the Hindu pantheon. His image is found throughout India and Nepal. Hindu sects worship him regardless of affiliations. Devotion to Ganesha is widely diffused and extends to Jains, Buddhists, and beyond India. Although he is known by many other attributes, Ganesha's elephant head makes him particularly easy to identify. Widely revered as the Remover of Obstacles and more generally as Lord of Beginnings and Lord of Obstacles. Ganesha emerged as a distinct deity in clearly recognizable form in the 4th and 5th centuries CE, during the Gupta Period, although he inherited traits from Vedic and pre-Vedic precursors. His popularity rose quickly, and he was formally included among the five primary deities of Smartism (a Hindu denomination) in the 9th century. A sect of devotees called the Ganapatya, who identified Ganesha as the supreme deity, arose during this period. The principal scriptures dedicated to Ganesha are the Ganesha Purana, the Mudgala Purana, and the Ganapati Atharvashirsa. A very popular god of Hindus. Hindu tradition states that Ganesha is a god of wisdom, success and good luck. He is also giver of different types of favours. The Hindu tradition calls Ganesha as the Vighneshvara. 'Vighneshvara' in Sanskrit language means one who is the lord of obstacles or difficulties. Thus, the Hindu tradition states that by worshiping Ganesha, one can remove all obstacle and difficulties.

Lakshimi -The Hindu goddess of wealth, prosperity

(both material and spiritual), fortune, and the embodiment of beauty. She is the consort of the god Vishnu. Also called *Maha Lakshmi*, she is said to bring good luck and is believed to protect her devotees from all kinds of misery and money-related sorrows. Representations of Lakshmi are also found in Jain monuments. Lakshmi is called Shri or Thirumagal because she is endowed with six auspicious and divine qualities, or Gunas, and also because she is the source of strength even to Vishnu. When Vishnu incarnated on earth as avatars Rama and Krishna, Lakshmi incarnated as his consort. Sita (Rama's wife), Radha (Krishna's lover) and Rukmini and the other wives of Krishna are considered forms of Lakshmi. Lakshmi is worshipped daily in Hindu homes and commercial establishments as the goddess of wealth. She also enjoys worship as the consort of Vishnu in many temples. The festivals of Diwali and Kojagiri Purnima are celebrated in her honor. Commonly seen together with Ganesha and Saraswati, depicting three parent aspects of 'the removing of obstacles' to 'prosperity and abundance' and the 'wisdom to use it'.

Saraswati - She is the consort of Brahma, also revered as his Shakti. Her figure is also popular in the Jain religion of west and central India. The name Saraswati comes from saras (meaning 'flow') and wati (*meaning 'she who has ...'*), i.e., *'she who has flow'*. So, Saraswati is symbol of knowledge; its flow (or growth) is like a river, and knowledge is supremely alluring, like a beautiful woman. She is depicted as a beautiful fair goddess with four arms, wearing a spotless white saree and seated on a white lotus. She is also known as Sharada, Vani and Vagdevi (all meaning 'speech').

Shiva - A major Hindu deity, and is the Destroyer or Transformer among the Trimurti, the Hindu Trinity of the primary aspects of the divine. Shiva is a yogi who has notice of everything that happens in the world and is the main aspect of life. Yet one with great power, he lives a life of a sage at Mount Kailash. In the Shaiva tradition of Hinduism, Shiva is seen as the Supreme God and has five important works: creator, preserver, destroyer, concealer, and revealer (to bless). In the Smarta tradition, he is regarded as one of the five primary forms of God. Followers of Hinduism who focus their worship upon Shiva are called Shaivites or Shaivas (Sanskrit Śaiva). Shaivism, along with Vaiṣṇava traditions that focus on Vishnu and Śākta traditions that focus on the goddess Shakti, is one of the most influential denominations in Hinduism. Shiva is usually worshipped in the abstract form of Shiva linga. In images, he is represented as immersed in deep meditation or dancing the Tandava dance upon Apasmara, the demon of ignorance in his manifestation of Nataraja, the Lord of the Dance.

Tara - In Tibetan Buddhism, a female Bodhisattva. She is known as the *'mother of liberation'*, and represents the virtues of success in work and achievements. In Japan she is known as Tarani Bosatsu, and little-known as Tuoluo in Chinese Buddhism. Tara is a tantric meditation deity whose practice is used by practitioners of the Tibetan branch of Vajrayana Buddhism to develop certain inner qualities and understand outer, inner and secret teachings about compassion and emptiness. Tara is actually the generic name for a set of Buddhas or bodhisattvas of similar aspect. These may more properly be understood as different aspects of the same quality, as bodhisattvas are often considered metaphoric for Buddhist virtues.

The most widely known forms of Tārā are:

Green Tārā - known as the Buddha of enlightened activity

White Tārā - also known for compassion, long life, healing and serenity; and as The Wish-fulfilling Wheel, or Cintachakra

Red Tārā -   of fierce aspect associated with magnetizing all good things

Black Tārā - associated with power

Yellow Tārā - associated with wealth and prosperity

Blue Tārā -   associated with transmutation of anger

Cittamani Tārā - a form of Tārā widely practiced at the level of Highest Yoga Tantra in the Gelug School of Tibetan Buddhism, portrayed as green and

often conflated with Green Tārā
Khadiravani Tārā - (Tārā of the acacia forest), who appeared
to Nagarjuna in the Khadiravani forest of South India
and who is sometimes referred to as the '22nd Tārā.'

Arch Angels

Ariel - "Lioness of God." She helps with qualities of bravery,
courage and focus. She will boost your self-confidence. She
helps bring about miracles of manifestation. Ariel helps teachers,
healers, and service workers. She protects the environment. She
works closely with nature spirits to heal animals in and near the
water. Ariel will also help you attract support needed for your
life's mission.

Azrael - "Angel of Death." Azrael brings comfort and love to
those who are grieving or dying. Azrael assists people crossing
over when they die. Azrael brings communication from those
who have already crossed over. Azrael also assists with grief and
other types of council that is needed. She also helps those who
are helpers. She works with grief counselors to shield them from
absorbing their clients' pain.

Chamuel - "He who is with God." Chamuel is considered
a powerful leader in the angelic hierarchy known as "Powers."
As a Powers Angel, Chamuel oversees protection of the world.
Chamuel helps us to see clearly in all areas of our life. He can assist
you in finding lost items. Chamuel can assist you with career and
employment issues. He can help you with your relationships and
soul partners. Chamuel will assist you in finding your path in life.
Call on Chamuel for comfort, protection, and intervention from
lower energies. Chamuel is the Angel of Peace both personal and
global. He can heal anxiety. He is very kind, loving and sweet.

Gabriel - "Messenger Angel." Gabriel loves to coach and help
you with writing. He can open doors for publication and will
help you in the enjoyment of your writing. He will push you
into action. Gabriel can set up opportunities for television and
radio work. Gabriel will help you to find strength and help you
connect with your personal power. He will reassure you that it is

safe to be powerful. He assists mothers and children on all levels of conception, childbirth, adoption and parenting. Call on him for help in any of these areas. He also helps you to connect with your inner child.

Haniel - "Glory of God." Haniel helps in connecting with divine magic and powerful cycles of the moon. Haniel helps to groom hidden talents and to find your true passions. She helps with clairvoyance and psychic abilities. Haniel helps you to appreciate yourself and build self-worth. Call upon her to bring harmony, grace, beauty and wonderful friends into your life. Haniel's energy is etheric, patient, quiet and mystical. She can also help you stay poised before and during important personal events.

Jeremial - "Mercy of God." Jeremial helps to open clairvoyance and prophetic visions. He helps you to do life reviews in order to recognize any areas of your life that you might want to make changes in. He helps you to heal patterns that are no longer working and can help you heal on an emotional level. Jeremial guides you to act in loving ways and to learn to treat yourself with respect and tender loving care. Jeremial assists you with harmonious changes by being merciful to all and helps you maintain a connection to God. He assists you with spiritual growth. He answers prayers. Jeremial is a healer and can assist you with any physical issues that you might have. Jeremial can block negative energies. He will help you to open your heart and live in compassion.

Jophiel - "Beauty of God." Jophiel assists you with creativity and assists artists with their gifts. Since she is the archangel of beauty, she can help you think beautiful thoughts and create more beauty in your life. Jophiel helps you to clear clutter both mentally and physically. This includes negative thinking and clearing negative energy. Jophiel encourages you to spend time in Mother Nature to clear out lower energies and be able to experience gratitude and peace in life.

Metatron - is the angel of sacred geometry and numerology associated with the Kabbalah. He helps you to clear and open your chakras and clean psychic toxins from your body. Metatron will help you with organizational skills. If you need help with organizing your schedule to make time for activities that you enjoy, call on Metatron. He can assist you with more time, money, ideas, and contacts, just to name a few. He will assist you in making choices to support your life mission and with your spiritual understanding. Metatron also will assist you with focus. He helps Indigo and Crystal children as well as parents and teachers of these children. He has a special love for children and will help them with any issues. He can also assist you in overcoming your procrastination and help you stay motivated.

Michael - "He who is like God." Michael is a leader among the archangels. He is in charge of the order of angels. Michael affords protection for you and your loved ones. Call on Michael to protect you whenever you feel afraid or vulnerable. He will escort lower energies away from your space. Michael works with you while you sleep and enters your dreams to clear away fears. Just ask Michael to clear away your negativity energy and fears. Michael assists light workers with their life purpose. He gives direction, courage, and motivation. Michael helps with the qualities of love, power, strength, unwavering faith, courage and direction. Michael has a fiery spirit and you will be able to feel the heat from his strong energy. He can assist you with spirit releasement. Michael also can fix electrical and mechanical problems.

Raguel - "Friend of God." Raguel assists you in being more clairsentience (to have gut feelings). He helps you to distinguish between your feelings and those of others. He guides you towards situations, people and places that have clear and loving energy. Raguel will help you to defend and empower those that are treated unfairly. He gives guidance to all involved to act in fair and just ways. He helps you to maintain harmony and order in your relationships. He is wonderful at resolving conflicts and can act as a mediator. He will help you to find creative solutions to your problems.

Raphael - "Heaven's Physician." He gives you guidance for a healthier life. Raphael can help you with anything requiring healing including relief from burdens, thoughts, and fears. He is a powerful healer, being able to heal physical bodies of both humans and animals. Raphael will support healers. He will assist you in eliminating cravings and addictions. Raphael can increase clairvoyance (third eye vision). Raphael works to enhance both physical and spiritual eyesight. Raphael often works with Michael to clear out lower energies. He can also give you Divine guidance through your intuition.

Raziel- Can help you gain deeper spiritual understanding and then help you apply it in practical ways. He will take your soul travelling in your dreams to help you discover truths and ancient wisdom that will then become a part of your subconscious and be with you when you wake up. Raziel is known as the wizard of the Archangels. He helps you understand ideas that defy normal logic. He will then assist you in letting go of limited thinking. Raziel assists with clairvoyance, divine magic and esoteric information. Raziel is also known for his abilities to help you manifest your desires. He is a very loving, kind and intelligent angel.

Sandalphon - His primary role is the delivering and answering of prayers. He is considered to be so tall that he extends from Earth to Heaven enabling him to carry your prayers to God. Sandalphon assists you in taking time to reconnect with peace. He will assist you in learning how to enjoy the present moment. Ask him to help you live in integrity with your gifts of prophecy and healing. He will enable you to fully awaken your manifestation abilities. He will encourage you to listen to gentle music. This is often his way of answering prayers. He is also known to help expectant parents determine the gender of their expectant baby.

Uriel - "God is light." Uriel is known as the Light of God because he illuminates situations. Uriel is there to help you with claircognizance (a knowingness). He gives insight to support your life purpose and will give you prophetic information and warnings. He will help you problem solve and give you clear signs to validate your thoughts and ideas. Uriel will light your pathway so you know which step to take next. Uriel is thought of as one of the wisest archangels. He can help you with practical solutions and even give you creative insight.

Zadkiel - "Mercy of God." Zadkiel teaches compassion and forgiveness. He helps you to release emotional toxins. He assists with clairaudience (clear hearing) through the brow chakra. Zadkiel assists with memory. This archangel guards the powers of invocation and affirmation. He responds to the deepest call from your heart and encourages you to intensify this energy through your desire. Zadkiel helps remind us to open our hearts and minds in gratitude to receive the presence and power of the Universe.

Native American Deities

Earth Keepers - Among Native American and other indigenous peoples their tradition of spiritual teachers are called 'Earth Keepers'. Earth Keepers accept the responsibility to honor the spiritual essence of this Earth and all her '*helpers*' among the angelic beings, ancestral beings, the nature spirits and the elementals. By honoring and giving support to these beings, they support the Earth. Like humanity, these Beings need the support of healing, and our gratitude and love for them brings out their best...just as it does with humans.

Spirit of the 4 Directions - These are as follows Sapa, Luta, Gi, and Okaga Ska. This would be West, North, East and South respectively. The colors being black, red, yellow, and white. Each direction has its own meaning and power. West '*Sapa*' is a place the thunder beings (wakinyan) reside and is considered a place of darkness. This darkness is in a good sense, like that of solitude or meditation and crossing into the spiritual realm. North or '*Luta*' is a place of renewal and represented by the color red. East '*Gi*' is a place of brightness, light, clarity and fire with the color being yellow. And South (color white) is a place or door between the spirit world and the visible realm. This circle represents the cycle of life from birth, youth, to elder and death. Some tribes vary the colors animal representations, and meaning, but one thing for sure, is that the spirits of the four directions are powerful and are waiting to be called upon for direction and help. Walking the wheel of the four directions in this life, can mean you have experienced many cycles of birth and death to former aspects of yourself. This is a natural thing from which we learn lessons and gain wisdom. When we gain enough wisdom we can help others walk the circle and follow ritual. We become elders in a figurative and real sense. Some are called and hear the calling. We carry the pipe, hawk or eagle feather, and drum so we may connect and heal with their use. We use sage a lot along with various other herbs.

Great Spirit - called Wakan Tanka among the Sioux and Gitche Manitou in Algonquian, is a conception of a supreme being prevalent among some Native American and First Nations cultures. According to a Lakotah activist, a better translation of Wakan Tanka is the Great Mystery. The Great Spirit or Great Mystery is generally believed to be personal, close to the people, and immanent in the fabric of the material world. Lakotah prayers refer to him as Grandfather; however, not all Nations assign gender, or only one gender, to the Great Mystery. A spiritual leader of the Hopi Nation, described the Great Spirit as follows: 'To the Hopi, the Great Spirit is all powerful. He taught us how to live, to worship, where to go and what food to carry, gave us seeds to plant and harvest. He gave us a set of sacred stone tablets into which he breathed all teachings in order to safeguard his land and life. In these stone tablets were inscribed instructions, prophecies and warnings.' *'Old Man'* is how the Great Mystery is *'known'* by the Blackfoot people. Old Man personally created all things and personally instructed the Blackfoot people on how to attain spiritual wisdom in daily life.

Spiritual Teachers

Dali Lama - A high lama in the Gelug or *'Yellow Hat'* branch of Tibetan Buddhism. The name is a combination of the Sino-Mongolian word (dalai) meaning *'Ocean'* and the Tibetan word bla-ma (with a silent 'b') meaning *'chief, high priest'*. In religious terms, the Dalai Lama is believed by his devotees to be the rebirth of a long line of tulkus who are considered to be manifestations of the bodhisattva of compassion, Avalokiteśvara. Traditionally, the Dalai Lama is thought of as the latest reincarnation of a series of spiritual leaders who have chosen to be reborn in order to enlighten others. The Dalai Lama is often thought to be the leader of the Gelug School, but this position belongs officially to the Ganden Tripa, which is a temporary position appointed by the Dalai Lama who, in practice, exerts much influence. The line of Dalai Lamas began as a lineage of spiritual teachers; the 5th Dalai Lama assumed political authority over Tibet.

Edgar Cayce - March 18, 1877 – January 3, 1945) was an American psychic who allegedly possessed the ability to answer questions on subjects as varied as healing, reincarnation, wars, Atlantis and future events while in a trance. These answers came to be known as "life readings of the entity" and were usually delivered to individuals while Cayce was hypnotized. This ability gave him the nickname "The Sleeping Prophet". Cayce founded a nonprofit organization, the Association for Research and Enlightenment (A.R.E.) in Virginia Beach that included a hospital and a university.

Enoch - The priest-scientist is a prediluvian patriarch, one of the most famous and seminal characters of the previous time cycle. Father of Methuselah and great grandfather of Noah, Enoch is credited in the Bible as architect of the original Zion, the legendary "City of Yahweh", as well as inventor of the alphabet and calendar. Enoch is also history's first astronaut, who "is taken aloft by the Lord" and shown "the secrets of earth and heaven". He returns to earth with the "weights and measures" for all humankind.

Gandhi - Mohandas Karamchand Gandhi (1869 – 1948), commonly known as Mahatma Gandhi, was the pre-eminent leader of Indian nationalism in British-ruled India. Employing non-violent civil disobedience, Gandhi led India to independence and inspired movements for non-violence, civil rights and freedom across the world.

Paramahansa Yogananda - (January 5, 1893 – March 7, 1952), born Mukunda Lal Ghosh, was an Indian yogi and guru who introduced many westerners to the teachings of meditation and Kriya Yoga through his book, '*Autobiography of a Yogi*' designated one of the '100 Most Important Spiritual Books of the 20th Century'. In his youth he sought out many of India's Hindu sages and saints, hoping to find an illuminated teacher to guide him in his spiritual quest. Yogananda's seeking after various saints mostly ended when he met his guru, Swami Yukteswar Giri, in 1910, at the age of 17. He describes his first meeting with Yukteswar as a rekindling of a relationship that had lasted for many lifetimes: Later on Yukteswar informed Yogananda that he had been sent to him by Mahavatar Babaji for a special purpose. Mahavatar Babaji taught Kriya Yoga to Lahiri Mahasaya, who taught it to his disciple, Yukteswar Giri and then to Paramahansa.

Lao Tzu - Best known as the author of the Tao Te Ching (often simply referred to as Laozi). His association with the Tào Té Chīng has led him to be traditionally considered the founder of philosophical Taoism (pronounced as '*Daoism*'). He is also revered as a deity in most religious forms of Taoist philosophy, which often refers to Laozi as Taishang Laojun, or "One of the Three Pure Ones". According to Chinese traditions, Laozi lived in the 6th century BCE. Historians variously contend that Laozi is a synthesis of multiple historical figures, that he is a mythical figure, or that he actually lived in the 5th–4th century BCE, concurrent with the Hundred Schools of Thought and Warring States Period. A central figure in Chinese culture, both nobility and common people claim Laozi in their lineage. He was honored as an ancestor of the Tang imperial family, and was granted the title Táishāng xuānyuán huángdì, meaning '*Supreme Mysterious and Primordial Emperor*'.

Leanardo da Vinci - A classical and historic renowned painter. Among his works, the Mona Lisa is the most famous and most parodied portrait and The Last Supper the most reproduced religious painting of all time, with their fame approached only by Michelangelo's The Creation of Adam. Leonardo's drawing of the

Vitruvian Man is also regarded as a cultural icon, being reproduced on items as varied as the euro coin, textbooks, and T-shirts. Perhaps fifteen of his paintings survive, the small number because of his constant, and frequently disastrous, experimentation with new techniques, and his chronic procrastination. Nevertheless, these few works, together with his notebooks, which contain drawings, scientific diagrams, and his thoughts on the nature of painting, compose a contribution to later generations of artists rivalled only by that of his contemporary, Michelangelo.

Leonardo is revered for his technological ingenuity. He conceptualized flying machines, a tank, concentrated solar power, an adding machine, and the double hull, also outlining a rudimentary theory of plate tectonics. Relatively few of his designs were constructed or were even feasible during his lifetime, but some of his smaller inventions, such as an automated bobbin winder and a machine for testing the tensile strength of wire, entered the world of manufacturing unheralded. He made important discoveries in anatomy, civil engineering, optics, and hydrodynamics, but he did not publish his findings and they had no direct influence on later science.

Melchezideck - Was a real person who lived during the time of Abraham about 2,000 B.C. He was a righteous and Godly leader over a very special piece of real estate, the ancient city of Salem, the city of God's Peace, later to be known as Jerusalem. He was an early priest-king and in the manner of many early leaders of those times. He presided over both the religion and the politics of his city. The significant thing about Melchizedek was not only the place of His rule and ministry, which was over the "Holy Place", but that he operated in two offices as both priest and king. Melchizedek has been recognized as a "type" or a forerunner of our coming Messiah who as we know presides eternally over this cosmos and its people in those dual mutually supportive offices as High Priest and King of Kings. As we read the account in Genesis 14:18,19,&20 we see that our patriarch Abraham gave Melchizedek tithes and Melchizedek blessed Abraham and his family. Melchizedek also brought out bread and wine which are the constant and continuing elements of a covenant meal among the covenant people of the God of Israel. The bread and the wine are the elements that are still laid out before us in our Christian communion services today.

Nostradamus - Born Michel de Nostradame in Saint-Remy-de-Provence, France in 1503. He studied medicine and became a physician, treating plague victims throughout France and Italy. It's believed he had a psychic awakening. He began to practice the occult and make predictions of the future, which he published in The Prophecies. Many people today believe his predictions have come true or will in the future. Over the history of the world one of the most revered seers of all time.

Spiritual Masters

Djwal Khul - A Tibetan disciple in the tradition of ancient esoteric spirituality known as The Ageless Wisdom tradition. The texts describe him as a member of the '*Spiritual Hierarchy*', or '*Brotherhood of Mahatmas*', one of the Masters of the Ancient Wisdom, defined as the spiritual guides of mankind and teachers ancient cosmological, metaphysical, and esoteric principles that form the origin of all the world's great philosophies, mythologies and spiritual traditions. According to Theosophical writings, Djwal Khul is said to work on furthering the spiritual evolution of our planet through the teachings offered in the 24 books by Alice A. Bailey of Esoteric Teachings published by The Lucis Trust; he is said to have telepathically transmitted the teachings to Bailey and is thus regarded by her followers as the communications director of the Masters of the Ancient Wisdom.

El Morya - Morya is considered one of the "Ascended Masters," also known as the '*Chohan of the First Ray*' (see Seven Rays). H. P. Blavatsky. Morya and Kuthumi were her guides in establishing the Theosophical Society. Blavatsky also wrote that Masters Morya and Kuthumi belonged to a group of highly developed humans known as the Great White Brotherhood. After Blavatsky's death, theosophists and others continued claiming to have met Morya or to have received communications from him. Theosophical writings offered vivid descriptions of Morya, his role in the Brotherhood, and his past lives.

Kuthumi - Is the lord of the Second Ray, and exemplar of wisdom. He is especially concerned with culture—art, religion, and education—and is the guardian of a vast museum located in the remote Tibetan valley where he and Master Morya reside. In one of his past incarnations he was the philosopher Pythagoras and in recent times he inhabits the body of a Kasmirian Indian. Like Morya, he travels frequently and many members of the Theosophical Society have reported seeing him. Blavatsky reportedly first met him in 1868. He also had a special relationship with A. P. Sinnett, one of the early theosophical leaders. Master Kuthumi was one of the three main communicators (the others being Master Morya and Djual Khul) of what were compiled as The Mahatma Letters, the ultimate source for many theosophical ideas

Merlin - Merlin first appears in extant records (Armes Prydein, Y Gododdin) from the early 10th century as a mere prophet, but his role gradually evolved into that of magician, prophet and advisor, active in all phases of the administration of King Arthur's kingdom. He was apparently given the name Emrys (or Ambrosius) at his birth in Caer Fyrddin (Carmarthen). He only later became known as Merlin, a Latinized version of the Welsh word, Myrddin, taken from the place of his birth. Merlin was the illegitimate son of a monastic Royal Princess of Dyfed.

Merlin's father, it is said, was an angel who had visited the Royal nun and left her with child. Merlin's enemies claimed his father was really an incubus, an evil spirit that has intercourse with sleeping women. The evil child was supposed to provide a counterweight to the good influence of Jesus Christ on earth. Merlin, fortunately, was baptized early on in his life, an event which is said to have negated the evil in his nature, but left his powers intact. The original story was presumably invented to save his mother from the scandal which would have occurred had her liaison with one Morfyn Frych (the Freckled), a minor Prince of the House of Coel, been made public knowledge. Legend then tells us that after the Roman withdrawal from Britain and the usurpation of the throne from the rightful heirs, Vortigern was in flight from the Saxon breakout and went to Snowdonia, in Wales, in hopes of constructing a mountain fortress at Dinas Emrys where he might be safe.

Unfortunately, the building kept collapsing and Vortigern's house wizards told him that a human sacrifice of a fatherless child would solve the problem. One small difficulty was that such children are rather hard to find. Fortunately for Vortigern's fortress, Merlin was known to have no human father and happened to be available. Later, Merlin appears to have inherited his grandfather's little kingdom, but abandoned his lands in favour of the more mysterious life for which he has become so well known.

After 460 British nobles were massacred at a peace conference, as a result of Saxon trickery, Ambrosius consulted Merlin about erecting a suitable memorial to them. Merlin, along with Uther, led an expedition to Ireland to procure the stones of the Chorea Gigantum, the Giant's Ring. Merlin, by the use of his extraordinary powers, brought the stones back to a site, just west of Amesbury, and re- erected them around the mass grave of the British nobles. We now call this place Stonehenge.

Quan Yin - also Guanyin, Kwan Yin, Is the bodhisattva associated with compassion as venerated by East Asian Buddhists, usually as a female. The name Guanyin is short for Guanshiyin which means 'Observing the Sounds (or Cries) of the World'. She is also sometimes referred to as *Guanyin Pusa* '*Bodhisattva Guanyin*'). Some Buddhists believe that when one of their adherents departs from this world, they are placed by Guanyin in the heart of a lotus then sent home to the western pure land of Sukhāvatī. It is generally accepted among east Asian adherents that Guanyin originated as the Sanskrit *Avalokiteśvara*, which is her male form. Commonly known in English as the Mercy Goddess or Goddess of Mercy, Guanyin is also revered by Chinese Taoists (sometimes called Daoists) as an Immortal. However, in

Taoist mythology, Guanyin has other origination stories which are not directly related to Avalokiteśvara.

Sananda - In ancient Lemuria, a master with great power incarnate only 3 times on the planet. Responsible for leading a group of followers away from mainland Lemuria to populate what is now Japan. Sananda was said to have intense natural transformative powers, including the power to heal, create or manifest with words. A radiance like the sun emanating from his body. Believed in some metaphysical communities to also have been an earlier incarnation of Christ.

Sanat Kumara - Also known as the Ancient of Days, is the Hierarch of Venus. Long ago, around the time of the caveman, Sanat Kumara came to the earth to keep the flame of life (the threefold flame) for everyone on the planet. This was during the earth's darkest days when the consciousness of the people had fallen to an all time low and no one honored God or the inner flame of the heart. It was such a dark time that a council of the Cosmic Hierarchy convened to discuss what could be done.

Sanat Kumara convinced the council to let him come saying he would keep the flame of the heart on behalf of the people until at least some started doing it for themselves. He was granted this request and prepared to go into exile when 144,000 light-bearers from Venus volunteered to come and support him in the mission. A special envoy went ahead to build the retreat of Shamballa on an island in the Gobi Sea. Today we know this area as the Gobi Desert. Sanat Kumara placed a focus of the inner flame (threefold flame) on the altar where it remained in the physical for many centuries. Although Sanat Kumara resided in this retreat he did not embody in the physical and remained in his higher body of light. He anchored a filigree port him in the mission. A special envoy went ahead to build the retreat of Shamballa on an island in the Gobi Sea.

Today we know this area as the Gobi Desert. Sanat Kumara placed a focus of the inner flame (threefold flame) on the altar where it remained in the physical for many centuries. Although Sanat Kumara resided in this retreat he did embody in the ray of light from his heart to each heart on the planet and continuously nourished it plus assisted everyone to be quickened by the consciousness of the Christ. After a period of time people began to respond and finally some of them started raising their consciousness and developing their inner flame. This allowed Sanat Kumara to return home to Venus

St. Germain - (also sometimes referred to as Master Rakoczi) is a legendary spiritual master of the Ancient Wisdom in the Theosophical teachings of C.W. Leadbeater, Alice A. Bailey, Benjamin Creme, the White Eagle Lodge, modern Rosicrucianism and the Ascended Master Teachings, responsible for the New Age culture of the Age of Aquarius and identified with the Count of St. Germain (fl. 1710–1784), who has been variously mysterious manifestation of the 'resurrected form' (or 'resurrection body') of Sir Francis Bacon. In subsequent described as a courtier, adventurer, charlatan, inventor, alchemist, pianist, violinist and amateur composer. As one of the Masters of the Ancient Wisdom, is credited with near god-like powers and with longevity. It is believed that Sir Francis Bacon faked his own death on Easter Sunday, 9 April 1626, attended his own funeral and made his way from England to Transylvania where he found lodging in a castle owned by the Rakóczi family. There, on 1 May 1684, Bacon, by using alchemy, became an immortal occult master and adopted the name Saint Germain and became one of the Masters of the Ancient Wisdom, a group of beings that, Theosophists believe, form a Spiritual Hierarchy of planet Earth sometimes called the Ascended Masters. Thus, according to these beliefs, St. Germain was a lifetime he did embody. What this master did was truly beautiful and demonstrates the love of an Ascended Master of Light for all of us.

Serapis Bay - Is regarded in Theosophy as being one of the Masters of the Ancient Wisdom; and is considered to be an Ascended Master and member of the Great White Brotherhood. He is regarded as the Chohan (or Lord) of the Fourth Ray. C.W. Leadbeater wrote that Henry Steele Olcott was given occult training by Serapis Bey when his own master, Morya, was unavailable. A series of alleged letters from Serapis to Olcott encouraging him to support Blavatsky in the founding of The Theosophical Society were published in the book Letters from the Masters of the Wisdom. Serapis Bey was incarnated as a priest in one of the "Temples of the Sacred Fire" on Atlantis who migrated to Egypt at the time of the destruction of Atlantis. Also believed that he was incarnated as the Egyptian Pharaoh Amenhotep III (who constructed the Temple of Luxor to the god Amon) and also as Leonidas, the King of Sparta, who was killed in 480 BC defending the pass of Thermopylae against the invasion of Greece by Xerxes I, Emperor of the Persian Empire. According teachings of Agni Yoga, Serapis Bey was in past lives the Roman King Numa Pompilius, the philosophers Confucius, Plato and Lucius Anneus Seneca. He is referred to as *'The Thinker'*.

The "Journey to the Akasha" Study Set
For Home Study and the Workshops Into the Akashic Records

Available at www.billfoss.net

Akashic Records, Healing, and Personal Guidance Phone Sessions

Bill works with you in person when available or by phone to unlock your greatest potential, give life path guidance, for personal healing and manifesting your goals and dreams in life. Looking into your personal Book of Life within the Akashic Records. This enables you to see tendencies from other lifetimes as they are played out in the multi-dimensional reality that makes up who you are. Channeled information from the Records, with the aid of your spirit guides, angelics, and ascended masters or spiritual gurus, reveal information that make up who you are on the otherside, as well as in the physical. This can bring clarity to your current situation. As you state your questions, Your answers will come from the Akashic Records and will give clarity to the reasons for the immediate events and circumstances as well as how to navigate more clearly and receive info for business and personal relations, spiritual attainment, and locations, Past, Present and Future.

Email your FULL NAME, BIRTHDATE & PLACE and a list of questions to: bill@billfoss.net
To book a phone session call
918-770-3810 or 714-706-0402,
"If you need help in getting to the next level on your journey, This will be beneficial for you."

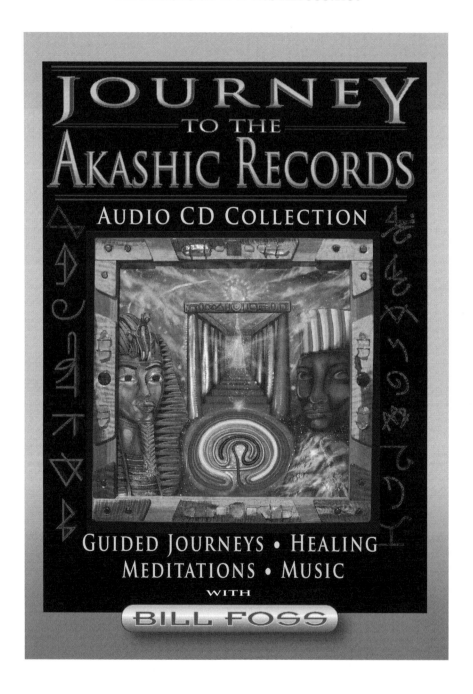

Music &
Meditation
CDs
Available

DOWNLOADS & CD's AVAILABLE AT THE WEBSITE

- **Akashic Healing Angels** - Guided Healing Meditation
- **Journey to the Akasha** - Guided Akashic Records Meditations
- **Magic of Merlin** - Akashic Records meditation
- **Letting Go into Bliss** -Background music from the Workshops
- **Super Divine** - 2 CD set, devotional music, chakra clearing,
      Akashic Records meditation
- **Chakra Music** - New age meditation music
- **Save the Planet** - New age/rock
- **The Wingmakers** - New age/rock

"Across The Universe through All Space and Time, the Creator has an Essence which flows through all things. Ever Present, Ever Watchful, Ever Compassionate. Waiting for the Moment when we come to recognize The Presence. Transforming our lives, others and the rest of our world into the Masterpiece as described by the Masters and indicated in all of the Sacred Texts and Ancient Teachings. May that Moment find You Now!"

The Secrets of Spiritual Success

Keys to the Art of an Abundant Lifestyle

Know Thyself • Service & Selflessness • Realization & Enlightenment
Power & Radiance • Opening the Senses • The Scene & the Unseen
Guidance & Counsel • Introspection & the External • Witness & Truth
Meditation & Prayer • Finding Love & Joy • Action & Awareness
Imagination & Intuition • Creativity & Visualization
Accessing the Soul, God & Self • Gratitude
Conceive, Believe & Receive

by BILL FOSS

The Secrets of Spiritual Success is a clear and concise road map providing an overview of understanding of 1000's of years of spiritual teachings, inquiries, and understandings. This book will help you to connect the dots more quickly in life, while adding to your studies already in motion or providing a great primer source to get started from. Whether you are a mystical student from beyond or you are new to expanded views and just looking for answers, this book was created to enliven and enrich your search, practices and studies. This book will turn on the lights for you and keep them on." Size 6" x 9" 237 Pages

Book • Workbook • Journal
Complete Study Set - Order at www.billfossworld.com

"The Keys of Spiritual Success" **Workbook**, companion to "The Secrets of Spiritual Success" is a collection of creative visualization and healing techniques, energy exercises, meditations, prayers. Exercises and insights to jump start your journey into your own long awaited or continued self inquiry and realization. Use this Workbook to Journal your subtle and not so subtle experiences as you open to greater understandings, fresh ideas, and new ways of being!" Size 8.5" x 11" 165 Pages

"The "Book Of Dreams" Journal is your gateway into creativity. This is your Journal, your space to create. What will you write, sketch, plan, or invent? Take the opportunity to go within and explore the vast regions, depths, and banks of Divine Creative Potential existing within you, all around you, throughout time, space & beyond. This is your chance to write down, plan and draw out your dream and make it a reality. Use this book as you will to expand your vision. It all starts here, and it starts with you so let's begin. Size 8.5" x 11" 165 Pages

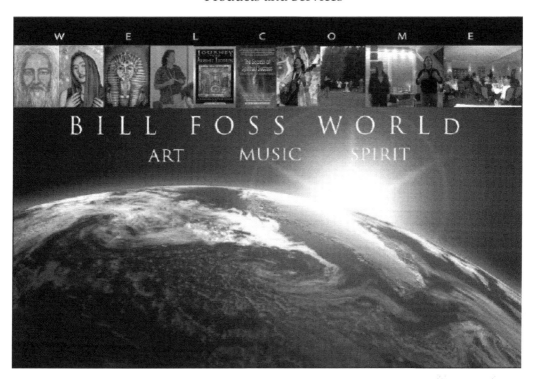

Art - **Paintings of the Spiritual Masters or a Personal Soul Portrait on Copper, Brass, or Steel**
Originals and Special Orders Available at www.billfossworld.com

ENERGY HEALING
CHAKRA CHEART

Chakra Charts - Copper or Brass hand made wall hanging 10 in. wide x 7 ft. tall on 7 panels.

Index of Art

Notes:

Notes:

Made in United States
Troutdale, OR
08/25/2023